Shadow Warriors

Shadow Warriors

Daring Missions of World War II
by Women of the OSS and SOE

GORDON THOMAS I GREG LEWIS

AMBERLEY

First published 2016

Amberley Publishing
The Hill, Stroud
Gloucestershire, GL5 4EP

www.amberley-books.com

ISBN 978 1 4456 6144 5 (hardback)
ISBN 978 1 4456 6145 2 (ebook)

British Library Cataloguing in Publication Data.
A catalogue record for this book is available from the British Library.

Typesetting: Nord Compo
Acknowledgments: Edith Maria Thomas and Moira Sharkey (research); Peter Durling (photo research)

"They were certainly young and attractive and well educated. Between them they spoke the languages of Europe, and beyond, as they fought for freedom and justice in a shadow war against the Nazi enemy. I selected them and read the reports of their instructors on their progress in the black arts of sabotage, subversion, and spying. When they qualified I accompanied them to a secret airfield to be flown on extraordinary missions, protected by the cover story which had been created for each one of them. They organized guerrilla groups, unmasked traitors, and shattered the morale of the enemy. Their own life expectancy was six weeks. They each were offered a suicide pill; not all accepted. They were my girls, like no other."

—Vera Atkins, intelligence officer in the French Section of the Special Operations Executive during World War II

"I hate wars and violence, but if they come then I don't see why we women should just wave a proud good-bye and then knit them balaclavas."

—Nancy Wake, SOE agent

"I discovered how easy it was to make highly trained, professionally closemouthed patriots give away their secrets in bed."

—Betty Pack, agent with the British Secret Intelligence Service and the Office of Strategic Services

"Air raid bombs that demolish homes and kill children bring out in every woman the right to protect, to seek out and destroy the evil behind those bombs by all means possible—including the physical and militant."

—Selwyn Jepson, SOE recruiting officer

Contents

Introduction

WORLD WAR II WAS the first time in history that women were trained as combatants and secret agents to be parachuted behind enemy lines. This was the war in which old gender rules changed, as intelligence agencies created specific training and roles for women. It was the war in which spy chiefs realized women's potential as couriers, wireless operators, spies, saboteurs, and even Resistance leaders. British prime minister Winston Churchill had rung the changes when he gave the order in July 1940 to "set Europe ablaze." The unit charged to do this was the Special Operations Executive, or SOE, a different kind of intelligence agency. Churchill called them "members of my underground army who collaborate and fight in the shadows."

They were spies and saboteurs trained as cryptographers, cartographers, analysts, and experts in recruiting, communication, and leadership to guide the resistance and partisans in the tense days of action in every theater of the European war.

In the United States, on June 13, 1942, six months after the Japanese attacked Pearl Harbor, President Franklin Roosevelt ordered the formation of the Office of Strategic Services, or OSS. The president's pen paved the way for American women to operate behind enemy lines along with the SOE.

These agents ranged from girls barely out of high school to mature mothers, from working-class women to the daughters of aristocrats, from the plain to the beautiful, from the prim and proper to wild high-livers.

Each of them was trained to blend in with the local population and even to disguise herself if necessary, by walking with a limp or wearing glasses. Burglars taught them how to pick locks and blow safes. Specialists showed them how to use rubber truncheons, tommy guns, Smith and Wesson automatics with silencers, and the killing knife with its polished and blackened blade. They were taught to throw grenades, jump from a fast-moving train, and plant a bomb on the hull of a ship. Those trained as wireless operators learned how to send secret messages and arrange for weapons to be dropped for the resistance fighters they would work with. All knew that torture and death were the price of failure.

They were brave and resourceful women, ready to place themselves in harm's way in order to serve their country. They worked undercover and carried out their assigned missions, sometimes with high-tech gadgets but none that could replace their own intelligence and determination. Their average age was twenty-five—some were younger, others older.

Their femininity could be a resource in itself, making the Germans less likely to search or arrest them if they were acting as message couriers or wireless operators. It also meant they were often in a position of making great self-sacrifice. For many of these women, going on active service meant leaving babies and children at home. Many paid the ultimate price for their bravery. All have individual stories that deserve a special place in the history of British and American intelligence during the Second World War. The clandestine war, and therefore the war itself, would not have been won without the courage and contributions of these shadow warriors.

....

On the same day Churchill gave the order to develop the SOE, Adolf Hitler made a speech in Berlin's Reichstag boasting that the Third Reich would last a thousand years. To thunderous cheers he reminded his audience that already in a matter of months the German blitzkrieg had conquered Poland, Czechoslovakia, Denmark, Norway, Belgium, and now France. Only England remained. In the skies over London the Royal Air Force fought a courageous battle against the Luftwaffe while thousands of citizens huddled in bomb shelters and subways at night, and when they emerged in the morning hundreds more wounded bodies and corpses lay in the rubble. Not since the Great Fire of 1666 had London burned so fiercely.

Britain stood alone, guarding its coast as the threat of invasion cast a dark shadow over the country.

Churchill's speech to the House of Commons outlined his vision of the future and ended with him saying:

> I expect that the Battle of Britain is about to begin. Upon this battle depends the survival of Christian civilisation, our own British life, and the long continuity of our institutions and our Empire. The whole fury and might of the enemy must very soon be turned on us. Hitler knows that he will have to break us in this island or lose the war. If we can stand up to him, all Europe may be free and the life of the world may move forward into broad, sunlit uplands. But if we fail, then the whole world, including the United States, including all that we have known and cared for, will sink into the abyss of a new Dark Age made more sinister, and perhaps more protracted, by the lights of perverted science. Let us therefore brace ourselves to our duties that, if the British Empire and its Commonwealth last for a thousand years, men will still say, "This was their finest hour."

That evening he told his War Cabinet how it would be achieved. "It is urgent and indispensible that every effort should be made to obtain secretly the best possible information about the German forces in various countries and to establish intimate contacts with local people and to plant our agents among them."

He told them the SOE not only would be a morale booster for the nation but also would show the world that Britain's resistance would determine the course of the war. "Our population will fight the Germans on the beaches and in the fields, in the villages, towns, cities, and ultimately, London. SOE will pave the way for victory."

Churchill appointed Dr. Hugh Dalton—a tall, bald man with a degree in economics—to be minister of economic warfare. In his customized suit, hand-sewn shirt, and his Marylebone Cricket Club tie, he embodied the British Establishment, a banker perhaps, or the chairman of a large company. A wealthy Socialist and an antiappeaser, he had devoted much of his time and money in the 1930s to warn of the threat Hitler posed, and he openly admired Churchill. Dalton knew his post, particularly its title, did not guarantee him a welcome among the budget trimmers in the Treasury or Foreign Office. Neither, he suspected, would the senior officers in the War Office see him as equipped with the military background to run the Ministry of Economic Warfare. Nor had his four years in the Great War told him anything about spying and counterespionage, let alone what they cost.

Churchill reassured Dalton he had chosen someone who had the military background to deal with Whitehall ministers, while at the same time create an underground army to send into Europe to wage war against the Nazis. He was Brigadier Colin McVean Gubbins, who had led a British Army force to Norway after the German Wehrmacht invaded that country in 1940. The Scots Highlander was the son of a family who had served in the British Army since campaigning for Oliver Cromwell in the seventeenth century. He had won a Military Cross in the First World War and possessed the virtues of command. He had courage, compassion, and was a natural leader of the young. He also held the conviction "that women can do the job as secret agents as well as men."

The prime minister learned that Gubbins had read a translation of Sun Tzu's *Art of War*, a military textbook that for two thousand years had been essential reading for China's military leaders. Churchill met Gubbins and discussed a key element of Sun Tzu's strategy: the infiltration of secret agents into enemy territory to gather intelligence and commit acts of sabotage. He saw Gubbins as "a mixture of patriotism and espionage." His name went into the file of "useful people" the prime minister kept, and he decided Gubbins should join the SOE in a key position.

In 1919 Gubbins had been sent to Russia, where he served under Britain's General Edmund Ironside and Russia's General Anton Denikin in the White Army. After the Red Army's victory in the Civil War, Gubbins returned to England to serve in Ireland. His experiences in Russia and Ireland gave him considerable insights into the nature of guerrilla warfare, and he wrote pamphlets on the subject including *The Art of Guerrilla Warfare*, *Partisan Leader's Handbook*, and *How to Use High Explosives*. They provided practical information on how to organize a road ambush, immobilize a railway engine, and kill the enemy. His writings had become required reading at Sandhurst and other officer training schools in the British Empire. Churchill had read every one of Gubbins's handbooks and decided he would have a crucial role in the training and selection of agents. Gubbins had told the prime minister about the roles women had played in Russia and Ireland as couriers, weapons carriers for men, and spies. When Poland had surrendered in 1939 it was women who protected the Polish general staff as they retreated from Warsaw to Bucharest.

The prime minister asked Gubbins to share his thoughts on the role that women could play in the SOE. Knowing Churchill's demands for any brief to be kept short, Gubbins confined himself to a page on why women with language skills should be recruited and given special training before being sent behind lines in occupied Europe.

"Women must be able to pass as locals and be sufficiently trained on how to survive among the German occupiers. They will pass on to Resistance fighters the knowledge they will have received. That must include guns and explosives. Being trained in wireless telegraphy will be essential. Armed combat and silent killing must be included in their training. They must be taught to a level that shows they are equally as capable as their male counterparts."

Churchill decided that women must be recruited into the SOE and trained as secret agents. He sent the memo to Dalton with the order that all recruiting officers were to keep a record of women's language skills and send the details to the Ministry of Economic Warfare.

Meantime the SOE had been listed in the government's classified telephone directory as the Inter Services Research Bureau with an address at 64 Baker Street. Only a black marble plaque at the entrance indicated its presence. The five-story building was a few doors from where Arthur Conan Doyle had given Sherlock Holmes his office, a connection that amused Churchill. Within months the SOE requisitioned country houses to become training schools, not only for men but for the women that Gubbins described in his memo. But how to find them?

He asked the Home Office immigration department to provide him with the names of women who had come to Britain from all over Europe to escape the advancing Nazis.

Gubbins arranged for the BBC to broadcast asking for photographs of "particular interesting areas in Europe" to be sent to the Ministry of Economic Warfare in Whitehall, London. Writers should attach a brief biographical note. Within weeks, scores of letters arrived.

A number were from women. They included shop assistants, typists, clerks, nurses, a newspaper editor's daughter, hotel receptionists, a professional dancer. Some had included vacation photos of themselves, mostly in France in prewar years. Several had a parent who was French, and they had been brought up and educated in France. Their letters indicated they were intelligent with a love for France as well as for Britain.

Gubbins chose Selwyn Jepson to analyze the letters to find suitable women to train as agents. He was a playwright, film director, and screenwriter and had served as an intelligence officer in the First World War. Afterward he had lived in Switzerland for a year, before spending four years in Rome and two years in Paris. He spoke their languages fluently. Gubbins told him that his selection of women to become agents would be a key part of the SOE's success. While their work would be like no other, he knew he must make sure the women had a full understanding of the risks they would face.

....

On May 27, 1941, Roosevelt, following the fall of Greece and Crete, addressed eighty-five million Americans in his weekly radio broadcast warning of the perils of Nazi victory in Europe. He declared, "A state of unlimited national emergency now exists." From coast to coast, no one was quite sure what the words meant. But soon there was a surge in military and naval construction programs. Isolationists also had a field day, led by the powerful Irish lobby opposed to America entering the war. Senator Worth Clark of Idaho urged in July that year that the United States should "draw a line across the Atlantic behind which Americans would shelter, taking peaceful control of their entire hemisphere, including South America and Canada." The proposal was widely reported in the German press as evidence that Roosevelt would stay out of the war.

....

In the American embassy in London, Ambassador Joseph P. Kennedy continued to display his contempt for his host country. It won him no friends in the White House or State Department, and Cordell Hull, the secretary of state, cautioned him about his views. But Kennedy persisted in his attempts to meet Hitler, a man he had come to admire. Meantime the US ambassador in Paris, William Bullit, also continued sending disparaging reports to Washington about Britain's prospect of surviving the war.

As the first bombs fell on London, Kennedy cabled the State Department to say that Britain was "not fighting for democracy. She's fighting for self-preservation. Democracy is finished in England. We should not give military and economic aid to the United Kingdom."

In 1940 MI5 continued to monitor the activities of Tyler Kent at the American embassy. He had arrived at the embassy in October 1939 from Moscow, where he had served since 1936 as the State Department code and cipher clerk, a post he now occupied in London. The twenty-nine-year-old son of the American consul in Beijing had started to express his anti-Semitism at meetings of the Right Club, a group of anti-Jewish Fascists who met at the home of Captain Archibald Ramsay, a distant relative of the Royal Family and a member of Parliament. Kent also shared with Ramsey cables that provided a clear insight into Kennedy's views that Churchill was a warmonger leading Britain to defeat. These caused consternation in the Foreign Office.

Lord Vansittart, chief diplomatic advisor to the British government, wrote a memo on January 22, 1940, to Foreign Secretary Anthony Eden: "Mr Kennedy is a very foul specimen of a double-crosser and defeatist. MI5 has noted that he flees with his family to the countryside whenever London is bombed. He is also making profitable investments on the stock market, a breach of State Department policy. Above all, he is anxious to break the relationship between Roosevelt and Churchill."

Kent also handled the Gray code, a cipher system the State Department believed to be unbreakable. It was the code Churchill used to correspond with Roosevelt. In one message Churchill told the president about the formation of the SOE.

Information continued to flow across Churchill's desk, and he shared it with Roosevelt. The president reciprocated by passing information he received from the US Navy. The intention was to allow sensible dispositions of their navies in both the Pacific and Atlantic. For Churchill there was also another motive: he hoped the exchanges would further enlist American sympathy and support for Britain—and ultimately bring the United States into the war.

Kent, in the solitude of the embassy's code room, continued to read the Gray code messages passing across the Atlantic.

On the morning of May 20, 1940, a team of Scotland Yard detectives entered his apartment overlooking Hyde Park. A forensic search, watched by the security officer from the American embassy, discovered fifteen hundred of the most recent Gray code cables. Kent insisted he had been acting in the "interest of my country to prevent American foreign policy leading it into the war." He was taken to the embassy and told by Kennedy that he was being dismissed from the Foreign Service. Stripped of diplomatic immunity, Kent was arrested, brought to trial at the Old Bailey, and convicted of theft and "dealing in documents of national security." He was sentenced to seven years imprisonment in Britain's grim jail on Dartmoor.

A devastated Kennedy cabled Roosevelt insisting he was unaware of Kent's activities. FDR waited until after his successful third term election before recalling Kennedy to Washington. Kennedy's own political ambitions would eventually succeed when he propelled his son John F. Kennedy into the White House.

When the United States entered the war after the attack on Pearl Harbor, President Roosevelt ordered the formation of the Office of Strategic Services, or OSS, America's first intelligence service, the nascent equivalent of the SOE. From its ranks, carefully selected women were sent to England to use their skills to support the women agents of the SOE. They were the first of four thousand women the OSS would employ.

....

The majority of those working in the intelligence communities at the outbreak of war instinctively believed that men made the best agents. The French Section of the SOE was to challenge that preconception. Women eventually made up a quarter of its force. Section heads realized that women could be less conspicuous in a country in which men of fighting age should have been working or might even have been picked up for forced labor in Germany. Being able to move around more easily made the dangerous task of carrying a concealed radio slightly less hazardous. Most women agents would work as couriers and wireless operators.

After the war many of these women, such as Violette Szabo and Odette Sansom, were rightly celebrated for their courage. They blurred the gender divide that had previously characterized war by not staying at home while the men went out to fight for their country's protection. Some, despite their exploits in open as well as clandestine warfare, stressed their femininity. New Zealand–born Nancy Wake's work with the French Resistance made her one of the Gestapo's most wanted agents in France, but after the war she stated, "What you've got to remember is that I was just a normal young woman." Wake learned what were considered "male skills" to take the fight to the enemy. But there were also women who openly used their sexuality to obtain information. Most notable of these was Betty Pack, who worked for both the SOE and the Americans, becoming the OSS's famed agent code-named Cynthia. Pack knew that men held the secrets she wanted and that sex was the way to make them divulge what they knew.

Even though the seductress spy appears in stories from most wars, the way in which Betty Pack got her information for the Allies may actually have put her in the shadow of the agents with the Sten gun. That said, Colonel Maurice Buckmaster, head of the French Section of the SOE, acknowledged, "My organization used quite a number of courageous women. They were not called upon to use their feminine charms in the way that Cynthia did. But I can well see the advantages of a good-looking woman spy using her feminine charms as an added weapon in seeking information."

Betty Pack argued that her methods were better than torturing or killing to obtain information.

....

The women who volunteered as agents might have been invited to volunteer, but that did not mean they did not face sexism and even derision. Yolande Beekman, an efficient and courageous agent who was executed by the Germans, had been dismissed by one SOE instructor as "a nice girl, [who] darned the men's socks, would make an excellent wife for an unimaginative man, but not much more than that." In a report on Eileen Nearne, who was twenty-two when she trained as a wireless operator, an officer used both her youth and gender against her. "In character she is very 'feminine' and immature," he noted.

The women's motivations for wanting to join the secret war were varied, but many quoted their family's experiences during World War I. Odette Sansom was six years old when her father was killed, and she grew up with her grandfather warning there would soon be another war. "I listened to that for years," she said. "The seed was there."

Violette Szabo's husband was killed in North Africa in October 1942. She said, "I am going to get my own back somehow." Yvonne Cormeau, who would become one of F Section's most adept radio operators, had seen her husband die in the London Blitz. "I was willing to do whatever I could," she said. "This was something I think my husband would have liked to do and, as he was no longer there to do it, I thought it was time for me to do it."

Sansom, Szabo, and Cormeau all left behind very young children when they volunteered. Sansom and Cormeau returned. Szabo sadly did not.

....

The time frame of this book encompasses somewhere between recent history and fading memory. However, there are sufficient acts of extraordinary bravery by those women and men of the SOE and OSS to provide an accurate, balanced, and compelling account of what happened when they parachuted in the moonlight to help disrupt the Third Reich. For the first two years of the war, the SOE operated alone. In 1942 the OSS became its partner.

Much has still been left unsaid about their work. In preparing this study we have consulted official records, memoirs, and private material, including diaries and letters, and followed the rule of double-checking previous material when it appeared to be contradictory and confusing.

The secret world of intelligence gathering has always fascinated us after reading about Gideon, the Old Testament hero who saved Israelites from a stronger enemy by providing them with better intelligence. But how was intelligence handled in one of the greatest and most terrible events in history, World War II? How was intelligence gathering carried out? Who were the men who formed the clandestine forces and realized women should be among their most important foot soldiers? And who were the women they chose?

After the war, the victors—the United States, Britain, and France, and later, Germany—microfilmed the records for their archives. In the Imperial War Museum in London are hundreds of hours of recordings on which the men and women who worked in intelligence gathering have recalled their memories of being behind enemy lines and carrying out nerve-racking sabotage operations. To this day their voices remain timeless testimony. They are reinforced by the Records of the Office of Strategic Services at the National Archives in Washington, DC.

Those sources are supported by the German depositories: the Military Archives in Freiburg im Breisgau, the Federal Archives in Koblenz, and the Federal Political Archives in Berlin.

In some cases documents are not always complete; parts of them may have been destroyed in the war or afterward, perhaps accidentally, maybe deliberately. But the stories of the men and women in the following pages explain why intelligence rose to its full importance in World War II.

Gordon Thomas
Greg Lewis
Bath, 2016

1

By All Means Possible

S INCE DAWN, BRIGADIER COLIN Gubbins had supervised the SOE's move into its headquarters at 64 Baker Street on July 15, 1941.

Born in 1896, his mother had given him a strong sense of duty and a piety governed by the demands of a responsive conscience. With it came his father's sense of justice, logic, and integrity in an orderly mind. War and action had filled Gubbins's own military life, during which he had learned that "thinking first before applying action was essential." His deep-set eyes and voice warned all comers not to cross him. They never lost their look of searching for information. He gave the impression that all he heard he would keep secret, unless it was an essential ingredient for the policies that guided both diplomacy and war and served the needs of the decision makers. Churchill was always the first to hear his latest secret—not something from the nonstop gossip mill in Whitehall but information that could involve a current event.

On that summer's day Gubbins went to his office on the fifth floor and stared out of a window at the ugly scars of a city at war—gaps in a row of buildings where a bombed shop or a café had stood, streets with sandbagged guard posts, and signs with arrows pointing to the nearest air raid shelter. In the sky hung barrage balloons to intercept the Luftwaffe if the bombers made another visit to be met by the Royal Air Force (RAF) Spitfires and the antiaircraft batteries stationed along the flight paths the Germans were known to use.

It would be after dark when the bombers came. By then the army engineers had promised Gubbins they would have finished installing a switchboard and checked its two hundred lines. He calculated the building would eventually need that number of phones by the time the SOE's training schools and other facilities had opened across Britain. Already in London twenty-five offices were staffed by men who had served under him in Poland and Norway. He had selected them with the help of Sir Hastings Ismay, the chief of staff, when unhelpful Whitehall departments had challenged their transfer into the SOE's headquarters.

Employees entered through an entrance with a black marble plaque mounted on the wall bearing the words INTER SERVICES RESEARCH BUREAU. Each person had signed the Official Secrets Act and been told that secrecy was their first duty; the smallest breach of the Act would result in arrest, trial, and imprisonment. In the creaky elevator that took staff up to their offices was a framed reminder. It depicted a finger on lips and the words NO TALK. NO SURPRISE. It was posted in every corridor and on the walls of every office.

To reinforce the need for secrecy, Gubbins created cover names for staff to use in any of their dealings with the War Office, Admiralty, or Air Ministry. They were to say they were calling from either the Joint Technical Board, the Special Training Headquarters, or the one Gubbins most enjoyed, the MO1 (SP), which staff joked stood for "Mysterious Operations in Secret Places," or simply MOSP. By the end of the war some people in high places in military departments had never discovered what the acronym stood for.

....

Winston Churchill had defined the MOSP as "tangle within tangle, plot and counter-plot, ruse and treachery, cross and double-cross, true agent, false agent, double agent."

To them he added the words of his favorite military strategist, Sun Tzu, the Chinese expert on guerrilla war: "The enemy must not know where I intend to give battle. For if he does not know where I intend to give battle he must prepare in a great many places. And when he prepares everywhere he will be weak everywhere." Both the MOSP and Tzu's words became the battlecry for the SOE.

The prime minister had sent both quotations to Gubbins. On that hot, somnolent July day, when the move into Baker Street was completed, he knew special means would be essential to defeating Adolf Hitler and the million German soldiers manning fortified defenses along the French coast, which Hitler boasted was the strongest since the Great Wall of China. He called it the Atlantic Wall.

The SOE would operate beyond it to provide the French people with their liberty, the first step to lifting the Nazi yoke off the rest of Europe.

....

Gubbins read every MI5 vetting report on his staff. A number were nationals of occupied countries who had fled to England. Their language skills and geographical knowledge of their countries made them suitable recruits.

But Britain was increasingly gripped by spy mania. B Section, the counterespionage department of MI5 headed by Guy Liddell, a cello-playing veteran spy hunter, faced a mounting task of checking reports that the nation was riddled with German spies who were embedded to prepare for Hitler's invasion. The fear was fuelled by spy novels, tabloid newspapers, and an obsession that the Kaiser had sent spies to England in the First World War and that these had remained. They were said to be disguised as nuns, traveling salesmen, bank managers, and "those gentlemen who are the best behaved in your town," the *Sunday Express* wrote. Robert Baden-Powell, the founder of the Boy Scout movement, insisted, "You can identify a spy from the way he walks—but only from behind."

"There is a class of people prone to spy mania," Winston Churchill told Gubbins, who dismissed it as a "Fifth Column neurosis." An ice cream vendor was poisoning his cones. A psychiatrist at a mental hospital was training patients to kill politicians. There wasn't a day when reports of nefarious activities didn't land on Gubbins's desk. They became stories to lighten his morning staff meetings.

Gubbins brought Margaret Jackson and Vera Long with him to Baker Street, both of whom had been his secretaries since the outbreak of war. He told Hugh Dalton, the minister of economic war, who was responsible for SOE salaries, that he wanted them paid on the same scale as lieutenants in the First Aid Nursing Yeomanry. In staff relations, as with so much else, Gubbins was ahead of his time.

In the First World War the FANYs were known as the first arrivals as they collected the wounded from the battlefields and drove them to the French coast to be brought back to England.

Gubbins decided that all female staff in the SOE would wear FANY uniforms. Those who would be sent into France would not wear them but would hold an officer's commission and their salaries would be banked for them in London until their return. However, he knew if they were captured they would almost certainly be executed as spies.

He had the gift of inspiring confidence that amounted to devotion, and both his secretaries typed some of the most secret communications of the war. More than once he asked either Jackson or Long to summarize important decisions made at meetings. Dressed in their FANY uniforms he would take them in turn to the War Office, or another Whitehall ministry meeting, to sit beside him and take perfect shorthand notes, which would be transcribed that night before they returned to their apartments farther down Baker Street. Next morning they would be at their desks in his outer office by 6:00 AM.

His workload grew, increased by the responsibility he carried for the lives of hundreds. At times his frustration boiled over, an anger that had started when MI6 had brought General Charles de Gaulle out of France in 1940 on Churchill's orders. Since then de Gaulle had been approaching Frenchmen living in Britain to join the Free French force he was forming.

At their first meeting, de Gaulle insisted to Gubbins his movement would become a secret army into which the SOE's French Section—F Section—should be absorbed. He reminded Gubbins he had come to London not only to establish a government-in-exile but also to use his "connections and reputation in France to prepare organized resistance." The Free French would be the vanguard. Gubbins replied that while the movement was welcome to work alongside the SOE, there was no possibility of F Section being absorbed under the general's command.

Gubbins decided he would make a change of the leadership of F Section. Its section head, H. R. Marriott, had developed "a false belief in his indispensability." Gubbins replaced him with Maurice Buckmaster.

Buckmaster was forty-one years old, a tall, thin man with a slight stoop. He had gone to Eton College, one of England's oldest and most prestigious prep schools, and had won a scholarship to study classics at Oxford. Afterward he went to France on a cycling tour and ended up on the staff of *Le Matin*, a Paris newspaper, as a reporter. Other jobs followed, including working in a public relations company that handled the accounts for the Ford Motor Company in France. In 1938 he returned to England and enlisted in the British Army. His knowledge of French led to him serving as an intelligence officer in the British Expeditionary Force sent to confront the German offensive sweeping across France. He was among the last units to be shipped out of Dunkirk and back to England in June 1940. He heard that a new organization was being created that needed French speakers with a military background.

"I called the War Office. Next day, I was told to come to London for an interview. It was with Gubbins. That's how I joined SOE on March 17, 1941. Gubbins placed me in the Belgium section. Five months later I was head of F Section," Buckmaster recalled.

Buckmaster's appointment resulted in the section becoming the first to send women behind enemy lines.

....

Gubbins spent time choosing heads of sections. Though all had undergone positive vetting by MI5, he decided selection would not be based on a candidate's family connections or school background, as was so often the route used by the armed forces.

With the patience of a headhunter, he made discreet inquiries about the service records of those whose names he had been given by members of his own network of military contacts. He had told them he was looking for men who had some experience in guerrilla tactics. Ideally they would have been at the Special Training Centre for commandos at Lochailort in the Scottish Highlands. Others had served under him in Poland or Norway.

Fluent in French, Polish, and Dutch, Gubbins tested each applicant's language skill, then talked about their family, military background, and any special qualities he noticed in their military records. Once satisfied, he offered a candidate a post as head of a section and told him to sign the Official Secrets Act.

The men and women selected as agents underwent three weeks of assessment in paramilitary training and psychological tests and a further five weeks of training in Lochailort. Courses included handling a range of explosives and learning the technique of silent killing with a dagger. Ten inches long, the double-edged razor-sharp blade was designed to slice through a person's throat in one stroke. Mannequins were used for practice. Those who showed an aptitude for Morse code were sent to a specialist training school to perfect their skills in sending encoded messages.

Field agents would be formed into small groups, known as circuits. Each would have an organizer who would recruit local resisters and be responsible for arming them and teaching them the techniques they had learned in the training school. Each circuit would have a courier to act as the link with other groups of local resisters and circuits.

"A courier will be constantly on the move, often by bicycle or train, traveling considerable distance to deliver messages. They run the risk of being caught by German patrols. A wireless operator must never operate a set for more than twenty minutes as the Germans have powerful detection vans which can detect Morse signals," Gubbins said.

The briefing ended with the impact of his next words.

I have been given by Churchill authority for SOE to send women as couriers and wireless operators into France. Women are less likely to be bodily searched and their messages can be hidden in their underwear. Because many are trained typists they will also make better wireless operators. They will all be assigned to the French Section. The Geneva Convention of 1929 offers no protection to women combatants, let alone for the war which SOE will conduct.

He then told them how agents would be recruited.

....

Selwyn Jepson was forty years old when Gubbins appointed him for the delicate, serious, and individual work of choosing secret agents. With dark, wavy hair and a voice that moved conversations along at its own pace with a nod or smile, the post fit Jepson's background. He was born in 1899 into a middle-class, respected London family. His father was a thriller writer and his mother a noted musician; his sister was a serious novelist, and a cousin, Fay Weldon, became a celebrated author. Jepson himself was a successful writer of books and screenplays.

Only Gubbins and Buckmaster knew why Jepson needed separate offices in different parts of London. One was where he interviewed men, and the other was where he selected women to be trained. None of the interviewees were ever brought to SOE headquarters in case they heard or saw something they did not need to know.

Jepson had his own office at SOE headquarters too, on the same floor as Gubbins. Within the building he became known as Captain Mosp, the SOE's chief recruiter for mysterious operations. His books had pride of place on a shelf behind his desk in his fifth-floor office. They had titles like *Puppets of Fate*, *The King's Red-Haired Girl*, and *The Death Gong*. Twenty-five of his thrillers had been published on both sides of the Atlantic. His screenplays had been turned into Hollywood movies like *Kiss Me Goodbye*, *The Love Test*, and *Money Mad*.

Jepson's office allowed him to look down on Baker Street as SOE staff came in and out of the building. Some worked in offices along the corridor, and he exchanged pleasantries with them as they rode up in the elevator. The thin man with the bowlegs of a jockey; a tall figure in an RAF uniform who addressed anyone as "hullo, old cock"; a fat man with an engaging smile, which shone through discolored teeth; a fair-haired girl in a FANY uniform, one of the secretaries—Jepson had come to know them, the men by their frequently conspiratorial air, the women with warm smiles. Like him they arrived early for work and left late in the evening.

In between interviews Jepson spent the day in his office reading the latest letters the Ministry of Economic Warfare had received as a result of the BBC broadcast asking for photographs of "interesting areas" in Europe. They were sent to the Air Ministry to be assessed for possible targets. The letters with the photos included personal details of the senders who had escaped to Britain from Nazi-occupied Europe.

By the end of the day Jepson had selected who he would invite to come for an interview. Afterward, those he accepted would be sent to Orchard Court, a large, modern apartment block where Vera Atkins lived. Gubbins told Jepson that Atkins had a quality that would be of value when assessing the character of a recruit, especially women. Her apartment became an SOE base to interview every man and woman Jepson selected for a follow-up interview.

Born in Romania in 1908 to a German Jewish father and a South African Jewish mother, her real name was Vera Rosenberg. She came to England in 1936, having anglicized her mother's name, Etkins, to Atkins, and had met Buckmaster, who had helped her naturalization and in 1941 had found her a job as a secretary in the SOE.

Gubbins appointed her as Jepson's assistant as recruitment was fast picking up, and soon a number of potential agents would arrive at Orchard Court for Atkins's follow-up interview.

Each interviewee was given a time to arrive at Orchard Court. The entrance was guarded by Atkins's doorman and butler, Andrew Park, who had worked at the Savoy Hotel before being recruited by the SOE. Dressed in a dark suit and tie, he would lead the way to the gilded elevator gates and up to the second floor to Atkins's apartment. Using his pass key he opened its doors and led the recruit down the hallway into a bathroom that Atkins used as a waiting room. Moments later he returned and led the person into Atkins's office. The routine never varied.

Before each interview Atkins studied the assessment report Jepson had prepared on each candidate. Some had escaped from France and had never been in England before. Others had relatives there who had helped them find work in shops and cafés. Until they had been interviewed by Jepson and signed the Official Secrets Act they had no idea they had been recruited for secret work, except that it would involve speaking French and not to discuss it with anyone. A few admitted to Jepson—"Mr. Potter" to them—they had worked on French Resistance escape lines. Some had just fled across the Channel.

Jepson's reports enabled Atkins to judge the character of each agent within a few minutes of meeting them.

Tall, slim, and in her midthirties, Atkins would smile, proffer her hand, and lead her visitor to an office armchair, before sitting opposite in another. Lighting a cigarette she would settle her blue-gray eyes upon the new recruit and began to explain why he, or more often she, had been chosen to be trained for "special work," adding that she would follow their progress day by day to the time she would accompany them to the airfield where they would get their final briefing for their secret mission into Nazi-occupied Europe. More than one recruit left her office excited and eager to begin work for this woman who exuded such confidence.

....

In the summer of 1940, the mood in President Roosevelt's White House was uncertain. Across the Atlantic, the RAF fought the Luftwaffe for mastery of the skies over England. The city of Coventry had been destroyed, and thousands of Londoners huddled in bomb shelters and subways, while Churchill continued to promise in his BBC broadcasts that Britain would never surrender and predicted "the time will come when the New World with all its power will step forth to the rescue and liberation of the Old."

The prime minister was too adroit a politician to say he was counting on the United States to openly support his optimism. Some of its radio networks had started to repeat BBC broadcasts from London with a new sound: the first four notes of Beethoven's Fifth Symphony, three dots and a dash, which created the Morse code for *V*—for *victory*. In occupied Europe the pattern was used to knock on doors, blow train whistles, and honk car horns. Churchill used two straight fingers to signal *V* for *victory*. The press attaché at the British embassy in Washington circulated a photo of the gesture to newspapers. The German embassy issued a press release: "Churchill should not think he can win the war by making a silly gesture."

The first of thirty-two thousand British children evacuated to the United States onboard the *Queen Mary* and *Queen Elizabeth* came ashore in New York singing the two new songs from back home. The fall of France had inspired "The Last Time I Saw Paris," and the London Blitz had led to "A Nightingale Sang in Berkeley Square."

The children found themselves welcomed into American homes equipped with appliances and consumer durables most had never seen before—refrigerators, radios, telephones, electric fans, and air conditioning. Hollywood provided 90 percent of the world's movies they were taken to see. Those who were sent from New York to places like Kansas learned it had more cars than all of Great Britain. There were skyscrapers in the cities and passenger planes to take them to their new homes across the nation.

American youth taught British children a new language: girls spoke of boys as "smooth" and girls were "neat" or "terrific." Their hosts took the newcomers to church on Sundays, and families would gather around the radio on Friday evenings to listen to President Roosevelt's fireside chats.

Newspapers, with advertisements very different from the ones in England, carried daily Gallup polls; one revealed the favorite adjective of that summer was *tantamount*—as in every Roosevelt order was "tantamount to declaring war." Key Pittman, the chair of the Senate Foreign Relations Committee, proposed that "British people should give up their home island and retreat to Canada."

Charles H. Lindbergh, who had become a national hero after flying solo across the Atlantic and a figure of sadness after his baby son was kidnapped and murdered, shared with the nation his views on the international situation at a New York rally in Madison Square Garden.

> We are in danger of war today not because people have attempted to interfere in America, but because we American people have attempted to interfere with the internal affairs of Europe. We need not fear foreign invasion unless American people bring it through their own quarrelling and meddling with affairs abroad. We are surrounded by people who want us to go to war. These are men seizing every opportunity to push America closer to the edge and want to lead us into conflict across the Atlantic and bring it to our doorstep.

The reporters gathered below the platform scribbled furiously while Lindbergh waited for the applause to stop before he continued.

"We have all heard Mr. Churchill's promise that Britain will go on to the end. That it will fight on the seas and oceans and in the air. That is fine for Britain. But we do not need it here."

Brushing aside questions, Lindbergh walked off the platform and was driven away. The next day, he resigned his commission as an Air Corps colonel. The speech was heavily criticized as being anti-Semitic. In response, Lindbergh insisted again he was not anti-Semitic, but he did not back away from his statement. Another Gallup poll reported that 90 percent of Americans would fight if America was invaded but only 10 percent would do so if America was not invaded.

In Jeanette, Pennsylvania, a gun club started to practice marksmanship so that its members would be ready to pick off descending Nazi parachutists. A hamburger chain changed the word *hamburger* to *liberty steak*. *Time* magazine quoted a new word—*blitzkrieg*. It was soon attached to every story from the war front in London. The House of Lords, adjacent to Parliament and Big Ben, had been hit by a bomb; Buckingham Palace had been struck by five bombs.

The thirty-second president of the United States knew that the United Kingdom was taking terrible punishment and the pound Sterling was falling on Wall Street. Roosevelt brooded about all this while convalescing from a severe sinus attack in the Caribbean sun aboard the cruiser *Tuscaloos* when a navy seaplane landed alongside to deliver a letter from Winston Churchill. It had been hand couriered by a Queen's messenger across the Atlantic and delivered onboard by the British ambassador, Lord Lothian. He would remember how Roosevelt carefully opened it with a knife, read it slowly, and then retreated to a sun chair on the deck.

"He sat there alone and read and reread the letter for two days. He took his meals in his cabin. When he did appear on deck to enjoy the sun he had the look of a man coming to an important decision," the ambassador recalled.

Churchill's letter asked if the president "working within the American Constitution could prevent Britain being stripped to the bone."

The answer to Churchill's appeal became known worldwide as the Lend-Lease Act. It was fortuitously numbered H. R. 1776 and was titled "A Bill Further to Promote the Defense of the United States, and for Other Purposes." It set out in the opening preamble "to provide aid to any country whose defense the President deems vital to the defense of the United States." It gave Roosevelt powers no other president had ever requested.

Before the bill became law, Roosevelt, his sinus condition cured, was back in the White House. As 1940 came to an end, he once more sent for William Joseph Donovan. Since 1936, the Wall Street lawyer had acted as the president's fact finder after Hitler came to power. Roosevelt told no one why he summoned Donovan.

....

A woman who was to become a key agent in the coming war was already on the MI6, the Secret Intelligence Service, payroll, and this after gaining her hunger for espionage during the Spanish Civil War.

Betty Pack was tall, slim, and beautiful, with bright auburn hair and deep green eyes. Born into a life of privilege in Minneapolis, Minnesota, on November 22, 1910, she had been christened Amy Elizabeth Thorpe, but everyone called her Betty. Her father, George, was a decorated officer in the US Marines, and her mother, Cora, had been educated at a number of top universities, including the Sorbonne in Paris. Throughout Betty's childhood the family moved around a great deal, settling first in Cuba and then Hawaii, where George was given command of marines at Pearl Harbor.

In 1922 George Thorpe retired, and the family, which by now included two younger siblings for Betty, moved to Washington. With time on his hands, George and his wife planned a grand tour of Europe. Arriving in France in the spring of 1923, the family traveled to Monte Carlo and then Rome, Naples, and eventually Germany. Betty then spent three months studying French at a boarding school for young women on the shores of Lake Geneva. Her trip gave her an excellent understanding of the French language and a love of Europe.

Back in Washington, she socialized with the city's elite, got to know Italian and Spanish diplomats, and was presented to Washington society in November 1929, a day before her nineteenth birthday. A few days earlier Betty, who had already had more than one sexual relationship, seduced Arthur Joseph Pack, a commercial secretary at the British embassy. Betty and Arthur had been guests at a weekend house party when he found her waiting for him naked in his bed. Arthur was thirty-eight and a veteran of the Great War, but he was no match for Betty. He was smitten, and by February 1930 they were engaged to be married. By then Betty was pregnant. The wedding was brought forward, and they were married at the end of April 1930. The couple then traveled to Britain. A son, Tony, was born on October 2, 1930. Some have speculated, perhaps unkindly, that Tony may not have been Arthur's son, and Arthur certainly acted coldly toward the baby, but this may have been due to his embarrassment over the obvious fact that the child had been conceived out of wedlock. Arthur advertised for a foster-mother, and Tony was taken away to be raised by a couple in Shropshire, England.

Arthur's career as a diplomat developed, and the couple moved to Santiago, Chile, where he accepted a post. They lived well and again mixed with high society, and on New Year's Eve 1934, Betty gave birth to a daughter, Denise. Betty learned Spanish, but still only twenty-one, she quickly grew bored with the much older embassy wives. To make life more bearable she took up horseback riding and joined the Santiago polo club, where she began an affair with a wealthy industrialist.

In 1935 Arthur Pack was transferred to the British embassy in Madrid. Life in Spain began well, with bridge nights and picnics in the Sierra de Guadarrama, but once again Betty grew bored. She and Arthur befriended a couple named Carlos and Carmencita Sartorious, who introduced them to the "authentic" Spain of bullfights and shooting. Betty and Carlos, an officer in the Spanish air force, began an affair, meeting in a borrowed penthouse apartment to make love. These liaisons went on for about a year while around them the country slipped toward civil war.

Just days before it broke out, on the orders of the British ambassador, Sir Henry Chilton, Arthur, Betty, and their daughter Denise left Madrid and traveled across the border to Biarritz in southern France. Together with Denise's nurse and her own child, they set up home in a rented villa. But as the fighting intensified, Arthur quickly became concerned for his embassy colleagues in the "summer embassy" in the northern Spanish city at San Sebastián, and on July 21, he set out on a four-hour journey to check on them. Two days later he had not returned, and Betty got her chauffeur to take her on a mission to find him. She was stopped in the border town of Irún and imprisoned by the Republicans. After an uncomfortable time in a basement jail, she managed to persuade her captors that she was not one of Franco's spies, and she and her chauffeur were escorted back across the border into France.

Betty was not to be dissuaded from trying again and set out on the same journey two days later. This time she met a more agreeable border guard who granted her a one-day pass and an escort of two militiamen. Betty reached San Sebastián and found her husband and the other embassy staff safe.

Arthur was angry that Betty had put herself in danger; but she reveled in it and even managed to smuggle five Franco supporters out of the city with her. She was back in Biarritz by late evening. It had been a wild and dangerous mission, bringing with it the same rush of adrenaline she had experienced from a love affair.

Her husband helped with the evacuation by ship of a number of Britons trapped by the war, then set up a temporary embassy in the border town of Hendaye. From there, Betty, whose personal loyalties were with the Catholic Church and Franco's forces, watched Irún burn. She mourned for Spain but also feared for her lover, Carlos, about whom she had heard nothing since they had fled Madrid. When a Spanish aristocrat friend suggested they visit Spain while Arthur was away on business in England, she eagerly accepted his invitation. In Burgos, Betty met the head of the Spanish branch of the International Red Cross and volunteered to smuggle in much-needed medical supplies.

Over the next few weeks she made two trips into Burgos with medicines. She also carried a letter addressed to Ambassador Sir Henry Chilton from Franco's foreign minister, Vizconde de Santa Clara Avedillo. It was an appeal to the British government to recognize Franco. Sir Henry reacted angrily to the letter, as the British government's sympathies were turning against Franco. He told Betty she was putting her husband's career in peril. She brushed off the criticism, but when she returned to Burgos with more medical supplies she found she had been denounced to Franco's military headquarters as a Republican spy.

Within the space of a few days Betty was accused of being a spy for the Republicans and for Franco. She vehemently denied the accusation of being a spy for anybody and managed to persuade the Nationalist officer sent to arrest her that the person who had denounced her was a wronged woman, and she escaped back over the border to the sanctuary of the British embassy.

Only Commander Don Gomez-Beare, who would become Britain's naval attaché in Madrid during World War II, knew that Betty, on visits to Burgos, was being "used as a useful informant . . . to British Naval Intelligence." She was reporting to Admiralty intelligence on conditions inside Nationalist-held Spain and on her conversations with the many high-ranking Nationalists in her social circles.

Betty Pack *had* become a spy. Within months, she would become an official recruit to the Secret Intelligence Service and a secret agent for MI6—a stepping stone to becoming an SOE and OSS spy.

2

The Clouds of War

ON SUNDAY AFTERNOON, JULY 14, 1941, William Donovan saw the reporters and photographers standing outside the Pan Am seaplane terminal on New York's waterfront. He slowed his stride and told them it was a business trip, smiling for the cameras. That had always been his way, the more so now that the war in Europe had led to him being engaged on behalf of President Roosevelt.

Donovan's colonel uniform had a clasp of brightly colored service ribbons on his chest and shiny silver oak leaf stars on the epaulets. The ribbons included the Distinguished Service Cross, the army's second-highest decoration, for leading his regiment in action during World War I in France. Beside it was the Medal of Honor, awarded for "performing extra heroism by leading from the front and refusing to be evacuated after wounded." When he had finally returned to New York on April 21, 1919, surrounded by his men, he was the most highly decorated soldier in American history. Still recovering from his war wounds in the leg, he had led his soldiers in a parade up Fifth Avenue to receive the key of the city from the mayor.

Now, at the age of fifty-nine, his hair silvered and neatly brushed to one side, his blue eyes as alert as ever, there was a determination on his face to honor the trust President Roosevelt had put in him.

Walking beside Donovan through the terminal to see him off was Canadian-born William Stephenson, another of the rich and powerful clients of Donovan's legal firm. A one-time amateur boxer and a Royal Flying Corps pilot in the Great War, Stephenson had become a millionaire entrepreneur first in Canada, trading in bear and seal skins, and then in Europe. In 1939 he had arrived in New York to expand his business. Needing a personal lawyer, he had received a recommendation from an old friend, the champion boxer Gene Tunney, to use Donovan. Sharing a common passion for boxing and other sports, Stephenson and Donovan had quickly become friends and enjoyed weekly martini lunches at the St. Regis Hotel or the 21 Club.

Donovan had negotiated office space for Stephenson on the thirty-sixth floor of Rockefeller Center in New York. The business was called the British Security Coordination. It was the cover name for MI5 and MI6, Britain's intelligence services, in the United States. Churchill had put Stephenson in charge of covert operations against German agents trying to sabotage any aid shipped to Britain.

That Sunday morning while they had brunched at the St. Regis, Stephenson said he had asked Lord Lothian, the British ambassador in Washington, to have his government ensure that Donovan met Churchill to discuss the idea that Britain and the United States should develop intelligence ties.

....

In those postwar years in the 1920s, Donovan, by then an established Wall Street lawyer, had been an outspoken critic of Roosevelt, then governor of New York State, accusing him of being a "big spending liberal." When Roosevelt was elected president, Donovan saw that in foreign affairs he matched his own views about the increasing threat Hitler posed in Europe since coming to power in 1933.

The lawyer had started to write letters to the president with observations from his own business trips to Europe. Roosevelt wrote back. Soon the exchanges became regular and they began to meet. Their common charisma and intellectual curiosity—one knowing how to use political skills in Washington, the other equally versatile in the legal world—drew them closer, as did their shared concern about Hitler.

On July 17, 1936, civil war broke out in Spain. General Francisco Franco brought home his legions from Spanish Morocco to oust the government in Madrid. That evening Donovan had dined with Roosevelt at the White House, and they had both agreed that the war clouds over Spain could lead to a wider conflict. Roosevelt had then asked his guest to become his personal envoy to scope out the situation in Europe. Donovan had immediately accepted.

The next day Donovan asked his secretary, Eloise Randolph Page, a debutante from Charleston, South Carolina, to arrange a standing reservation with Pan Am—seat 5 in first class—which was to be kept free for him on any of its transatlantic flights. His favorite menu should always be available: turtle soup, steak, and ice cream. Tea or coffee was his choice of beverage, and he never smoked and rarely drank alcohol. In his office he started to keep an overnight bag so he'd be able to leave at short notice in case of events developing in Europe.

On March 7, 1936, Hitler had sent troops marching into the demilitarized left bank of the Rhineland. The soldiers were under orders to withdraw promptly if their presence was challenged by either Britain or France. Neither country had done anything. They were both preoccupied with the war in Ethiopia. Poland had secretly proposed to France that they jointly attack Germany. Paris declined. In London, Foreign Secretary Anthony Eden condemned Hitler for repudiating the Treaty of Versailles: "One of the main foundations of the peace of Western Europe has been cut away. If peace is to be secured there is a manifest duty to rebuild."

Two years later, Hitler sent German troops into Austria, the Anschluss. Six months later came the annexing of the Sudetenland in western Czechoslovakia, followed by German tanks rumbling into Prague. On Friday, September 1, 1939, Luftwaffe dive-bombers and the Wehrmacht combined tactics to launch blitzkrieg to invade Poland and overrun its poorly prepared forces. World War II had started.

....

On his missions for Roosevelt, Donovan had visited Benito Mussolini in the Italian dictator's Venetian palace in Rome. He was escorted across a chamber he guessed was twice the size of the Oval Office. Mussolini sat behind a massive desk at the far end. Donovan's law school—trained eye for detail noted, "He put aside papers he was reading and, chin bulging, dark eyes fixed on me as I approached, he eased himself out of his armchair, nodded his shaved head, welcomed me in English and indicated a chair to one side of his desk where I would sit. Beneath his portrait sat a woman with a notebook open on her knees."

Earlier Donovan had received a different welcome from German diplomats in Berlin's Foreign Ministry when he had asked if it could be arranged for him to meet Adolf Hitler.

"They looked at me in astonishment and said the Führer was always busy. But if Herr Roosevelt wanted to meet him that could be possible if he came to Berlin. In the meantime it had been arranged for me to tour the city," Donovan later wrote.

His guide in Berlin had been Colonel Walter Warlimont, a member of the Wehrmacht General Staff. They had spent an afternoon in his apartment overlooking the Tiergarten. His host had spoken openly about Hitler's skill in spotting and exploiting the weakness in opponents and how he had consolidated his power by outmaneuvering the conservatives who had thought with naive arrogance they could control him. He had dealt with them with new laws and mass imprisonment. Hitler had halted the rise of unemployment by introducing conscription and rearmament. Neither Britain, France, nor the United States had objected.

Mussolini wanted to know whether Donovan had served alongside Italian troops in World War I. What did he think of them? Donovan was blunt. They appeared to lack discipline in the ranks. Mussolini assured him the Italian army had been changed at his orders. Their success in Ethiopia showed that.

Mussolini had more questions. Was Roosevelt popular? Donovan said he was. If there was another war would America expect Italy to remain neutral? Or would America remain neutral? Donovan said it would depend on what had caused the war. Mussolini laughed, came around the desk, said it was a good answer, and embraced Donovan.

That evening in the Vatican, Donovan met Francis Cardinal Spellman, the archbishop of New York. After Donovan described his meeting with Mussolini and his visit to Berlin, Spellman said it was time for America not to shrink from its obligation as a world power.

In his hotel bedroom that night, Spellman's words became the last ones in Donovan's report to Roosevelt on his visit to Rome.

....

Now, on that Sunday afternoon as he shook hands with Stephenson and boarded the Clipper seaplane flight to London, both men knew Donovan faced a difficult mission. He had told Stephenson the question uppermost in Roosevelt's mind was that while he hoped Britain would survive, could he be sure? Donovan was to find out if Britain could withstand the Luftwaffe and a cross-Channel invasion—and what help it would need from America.

As the flying boat headed out over the Atlantic, Donovan knew there was another matter Roosevelt had not yet decided upon. Apart from the Federal Bureau of Investigation, the United States had no real intelligence service like Britain's SOE. The FBI did little more than wiretap Teamster leaders or suspected Communists. Though the army, navy, and State Department had intelligence gathering units, Donovan had long seen them as dumping grounds for policemen, army officers, and FBI agents waiting to retire. The president had promised he would consider the matter. In the meantime he had suggested Donovan should formulate his proposal on paper for "a spy service" after returning from London.

....

In his office in Baker Street, Selwyn Jepson continued to assess the biographical details people had been asked to submit with photographs of places they had been to in Europe. He first divided the letters into piles: those written by men and those by women. He then separated them into those who spoke French and those who spoke other European languages. The French pile was noticeably larger. There was also a pile for those who said they were British-born, were married, and had children. Another pile contained various nationals, including Austrians, Belgians, Dutch, and Americans. Some of the writers were not suitable. Those letters were dismissed.

The piles were neatly laid out on Jepson's desk, and every morning he added to them, to select the men and women he would write to. He wanted those whose courage would be as important as their social background. He knew that while bravery would be important, some would be braver than others. The severe test would come if an agent were caught by the Gestapo. Would they be able to hold out for the forty-eight hours which it was calculated would allow enough time for their contacts and comrades to go underground? By the end of that period, Jepson believed an agent would be unable to reveal anything of value after being interrogated and tortured.

Gubbins had told Jepson every agent must be told about an L-tablet, a cyanide pill, which would be offered at the start of every mission but could be refused on religious or moral grounds.

Each potential agent received the same letter asking him or her to come for an interview "connected with the war effort." It was signed Captain "E. Potter," Jepson's chosen alias. Men were asked to come to room 505 in Sanctuary Buildings in Great Smith Street, close to Westminster Abbey. Women were called to room 15 in the Victoria Hotel in Northumberland Avenue, near Trafalgar Square. Both buildings had been requisitioned by the War Office, and Jepson had selected the rooms.

Jepson decided an interview could be spread over two or three sessions. During the first he listened to their stories, checking details on their vetting reports from initial research by MI5 and MI6 into their background. He hinted about them working in France or other countries in occupied Europe, which could be dangerous. Some interviewees, he expected, would volunteer immediately. At the second meeting he explained in detail what it meant to work for the SOE—the danger and possible death. The decision was theirs, but they had to keep it secret from everybody, including their family, and they should think it over carefully before deciding. Several women were married and had young children; Jepson assured them that the children would be safe and there would be regular reports on their progress. Contact with husbands could be maintained through a postbox address they would be given in due course.

At the last interview they gave him their final decisions and signed the Official Secrets Act. He then arranged for them to go and see Vera Atkins at Orchard Court.

....

While Donovan was flying across the Atlantic to England, Stewart Graham Menzies, the head of MI6, sat in his office at 54 Broadway, since 1924 the headquarters of the Secret Intelligence Service, the SIS, overlooking St. James's Park. On that July evening, Britain's senior intelligence officer was preparing a schedule Churchill had asked him to organize for the three-day visit of President Roosevelt's envoy.

The desk behind which Menzies sat was built from the mahogany panels from the cabin of Admiral Lord Nelson's *Victory*, and the longcase clock standing in one corner was made by the founder of the service, Mansfield Smith-Cumming. Tradition demanded that both pieces of furniture should remain in the office from one chief to another, each one known as "C."

Menzies knew in the backstabbing atmosphere of Whitehall some government ministers saw him as a shadowy figure who exercised undue influence over Churchill, himself always an admirer of intelligence. In the two years since he had accepted the position as the SIS chief, Menzies had survived criticism that his spies had failed to anticipate Mussolini's invasion of Abyssinia or more recently to provide an accurate figure for German rearmament.

Donovan's visit would be an opportunity to ensure his briefing would leave the envoy in no doubt that Britain was going to fight a merciless war with the help of its empire—and would welcome the support of the United States. Stephenson had sent a coded cable to

Menzies after seeing Donovan catch his flight, saying he was certain that not only would Roosevelt authorize "full support for Britain" but that Donovan planned to convince the president that the United States should have an intelligence service modeled on the SOE. It was another item to add to the briefing paper Menzies was preparing.

It included details from the Air Ministry of aircraft production and, from the Admiralty, the deployment of ships on coastal patrols and hunting U-boats. Government economists and leaders of industry had provided figures of factory output and the Ministry of Food details of agricultural production and fishery catches.

At the top of the list of people Donovan was to meet were the king and queen for lunch at Buckingham Palace. There would also be a visit to an RAF fighter squadron and the control center for London fire and rescue teams. A day had been set aside to show Donovan how far Britain had already gone to help occupied Europe resist the Nazis. His guide would be Gubbins.

The visit would conclude with dinner with Churchill. The prime minister had told Menzies he wanted Donovan to fly home with a clear understanding that, after all he had seen, he should convince Roosevelt not only that Britain would defeat Hitler but that it would do so more quickly with American support.

....

In Washington, General Friedrich von Boetticher—since 1933, the military attaché at the German embassy—continued to compose his cables to the Auswärtiges Amt, the Foreign Ministry, on Wilhelmstrasse in Berlin.

He had become friends with many American generals, including George S. Patton. These relationships enabled him to observe numerous troop maneuvers, visit important sites, and attend lectures, which gave him a detailed picture of US military capabilities. Since the beginning of the war, Hitler wanted personal reports and precise details of the growth of American arms.

Boetticher sent his messages every three or four days, filled with information he also culled from the American press or radio broadcasts:

Australian troops had arrived in Egypt; a speech in Ottawa by Britain's air chief marshal Hugh Dowding revealed that RAF fighters had "detectors" to spot Luftwaffe crossing the Channel; American forces would be 1.4 million strong in 1939. The information came from the annual report to Congress on the armed forces and had made headlines a few days earlier.

It earned him a telegram of thanks from Hitler. Like his führer, the attaché peppered his cables with attacks on American Jews: "They run America within the framework of the Jewish conviction regarding the power of business and money" and "President Roosevelt is the exponent of the Jews."

In a follow-up cable the attaché predicted that his sources had indicated "There is no danger of an intervention in the war by the United States."

....

After Donovan settled into his suite in the Savoy, Menzies sent a staff car to bring him to dinner at his home at 21 Queen Anne's Gate, bordered by the Houses of Parliament and Westminster Abbey.

Menzies had furnished the spacious apartment in a style that reflected his family's status as courtiers for the British throne down the generations. There were paintings and photographs of ancestors whose privileges and power had helped to create the British Empire. On side tables were silver-framed pictures of his own days at Eton and his travels through Africa and Europe. He spoke French and German fluently and had become admired as a horseman, riding with the aristocrats of the Beaufort and Quorn foxhunting packs. In World War I he had served on Sir Douglas Haig's staff as an intelligence officer at army headquarters. A photograph hung in the entrance hall of him in the days of the war, resplendent in the uniform of a captain in one of the British Army's most prestigious regiments, the Life Guards, with the Distinguished Service Order and Military Cross ribbon he had won at Ypres.

Returning to England after the war he had become a man-about-town with a succession of pretty society women on his arm. He was also rumored to be the son of his mother's affair with King Edward VII. She had been a lady-in-waiting to the Royal Family. His connection in the political world grew and included Churchill, who recommended that Menzies should be recruited by MI6. Its founder—Mansfield Smith-Cumming, a plump, balding figure with a gold-rimmed monocle—wrote all his orders in green ink and signed them with *C*, for *Chief*.

Menzies had always hoped to one day continue the tradition by becoming chief himself, as he steadily worked his way up through the MI6 departments in Broadway. From time to time he was sent on missions to various stations in the empire; India, South Africa, Australia, and New Zealand were included in his sea voyages. In 1935, an experienced officer, he became the head of Section Two, responsible for all overseas stations. By the end of the year he was promoted to be the deputy director of the SIS. It was a time when its chief, Hugh Sinclair, also used his green ink to battle against the peacetime budget cuts by the Treasury. Only Berlin and Paris stations were kept at full strength.

Early in 1936, Sinclair told Menzies that he had been diagnosed with lung cancer. Menzies had developed a liking for his chief and urged Sinclair to consult the best cancer specialist in London. While Sinclair was in the hospital for tests, Menzies took over the SIS, sitting in Sinclair's office, reading well into the evening what crossed his desk, and signing reports to Lord Halifax, the foreign minister, in green ink with a bold *C*. They mostly concerned the growing threat Hitler posed.

In the spring of that year Sinclair appeared in the office, a wan-faced figure. He asked Menzies to remain in charge while he convalesced and to arrange for the SIS codebreakers to be moved to the country mansion that had been purchased before he had been hospitalized. As Menzies supervised the move to Bletchley Park, Sinclair collapsed and was again hospitalized. In 1938, while still acting head of the SIS, Menzies found himself plunged into the Sudeten crisis over Hitler's threats to Czechoslovakia, and he accompanied Prime Minister Neville Chamberlain to Munich to meet Hitler and try, in Chamberlain's words, to bring "peace in our time to Europe."

On November 4, 1939, Sinclair died. By then war had broken out and Menzies had been already confirmed as the third chief of the SIS.

....

Over dinner on that July evening in 1941, Donovan's lawyerly questions drew out Menzies's background. Donovan suspected that his host was happy to share with him so that he could tell Roosevelt. As the evening passed the conversation became more concerned with the war. Menzies admitted that while the possibility of an invasion had once been a major concern, Britain's coastal defenses had been prepared. He then turned to the SOE. Its creation had led to a different concept of how the war would be fought. Sabotage and subversion would have an increasing role to support the bombing raids on Germany. The SOE would use a range of esoteric actions to create mayhem and confusion in Europe. Menzies was frank: some of those actions would be outside the work of both MI6 and MI5.

Donovan would recall how Menzies had paused before he said: "Churchill not only wants SOE to infiltrate occupied Europe with its specially trained agents, but he also wants to get women trained as agents. We have never done that before."

That night in his hotel suite, Donovan made notes about the meeting with Menzies. Under the function of the SOE, he wrote "women" and circled the word. It was his way of reminding himself to further explore their role.

....

Next morning Gubbins collected Donovan from the Savoy. In their uniforms, both cut imposing figures. As the staff car drove away from the hotel, Gubbins said they were off to see "Churchill's wizards."

Their first stop was a guarded warehouse in a bombed street in London's East End. Gubbins explained the people working there were forgers, creating a range of faked currencies of the occupied countries, as well as the German Reichsmark.

The operation was supervised by the Treasury and included printers from Waterlow, the company that produced Britain's banknotes. A
number of the forgers had been released from prison on parole with the
permission of the Home Office to carry on their counterfeiting skills
as part of the war effort. There were refugees from Europe. Some were
Germans, or Jews who had fled from Austria, bringing with them the
printing plates they had used to forge money.

As Gubbins led Donovan around the various work areas, they paused
to watch the process that produced the fake currency notes. The paper,
provided by Waterlow, was briefly dipped in a solution of very weak tea,
then placed under blotting paper and passed under huge hot irons, which
dried it in seconds. The paper was then trimmed to size, rubbed with a
rag cloth, and placed on one of the plates to forge the note. Hundreds of
different currencies were continuously produced and checked before the
fake notes were placed on a conveyor belt and sent to the packing area,
where bundles of various notes were boxed up. Porters wheeled them
to a storeroom where they would be kept until they were dropped by
the RAF for the Resistance to destabilize the Reichsmark. Donovan and
Gubbins were each given a fake banknote as a memento before they left.

Their next stop was a laboratory near Tower Bridge. Its chemists
had produced a superstrength itching powder that would be smuggled
into a clothing factory supplying underwear for U-boat crews. Resistance
workers would sprinkle the powder on the garments before they were
sent to the submarines. Within days at sea, crews would be scratching
themselves nonstop.

The powder had also been introduced into German-controlled
brothels in occupied Europe. The whorehouses were supplied with
contraceptives by the German army. The brothel keepers opened the
packets and dusted the condoms with powder.

During the afternoon Gubbins brought Donovan to workshops in
various parts of the city. One produced invisible ink and fake documents. Another factory that made test tubes for hospitals had been
converted to make explosive devices. One was called limpet. Named after
the mollusks, which fasten themselves on rocks, the device had been

designed to attach to the hull of a German ship. A team of engineers had developed what they called the "time delay pencil," a copper tube containing a glass ampoule of explosive liquid connected to a spring-loaded firing pen. Small and reliable, the "pencils" were color-coded to indicate different timing intervals. For assassinations the pens were fitted with silencers and fired special bullets.

In the basement of the Natural History Museum in Kensington, Donovan and Gubbins watched medical students stamping foreign manufacturers' names on flashlights, batteries, wire cutters, compasses, and magnets before packing them in containers.

By that evening Gubbins had taken Donovan to more than twenty places where a wide range of supplies and weapons were being prepared and packed for the Resistance. They had then driven to an RAF station on the outskirts of London to meet on-call pilots waiting in their crew room for the signal to scrabble to intercept Luftwaffe bombers heading from France across the Channel toward London. The visit had ended when Donovan was taken to the main air defense center for the city. On a plotting table and wall maps, WAAFs—members of the Women's Auxiliary Air Force—continuously recorded information from airfields and observers along the coast.

....

The nightly blackout started when Gubbins brought Donovan to the guarded, sandbagged entrance to the Cabinet War Rooms in Westminster. A soldier saluted, checked their names on his clipboard, and motioned for them to enter. In a small waiting area, a FANY, her belt shining in the overhead light, greeted them with a salute, opened a reinforced door, and led them down a corridor. Its walls were shored up with heavy timbers. Gubbins told Donovan the ceiling was reinforced by four-foot-thick concrete.

Their escort led them past a portrait of the king, George VI, and a lithograph of London Bridge. At the end of the corridor, a WAAF waited outside a closed door. She opened it and stood aside, and Gubbins led Donovan into a conference room. At the far end of a polished table sat Winston Churchill in a leather armchair. He rose and greeted his guests warmly and motioned for them to sit on either side of him at the table, which was set for dinner.

On the wall were several maps of Europe, and Donovan realized this was the room Menzies had told him about, where Churchill and his key aides planned strategies to defeat Hitler. The prime minister poured them each a measure of whiskey and handed one to Donovan with an impish smile, noting that it was an Irish vintage, not the usual Scotch he drank. Donovan suspected it was Churchill's way of saying an Irish American was welcome, even if Ireland remained neutral. He made a mental note to ask Roosevelt to send Churchill a gift of the finest American liquor.

Churchill led the conversation as the meal was served. Had Donovan been impressed by what he had seen so far? He replied he was very impressed. Churchill's smile showed it was exactly what he had hoped. Showing his own hold on history, he said that the British philosopher Thomas Hobbes had said, "Force and fraud in war are the two cardinal virtues." The prime minister added Britain would use both.

Donovan saw an opening to develop his reason for being in England: it was time for both Churchill and Roosevelt to join forces and "come up with a game plan to defeat Hitler."

For more than an hour, with support from Gubbins, a steady agreement developed. From what Donovan would later say had started from "minus zero," he increasingly saw that Churchill not only would be an ideal partner for Roosevelt but could support his own idea of America having its own intelligence service and also provide it with the experience of both MI6 and MI5.

It was in the early hours when Donovan returned to the Savoy. As they said good night Gubbins said, "You played a blinder, Bill."

Donovan spent the rest of the night writing a report of the dinner and his day tour of the workplaces of "Churchill's Wizards."

....

Next morning Menzies joined Donovan for breakfast at the Savoy and handed him a pouch of documents explaining that Churchill wanted

Donovan to be "taken into our confidence to fully brief President Roosevelt." The pouch contained secret war planning documents and a copy of the memo Gubbins had sent to Churchill about the role women could play in the SOE.

Later that afternoon, sitting in his favorite seat in the seaplane for the flight home, Donovan speed-read the documents, a technique he had mastered before making a closing speech to a jury. Somewhere over the Atlantic he memorized what he would tell FDR.

Could what he had seen and learned during his visit be adopted into the intelligence service he envisaged for America? He knew that, since his youth, FDR had enjoyed reading spy stories. Stephenson had called him "a real cloak-and-dagger boy." Gubbins had said as much about Churchill. In his notebook, Donovan began to describe the kind of intelligence service America needed. He began with a definition. "Strategy without information upon which it can rely, is useless. Likewise, information is useless unless it is directed to a strategic purpose."

He wrote what Menzies had told him about interservice collaboration between MI6 and MI5 with the SOE, and noted that the existing arrangements between the US Army, US Navy, State Department, and the FBI would benefit from such mutual collaboration.

Before coming to London, Donovan had read the history of intelligence in war. How Hannibal, the Carthaginian military genius, had used his spies to rule the Mediterranean after beating the Romans; how Julius Caesar had sent spies to scout the land; how the codebreakers in Renaissance Venice had solved the dispatches of foreign diplomats; how through the centuries feudal rulers had used their spies as military strategists; how Helmuth Count von Moltke had created Germany's first Intelligence Bureau to get information he lacked about its enemies, and how it became the forerunner of the Abwehr, the German secret service Hitler had now claimed as his own.

Donovan had read about Mata Hari, the dancer who became an eponym for the spy, and as the plane headed for New York, he read Gubbins's memo on how the SOE would deploy women. Could they be incorporated into the intelligence service he envisaged? Could he expect them to do what the SOE was going to ask of its women?

....

In August 1941 a tall, distinguished-looking lady in her thirties, with shining red hair and a limp, arrived in the town of Vichy in France and headed to the police station to formally register her presence. In a Maryland accent she told the police her real name—there was no attempt at subterfuge—and explained she would be working in the area for the *New York Post*. Over the coming weeks she would quickly ingratiate herself with businessmen, police officers, and doctors, as well as black marketers and brothel owners. Her name was Virginia Hall.

Born in Baltimore on April 6, 1906, the youngest child of a wealthy family, Hall had graduated from schools and colleges in America as well as the Sorbonne in Paris. Her ambition was to become a career officer in America's Foreign Service. To kick-start her dream she had accepted a job in the mail room in the State Department Consulate in Warsaw. Hoping for promotion, she next accepted a higher-grade position in the Consulate in Turkey. Her duties were similar, her social life better: garden parties and snipe hunting in the mountains on weekends.

On a hunt she suffered a shooting accident when a gun went off and wounded her left leg, which then had to be amputated below the knee at the American Hospital in Istanbul to save her life. She was flown back to Baltimore to have an artificial leg fitted, together with a wooden foot with a rubber sole that would smooth out her gait as she walked. She named her false limb Cuthbert. Within a month she could walk again.

Hall wrote to the State Department asking to be once more posted to an embassy or consulate. "Any post in Spain is my choice. I want to learn Spanish. My second choice is Estonia or Peru." She was told there were no vacancies in any of her wish-list locations. But a "note has been made of your preference." Hall decided she would go to Paris.

Before leaving she had called a contact on the *New York Post* and offered to provide stories on the situation in Europe. She had hoped that the life of a reporter might replace her dream of being a Foreign Service officer.

....

In Paris, with France and Germany by now at war, she joined the French ambulance service. When the French signed an armistice with the Germans she escaped to Spain and then England, where in late 1940 she met Nicolas Bodington, a former Reuter's news agency journalist who was now second-in-command at F Section. Her linguistic skills and resourcefulness immediately attracted her to Bodington, and they discussed ways in which she could help.

In London, on a summer evening he had invited her to a cocktail party. The hostess was Vera Atkins. Andrew Park, the butler–turned–SOE recruit, served the drinks. The guests were a cross section of actors, journalists, and officers in the army and air force. At some point in the evening Atkins took Hall aside and asked her to tell her what Paris was now like. Hall had long given up being circumspect and said she would like nothing more than to go back and see the "filthy Jerries driven out." Atkins did not comment.

That night when the guests had left, Atkins sat at her desk, wrote a memo, and filed it in a folder marked PROSPECTS. It read: "Miss VH, an American, talked at my party last night of wanting to go back to France via Barcelona or Lisbon. She would join the Quaker organization as a cover. She also had an accreditation as a Foreign Correspondent for the *New York Post* as another cover."

On that August morning in 1941, the memo was the reason Hall had gone to the Vichy police station and registered her nationality and her journalist profession.

....

Hall had been given a crash course in weapons, communications, and security. She flew to Barcelona via Lisbon, and then continued by train to Vichy. She carried out an intelligence survey of the spa town which, because she had no wireless operator, was brought back to England by a fellow agent, Jacques de Guélis. Hall then moved into the Grand Nouvel Hotel in Lyon, establishing herself as the key liaison officer for the SOE's early activities in France. She found the first safe houses and recruited new resisters, helped an evasion line for shot-down airmen, met arriving agents—including Peter Churchill—and continued to cultivate her contacts in the Vichy regime. She was a key spy for the SOE before she became the OSS's greatest female spy in France.

Radio operator Brian Stonehouse had had the most unfortunate arrival in France. He had parachuted into the Loire Valley only to find his radio had been caught up a tree. He spent five nights in the woods trying to get it down, then found that it did not work properly. He would recall, "I was told not to go near Virginia unless it was a matter of life and death because she was being watched by French police and, I presume, the Germans as well. But things got so complicated in Lyon that my courier and I went to see her and she was very helpful in getting us started and organized."

Hall helped him find shelter. He was soon joined by another female agent, Valentine "Blanche" Charlet, and together they went to work. Hall had built up a substantial network, and Charlet now took over much of it to allow the American to lay low.

Born in Belgium, Charlet was forty-six and running an art gallery in Brussels when the country was occupied. Among her clients had been English buyers, and she had fled to London, where she found a job as a receptionist in a West End hotel frequented by Buckmaster. He had already recruited two other women from the staff, Yvonne Rudellat and Andrée Borrel. Charlet's fluent French had made her his third to join F Section.

Hall saw that Lyon had become an increasingly dangerous place to be based. The Resistance activity in the area had caused the Germans and the Vichy government severe devastation. The curfew was being rigidly enforced and safe houses were being blown. On October 24, detector vans picked up Brian Stonehouse's radio signals, and the Milice, the French militia, arrested him and Charlet when she arrived for a prearranged meeting. Both were handed over to the Gestapo.

To maintain her cover, Hall filed a number of stories for the *New York Post*, each creating a picture of the changing nature of life in Vichy France. On September 4, 1941, she wrote, "The years have rolled back here in Vichy. There are no taxis at the station, only half a dozen buses, and a few one-horse shays. I took a bus using *gazogène*, charcoal instead of gas, to my hotel. I haven't seen any butter and there is very little milk."

Another story revealed the new restrictions on Jews, forbidding them from a number of occupations, including barber, merchant, and real estate work. On January 22, 1942, in one of her last news stories, she said theft of food had become commonplace as the people went hungry. "The average weight loss today is 12 pounds per person not only from lack of food, but increased physical activity and mental strain," she reported.

Following Pearl Harbor, Hall was classed as an enemy alien and her work moved underground. In the summer of 1942, she took on a new identity, Marie Monin, and became increasingly aware that the Germans were pursuing her. Soon after, she discovered she was on the most-wanted list of Schutzstuffel (SS) Obersturmführer Klaus Barbie, who had recently arrived in Dijon.

Hall's work for the SOE in France had begun almost a year before Buckmaster formally started to infiltrate women into the country. In November 1942, when the Germans crossed the demarcation line, ending any pretense of Vichy's independence, many agents and *résistants* chose to flee south toward the Pyrenees. The Gestapo closed in on Lyon, with officers ordered to track down Hall, the operative the Resistance called "*La dame qui boite*" ("the limping lady"). "The woman who limps is one of the most dangerous Allied agents in France," declared the Gestapo order. "We must find and destroy her."

By the time the Gestapo reached Lyon, she had gone south to the Perpignan. She then made a grueling forty-eight-hour climb over the Pyrenees and down into Spain. By the time she reached Spanish soil, her left leg was a bleeding stump.

Back in London she resolved that her war was not over. She told Buckmaster that her own country would soon land agents in occupied

Europe. She would be emblematic of the growing cooperation between the SOE and the Americans. The SOE sent her on a wireless training course and prepared to send her back into France.

....

The morning after Donovan read Gubbins's memo on the SOE's use of female agents on the flight back to Washington from London, he was shown into the Oval Office by Grace Tully, Roosevelt's secretary. She told him that the president had scheduled him a full hour before he chaired a cabinet meeting on defense and foreign affairs.

After FDR greeted him, Donovan began by describing London at war—the spirit of the people, the blackouts, the air defenses—and moved on to Menzies and Gubbins, deftly painting portraits of their lifestyles and how impressed he was with the plans for the SOE and the idea to use women.

Roosevelt listened attentively, occasionally nodding and chuckling at what Donovan called the prime minister's "complete frankness" and the unprecedented access he had been given.

The president asked, "So what does Churchill want?"

Donovan told him Churchill needed more planes to search for and bomb the U-boats in the Atlantic and more bombers to be fitted with America's Sperry bombsights to hit more German targets in the Ruhr. Above all, he wanted destroyers to protect convoys bringing supplies to Britain, especially from Canada and South America.

Roosevelt paused before saying it was a large order to fulfill but it would be done. He said after Donovan had gone to London, Stephenson had come to Washington and had been lobbying those in the administration who agreed it was essential for the United States to find every way to partner the United Kingdom.

As his scheduled hour came to an end, Donovan turned to the subject he wanted to raise. He said America needed an organization capable of collecting and analyzing information and data that could threaten national security. It should be like Britain's SIS.

The president said the idea of a new intelligence department was very much along the lines he had been considering. The promise of support from British intelligence was important, but an American organization would need someone who knew the setup in London and had met practically every European leader in prewar time. Roosevelt offered Donovan the job.

Donovan accepted.

The president called in Grace Tully. She should prepare an executive order for him to sign to create a new office. It would be known as the Coordinator of Information, COI. All government departments would be required to cooperate. Its director would be William Donovan, who would report directly to the president.

3

The Magician's Airfield

GUBBINS SUGGESTED TO WINSTON Churchill that the SOE should consist of three groups: agents recruited to harass the enemy, instructors to train them, and scientists and technicians to invent and manufacture devices for undercover warfare. The training schools and research and development sites would be in country houses requisitioned at the outbreak of the war. The prime minister came to regard them as "my Academy of Ungentlemanly Warfare" with Gubbins as its headmaster.

Many of the instructors were British soldiers who had returned from Dunkirk and Norway initially to be trained to defend the British mainland against the German forces assembling across the Channel. When the threat of invasion faded, Churchill told the War Cabinet that the troops would be used to train SOE recruits and "provide a swift means of our return to the coast of France."

Gubbins had decided the perfect place for training schools was in the West Highlands of Scotland. Its mountains, ravines, and lochs had for centuries been breeding grounds for generations of fierce-fighting, tartan-kilted warriors. Thousands of Highlanders had served in British battalions in the Great War, on the Western Front, Gallipoli, Macedonia, and Salonika. Some had served under Gubbins in North Russia in 1918 to deny both German and Bolshevik forces access to the ports of Murmansk and Arkhangelsk. He had handpicked a number of them to become SOE instructors. Some would be sent to Canada, where the first training camp overseas was to be based.

....

The camp was set up after William Stephenson, Britain's intelligence chief in North America, had proposed to Donovan that although the United States had not yet entered the war, Americans should be trained alongside SOE agents in preparation for the fast-approaching time they would be needed. They should be taught "to be calculating and reckless with disciplined daring."

On December 6, 1941, Stephenson flew to Ottawa to lease 260 acres of Canadian government–owned land on the north shore of Lake Ontario at Whitby. It had been a training camp for soldiers. With accommodation and facilities for five hundred men and women, it was located between the sleepy towns of Oshawa and Whitby. On the leasing agreement between Canada and Britain it was identified as "Military Camp 103." Within the SOE it was referred to as Camp X.

Its acres of Canadian farmland were separated from the United States by forty miles of cold lake water and guarded by the Royal Canadian Mounted Police and British commandos. After the lease document was signed by Stephenson and the Canadian government, it was sent to the Crown Office in London, and the land was registered as British property.

Soon one-man submarines and underwater demolition devices were being tested in the lake. Radio aerials were erected that linked Camp X to London.

As well as instructors from SOE training camps in Scotland, WAAFs, FANYs, and cooks had been flown in from England to service the staff and recruits. Camp X had its own cinema, athletic fields, and an airfield and aircraft for parachute training.

Among the instructors was William Fairbairn. He was tall, with thick lips and hair so fine it appeared to be hardly there at all. He spoke fluent Mandarin, a language he had mastered during thirty years with the police in Shanghai, China's most chaotic and violent city. His body, arms, and legs were covered with the scars of knife wounds inflicted during street fights while he made arrests. A master in the art of jujitsu, he was also an expert pistol shot and a strict disciplinarian, who commanded a strong sense of loyalty from those who followed him.

When Fairbairn had joined the city's police force, Shanghai was known as the "whore of Asia" with its estimated seven thousand prostitutes, many working in opium dens in a city where the annual gambling turnover was estimated at four times that of Monte Carlo. Its criminals specialized in kidnapping and armed robbery, and hurled homemade bombs at the police in what became nightly battles.

Fairbairn had opened a training school to teach the police. He had furnished it like a Chinese gambling house: dark inside with creaking wooden staircases and dummy figures in the rooms each holding a gun. These were booby-trapped with firecrackers and triggered by trip wires on the floorboards. Fairbairn had told his trainees they must take in the situation in a flash and shoot to kill. The old building echoed day and night with gunfire hitting the dummy targets. Within months the Shanghai Municipal Police Force became the most feared across Asia.

Fairbairn had furthered his own reputation as the author of a bestselling textbook, *Scientific Self Defense*. Required reading for all his police officers, it also had become widely read in the United States under the title *Get Tough*. It had a preface by the Hollywood star Douglas Fairbanks: "I do not know of any more interesting book to study and the author has an intensive and practical knowledge of his art. I commend this book to all those who have not been born with great physical strength."

In trenchant prose, its pages detailed how to deliver blows with the side of the hand, how to kick, and how to make use of knees, elbows, and finger jabs.

Gubbins had read the book by the time Fairbairn had returned to England in 1940. He had sent for the police chief and offered him a post as an SOE instructor with the rank of a major and a brief to go to Scotland where six SOE training camps had been set up. Fairbairn was to teach close-quarter combat, knife work, shooting, and hand-to-hand fighting. "It will be essential to confine the teaching to what is simple, easily learned, and deadly," Gubbins had told him.

Fairbairn had described how he would teach recruits how to shoot accurately in the dark, when all that could be seen was the shadow of a target, and how to fire in two-shot bursts—what he called his double tap system—to make certain an opponent was dead. They would be instructed in using catapults to fire stones or nails against a sentry and how to deliver stunning blows to the solar plexus, neck, or under the nose. He would also show them how to use the coshes he had developed for his officers to use in Shanghai.

Each cosh was a metal tube with a spring inside attached to a lump of lead at the end. Fairbairn had demonstrated to Gubbins that as he swung a cosh at a tailor's dummy, the spring ejected the lead against the target. Gubbins had ordered boxes of coshes to be made and special dummies produced for agents to practice on.

....

When Fairbairn had arrived at Camp X, he assembled his class and repeated what he had told trainees in the SOE camps in Scotland.

"Some of you are going to be shocked by the methods you will be shown. In war you cannot afford the luxury of squeamishness. The methods you will be taught I have developed over years."

On the classroom blackboard he wrote his rules. "You must practice every day what you have learned and become instinctive and automatic in all your movements. You must perform your action with maximum speed. You will always remember you are being trained to disable and kill your enemy. The knife you have each been given is your silent weapon. Its blade is double-edged and the grip designed to protect your hand when you use it to stab or cut a throat. All this you will learn. I teach Gutter Fighting. Fair play is not on the curriculum."

Like instructors at training camps in the United Kingdom, those at Camp X made weekly reports that evaluated the trainees' progress in loading and dismantling a weapon in the dark and placing bombs inside vehicles. There were also assessments of their fitness after cross-country runs, long-distance swims, and obstacle courses that were constantly waterlogged in which trainees sank up to their knees in mud.

Instructors paid close attention to recruits at the shooting ranges. Live rounds were fired, bullets zipping over the heads of trainees as they stormed a derelict building where metal pop-up targets, fashioned in the image of German soldiers, had to be hit. Failure to strike every target led to being hauled out of bed to repeat the attack in the middle of the night.

The classroom sessions included memorizing the different ranks and uniforms of the Gestapo and Wehrmacht; the French Milice; the Feld-gendarmerie, the equivalent of the British military police; the Geheime Feldpolizei, the secret field police; the Sicherheitspolizei, the security police; and the Kriminalpolizei, the criminal police.

Those who graduated from Camp X were told they would be sent to England to undergo further training at what were called "finishing schools." Gubbins had told Maurice Buckmaster, the head of SOE's F Section, he would have first call on secret agents from those schools.

....

On Sunday morning, July 10, 1942, a camouflaged car drove through an area of the Surrey countryside in England known as the Hog's Back. The driver was in her late thirties and wore a FANY uniform. She had been a housemistress at a girls' boarding school before she had been recalled to the FANYs a year earlier. Sitting beside her was an officer in the uniform of a major in the Coldstream Guards, one of the oldest regiments in the British Army.

Roger Christopher de Wesselow looked about sixty, ten years older than his age. He had survived the First World War, where he had been a brother officer of Gubbins. Their relationship was the reason he was chosen as commandant of the training school for the French Section at Wanborough Manor in West Surrey.

In his baggage was a history Gubbins had given him of the manor's past. After centuries of surviving the reigns of the Tudor kings and Elizabeth I, it had been renovated in 1527 and had become a sanctuary for Cistercian monks, who had grazed sheep on the manor land and sold the fleeces in the London wool market. For centuries afterward it had been the home of the Earls of Onslow. When the noble line died out, a succession of owners bought the estate. The outbreak of the Great War in 1914 led to its owner, Sir Algernon West, suggesting the manor could become a convalescent home for wounded officers. The War Office had ignored the offer. When West died in 1921, a millionaire timber merchant bought the estate as a family home and hired a team of landscapers to restore the grounds and build a swimming pool. The rich and famous became regular guests, but the Depression saw the merchant sell the estate along with the title of Lord of the Manor that went with it. The new owner was still there when World War II started. In 1941 he was served with a requisition order. Since then the manor had remained empty until a few months earlier, when a team from the Ministry of Works had moved in to refurbish the mansion as F Section's training school.

De Wesselow's driver had collected him from what had been his base for months, an orphanage on Wandsworth Common in London, which had been requisitioned to serve as a holding camp for various nationalities, the majority of whom spoke French. He had been one of the intelligence officers who had questioned them as potential agents. Buckmaster told de Wesselow he was appointing him to run the training school. Days later de Wesselow had received an MI5 security file on the driver. It was marked FULL CLEARANCE.

De Wesselow had told the driver she would be the housekeeper of the training school. There would be a kitchen and laundry staff. A quartermaster would be responsible for all supplies. Visitors and phone calls were forbidden. Staff who wanted to send letters should bring them to his office. The spoken language would be French with English kept to a minimum.

By the time the car reached the north end of the Hog's Back, de Wesselow had satisfied himself that her fluency in French was as good as his own. It was noon when the car passed the boundary marker stone of Wanborough parish. Beyond were its cottage houses and barns. Parishioners were emerging from the village church, which had stood for twelve centuries. The worshippers were mostly women and children; the armed forces had enlisted the men and teenagers of Wanborough. Some had been posted overseas; others were in the Home Guard.

Farther along the road, beyond the church graveyard, was the manor. At the estate entrance was a guard hut. A soldier checked their papers and waved them in. Wanborough Manor was entering a new phase in its history. That Sunday evening de Wesselow telephoned the switchboard at 64 Baker Street to inform the duty officer that the SOE training station was operational.

....

Sixty miles north of Wanborough Manor was SOE Experimental Station XV. Before the war the roadhouse, known as the Thatched Barn, was a popular stopover on the road out of London for door-to-door salesmen, lovers on their way to a weekend in the countryside, and truck drivers loaded with goods for the Midlands. It stood in its own grounds with bars and a popular restaurant, bedrooms, and a swimming pool. It had been requisitioned at the outbreak of war, and a high wire security fence had been erected around the property with a large notice announcing, GOVERNMENT PROPERTY. TRESPASS FORBIDDEN. The gated entrance had a guard hut manned around the clock.

The new occupants were middle aged and experts in their professions. They came from university science departments and research institutes or had been employed by the Air Ministry and the Admiralty. Some had worked at Woolwich Arsenal, Britain's weapons research center, or at Porton Down, the country's chemical and biological warfare establishment, established in 1916 to develop defenses against gas and germ warfare. All had signed the Official Secrets Act. The experts would be paid their usual salaries but would be exempt from income tax. They would all be commissioned with various ranks as officers into the army, navy, or air force during the war.

All had degrees in chemistry and biology, and their work would be to use a mixture of chemicals. Potassium and chlorine would be combined with sulfuric acid to create time switches to detonate bombs that would blow a train engine off the rails; incendiary bombs would be fitted inside fountain pens, filled with a liquid chemical that would demolish a room.

Between them they converted the Barn into workshops with Nissen huts around the grounds. The Ministry of Munitions had built a magazine to store explosives to be used in experiments. A hut had been equipped with drawing boards on which weapons were designed. Another hut contained a printing press to run off instructions on how to use new weapons. A small team of FANYs typed the instructions in French. A middle-aged woman sat at a desk and proofread the typing. The instructions would be later dropped by the RAF to the Resistance.

In other workshops technicians worked in an atmosphere of good humor as they adapted scientific principles to produce limpet mines, incendiary liquids, and plastic containers to carry messages by secret agents. Those had been designed to be hidden in the anal and vaginal orifices of the human body and had been tested on FANYs on the Barn staff.

In the swimming pool, the first midget submarines were tested. In a workshop, technicians who had built motorcycles for prewar international races created a small motorbike that could be folded to fit into a parachute container to be dropped to agents. In another workshop, women made a device designed to explode under pressure when camouflaged inside a small stone, a lump of mud, or a cow pie. The tire busters were intended to be placed in the path of a German convoy.

Every day a van arrived with boxes of dead mice and rats. The two vets on the staff scooped out their innards, replaced them with plastic explosives, and sewed them up. The rodents were to be placed near furnaces in German weapons factories in the expectation the corpses would be thrown into the furnace.

In another hut, explosive coal was prepared. Each lump consisted of a hollow shape that could be packed with explosives and painted black. These could be dropped with other arms and supplies to the Resistance, who could hide them among the fuel supplied for locomotives. The charges were capable of destroying an engine's boiler.

Elsewhere in the grounds of the Thatched Barn were blast walls behind which incendiaries were tested. Behind one wall was a small pond into which researchers tossed bars of soap that exploded in the water. The soap was being tested to leave in German barracks' washrooms.

Marjorie Hindley worked in the Gun Room, where she was one of the women assembling silencers for guns. They were tested on a small shooting range at the back of the hut. For Hindley, "The work was motivated by keeping company with so many talented people."

It was a view echoed by the staff of Experimental Station XV as they gathered in the evening in the bar and sang wartime songs around the piano.

....

Gubbins started each day with a meeting with his operational staff to discuss the overnight reports from training schools and their recommendations as to who should be sent to one of the Finishing Schools to complete their preparations before being sent into occupied Europe. Meetings ended with discussions on the latest reports from the research and experimental stations and their latest gadgets and weapons.

Station VI-A was housed in what had been a prewar factory producing cheap clothes for the mass market. It now produced French clothing, which was copied from French newspaper photographs and catalogs; the garments had to be perfect down to the last stitch and button for an agent to wear and pass scrutiny by the Germans.

Station VII-E had been a factory making cough mixtures for High Street shops. Now it produced German bicycle pumps that exploded when used. Stations VII-B and VII-C before the war had produced materials for the building trade. Now they assembled radio transmitter sets for wireless operators, which contained seventy-foot-long aerials and specially tuned crystals to avoid German detection vans when transmitting. Gubbins had visited the radio training school at Thame Park in Oxfordshire and told the staff their work and equipment was "the most valuable link in our chain of operations." He had met, for the first time, the women who would be trained to be secret agents.

....

In Washington, DC, Donovan continued to plan the role women would play. Some he decided would "be the invisible apron strings sat behind desks and filing secret reports or answering the telephone. Tasks like that would ensure the flawless performance of my organization."

But he envisaged there would be more in the future for women to do. They would be a key part of the five branches he had already created on paper. There would be Research and Analysis (R&A) for the collection of overt and covert material for use in planning subversive operations. Special Operations (SO) would carry out sabotage and guerrilla warfare. Maritime Unit (MU) would carry out attacks on enemy shipping. Counter Intelligence (X-2) would work closely with the SOE. Morale Operations (MO) would use persuasion, penetration, and intimidation by disguising the truth, slanting stories, and spreading rumors against the enemy. Donovan had devised the branches to protect America once it entered the war.

The women he would select would have linguistic skills that would allow them to operate in occupied Europe, train and organize Resistance groups, unmask traitors, and destroy the morale of the enemy.

"They have much to learn, how to burgle, blow safes, and steam open letters," Eloise Page, his secretary, would recall him telling her as she typed his ideas for the future. "He could be an unreasonable man with an Irish temper, but he could also charm the birds off the trees as he kept on dictating his ideas for me to type as the night wore on," she remembered.

....

SOE agents received their wings after parachute training at Ringway Airfield, Manchester. Each had to make five jumps, two at night, in a camouflaged jumpsuit and padded helmet. The suit pockets contained a folding shovel, flashlight, pistol, dagger, medical kit, and money (paper and coins). The suits had a full-length zipper to allow the jumper to "walk out" upon landing. Beneath their suits each agent wore his or her civilian clothes, made by Station VI-A.

Agents at the training schools in Scotland were shown how to live off the countryside by trapping rabbits and cooking various plants, which would later help them to subsist in the Pyrenean foothills and other areas. They also became experts in using plastic explosive. The color of butter, it had a distinct almond smell. Agents were shown how to disguise the explosive by molding it into a chocolate bar shape and breaking off a piece to embed it in a target. The hills of Inverness echoed with explosions as old trucks or deserted sheds were blown up as part of their training in guerrilla war tactics.

In the winter the slopes of the Highlands saw SOE trainees undergoing various tests on the iron-hard snow, their skis crunching as they hauled a sleigh through an obstacle course known as Sniper Valley, where live rounds were fired at targets in the image of enemy soldiers.

Yvonne Baseden, slim and gifted with a natural grace, had joined the WAAF at the age of eighteen after leaving a convent school. Posted to the Air Ministry in London, the only daughter of an engineer in the Royal Flying Corps and of a French château owner, she was assigned to translate technical documents from French into English. She had applied to join the SOE and had been selected to become a wireless operator and had been sent to Scotland. She would recall, "Lectures were held in a hut on an island in a Highland river."

Agents had to wade through the ice-cold water to reach the hut to be briefed on their next exercise as they sat in wet clothes. "We were either wet up to the waist or perhaps even the chest. Discomfort went with the training." Baseden would be among the first twenty women agents.

An eclectic group of trainees, men and women whom Selwyn Jepson had recruited, were being made ready for operational service. The last stage was to send them to Finishing Schools.

....

Schools were established among the tall trees and around the medieval ruins of Beaulieu Abbey and its cloisters on the estate of Edward, Lord Montagu Beaulieu, deep in the New Forest of Hampshire. It had been among the first properties requisitioned for SOE use because its cottages, lodges, and large private houses provided ready-made accommodation for agents and their instructors. FANYs performed the duties of housekeeping.

There were twenty officers on the teaching staff and a dozen more listed as "house masters," one for each school. They sat with trainees at meals and accompanied them on their walks through the estate to enjoy the peace of the cloisters while students were encouraged to discuss their class work. The house masters reported the conversation to the teaching staff to judge agents' progress.

Their syllabus had been created by Gubbins and the Secret Intelligence Service, MI6. Gubbins had established a strong working relationship with its head, Stewart Menzies. The courses at Beaulieu had been designed not only to expand upon what agents had learned at other training schools but to ensure they understood that life in occupied France was regularly changing. Women were no longer given a cigarette ration; coffee was only available in cafés or restaurants without milk, and to put milk into a teacup would be a giveaway that an agent was English. To look right, and not left, before crossing a busy French road was another mistake that would be spotted, along with cycling on the wrong side of a road.

It was stressed to agents that they must live how the person of their cover story would live, according to their social class or income. A wireless operator, Yvonne Cormeau, was warned by a peasant woman while posing as a farm worker: "The farmer's wife told me, 'Don't wear a watch. No woman who looks after cows would be able to afford a watch.'"

An entire class was shown how to spot if an agent was being followed and how to use the right level of self-confidence if stopped by a German patrol and ordered to produce papers.

While French women did not smoke in public, women agents were taught to write a message on a thin roll of onionskin and insert it into a cigarette with a needle. To test this method of passing messages, agents were selected to work in pairs. One was told to take a few puffs while his partner waited at a prearranged place. The smoker would extinguish his cigarette as he approached his partner, drop the butt, and walk on. His partner would discreetly pick up the stub, pocket it, and remove the message. The test was constantly repeated until their tutor was satisfied they had the confidence to do it in France, in the street. All agents, male and female, learned how to choose hiding places where messages could be left among the Beaulieu Abbey ruins, placing them under a stone or in the cracks of a cloister wall.

Upon arrival each potential agent underwent a clinical interview by one of the psychologists at Beaulieu to assess any sign of nerve failure in an agent that the training staff had noted during a previous course and that suggested an agent could be a security risk to send into France.

"[The agent] would have known the other agents on a course, even if their names were aliases. Caught by the Gestapo the agent would be tortured for their identities and missions and the training they had undergone. Beaulieu and SOE would be at serious risk," recalled psychologist Andrew Knott.

To avoid that happening, agents who received adverse security reports that did not encourage trust in them were sent to what was known as the "refractory cooler" in a remote part of the Scottish Highlands at Inverlair. Guarded by prison wardens, they were held there until all the other agents they had known at Beaulieu were judged to be safe when the time came to send them to France. Those held in the refractory were constantly reminded of the Beaulieu motto: "He that has learned a secret should not only hide it, but hide that he has it to hide."

Only when the reminder had been drummed into him at Inverlair was a failed agent posted to a military unit to fill the general manpower shortage. Some found themselves on coastal guard duty looking out toward the France they would never go to.

There are no records that female agents were ever sent to the "refractor cooler." Vera Atkins would recall it "was a matter of pride that I made sure that every woman, from the moment she was selected to the moment she landed in France, that she never committed a breach of security."

....

After its formation, Gubbins had come to terms with the fact that the SOE would be resented by some government departments, especially the Foreign Office where staff dismissed it as "having a philosophy of action for action's sake."

Such infighting was conducted at the highest level, nowhere more so than Gubbins's relations with the Air Ministry over the matter of providing aircraft to fly agents to France. Sir Arthur "Bomber" Harris, the commander in chief of Bomber Command, had an obsessive belief that his bombers would win the war. More than once at staff meetings he had said, "SOE should be regarded as no more than an unorthodox instrument."

Gubbins knew that Harris had refused to support the request of Resistance groups in Poland and Czechoslovakia for RAF long-range aircraft to fly to those two countries and drop supplies to support sabotage and subversion. Harris felt such missions would "be at the expense of RAF bombing operations on German targets." Harris had written to Charles Portal, the chief of the Air Staff, that "parting with even a few of my precious aircrews will decimate my reserves. My bombing offensive is not a gamble; it is a gilt-edged investment. I cannot divert aircraft from a certainty, to a gamble which may be completely worthless."

The decision had caused great upset for the Polish and Czech governments-in-exile. Their pilots had arrived in Britain to fight in the Battle of Britain and had volunteered to become aircrews for bombing raids on Germany. Their request to be allowed to fly RAF planes to their homelands to supply the Resistance was largely ignored. Gubbins, who admired them, found he was fighting his own battle with the Air Ministry.

Portal, never a fan of Gubbins, wrote to Gladwyn Jebb, who was the link between the SOE and the Foreign Office, "I think that the dropping of men dressed in civilian clothes for the purpose of killing members of the opposing forces is not an operation with which the Royal Air Force should be associated." The SOE agents were simply "assassins," he stated.

Copies of the correspondence found their way to Menzies's office at 54 Broadway, the London MI6 headquarters. From the start of their friendship, the spymaster had shown an instinctive understanding of the problems Gubbins faced. They would meet once a week at White's Club in Piccadilly, where they were both members, and after dinner they played backgammon. He had shown the correspondence to Gubbins, who handed it back with a dismissive shrug.

Both knew that the SOE's enemies in Whitehall were still busy planting rumors that Churchill was considering placing the SOE under the chief of staff or the Foreign Office. In the corridors of power in the War Office and Air Ministry, the talk was that the SOE had still to justify the prime minister's call to set Europe alight.

Gubbins and his staff had been sarcastically dubbed the "Baker Street Irregulars" by those who strongly disapproved of the sort of action that the SOE was pursuing and which Portal called "the fanatics whose role has not been worked out."

Gubbins told Menzies he would need aircraft as soon as possible to send his agents into occupied Europe. The Lysander was a single-engine, high-wing monoplane that had been designed as a spotter aircraft for the Royal Artillery. Gubbins was told while they were useless for the task for which they were built, they could be adapted to land and take off at night from a field, making them ideal to drop or pick up agents. Menzies said he would raise the matter with Churchill.

....

In a reshuffle of his cabinet, Churchill moved Dalton from the Ministry of Economic Warfare to the Board of Trade. His replacement was Lord Selborne, fifty-four years old, a small, stooping figure with protruding gray eyes, who would smile at any attractive woman who caught his attention. From their first meeting he told Gubbins, "I will have no desire to interfere in the everyday work of SOE. Just tell me what you need."

Gubbins said he wanted Lysanders and an airfield for them to operate from. It must be near London and take into account prevailing winds that would affect flights to and from Europe. It would also need to be large enough to accommodate any other aircraft the SOE would need. Selborne replied it was a reasonable request. It was the start of a relationship in which there would be a mutual liking and respect.

Gubbins had not long to wait before Selborne told him that Churchill had authorized the secretary of air, Archibald Sinclair, to provide seven Lysanders for the SOE's exclusive use, together with an airfield.

The Lysanders were listed as a Special Duties Squadron and given the number 138. The squadron with that designation had been originally formed six days before Armistice Day in 1918, and its planes had not taken to the air in anger over France before its pilots had returned to England and their squadron became a dusty file in the Air Ministry archives. Gubbins arranged for it to have a new squadron badge: a gleaming sword cutting a knotted rope and the motto FOR FREEDOM. Gubbins told Selborne it represented the role the Lysanders would have. He stipulated that their pilots should have a minimum 250 hours of flying experience.

RAF squadron commanders combed through their files to find pilots and ground staff to transfer to 138 Squadron at its temporary base on Newmarket Racecourse near Cambridge. The pilots would be young, all with strong personalities, and would fly their Lysanders to the racecourse.

A briefing officer told them their work would be governed by the phases of the moon since they would need its light to map-read their way to small fields where tiny pricks of light would guide them to touch down in occupied Europe. A young pilot officer, nineteen-year-old John Bridger, would recall "the sudden thrill in the briefing room as we heard what we were going to do." Until then he had piloted a Beaufighter and always had a navigator to guide him. Now he would have to navigate himself by moonlight.

The briefing officer produced copies of the Official Secrets Act and told them they had all to sign one. Now was the time for anyone to ask to be posted back to his old squadron. No one moved. He then told them that they would eventually be carrying agents who were now being trained for their missions. The briefing concluded with the officer saying the flying skills would be constantly tested; those who failed would be posted back to their squadrons. Only the best would fly with 138

Squadron. They would have a month to turn into competent Special Duties Lysander pilots.

That night in the officers' bar those who had arrived at Newmarket as strangers to each other began to bond. They came from all over Britain, a cross section of men from the coal mining villages of Wales, a farmer's son, and graduates of Britain's public school system.

The following night under a waxing moon, they began an endless round of night flying at low altitude in the Lysanders over darkened villages, scattering cows in the process as they swooped over hedges to land in a field and then take off in seconds. Night after night over southern England, the pilots learned to find their way to an assigned field on their maps, where an SOE instructor waited with a flashlight to guide them down, noted their landing skills, and the speed with which the Lysander took off again. Back at the airfield their abilities were evaluated. They were given more road maps to study, by which they would navigate. Their Lysanders had been painted matte black to make them invisible at night. A ladder had been added on the port side to allow a passenger to climb in and out.

The training flights were extended over the hills of Wales where RAF aircraft, acting as German night fighters, sought the Lysanders. The pilots had to fly low enough to prevent the fighters from getting into a position to attack them. Back at the base there were more lectures and, this time, road maps of Europe to study. They were told those would be their flight paths to the fields where reception committees of the Resistance would be waiting with their signal lights. They were also told they would be called the Moon Squadron pilots.

....

Meanwhile the air minister's surveyors had settled on an area where the SOE airfield would be built. It was close to the borders of Cambridgeshire and Bedfordshire and about fifty miles north of London. There were few agricultural communities, the largest being the village of Tempsford, and the chosen site was Gibraltar Farm, named after Britain's victory in the Napoleonic Wars. The ground was flat and the soil free of rocks or stones; the surveyors agreed it was the ideal spot on which to build the airfield. On their maps it was classified to be built to "RAF Class 'A' Standard."

Excavators, plows, and steamrollers began work. Draftsmen swarmed over the site marking out foundations and runways. Linemen maneuvered huge cable drums to connect lines. Work gangs uprooted trees and grubbed up acres of bushes and stacked them in huge piles to burn. Day and night, smoke drifted across the countryside, forcing the housewives of Tempsford not to hang their washing outside. No one complained. The site work had brought a new prosperity to the village shop, post office, and its two pubs. Villagers dug up their flower beds to grow vegetables that were sold to the field kitchens that fed the workmen on the site.

As building progressed, Churchill issued an order that the airfield must be disguised to resemble anything but an airfield. He cited the words of Carl von Clausewitz: "War has a way of masking the stage with scenery." The prime minister added: "There is no better man to do that than Maskelyne."

....

For sixty-five years the Maskelyne family had played to packed houses in their own theater on Regent Street in London's West End. Jasper Maskelyne had been born into the world of illusions.

His own childhood had been spent in the workshop beneath the stage, learning such tricks as how his father made an assistant sealed inside a cabinet vanish only to appear flying across the stage into the wings. His father had told him that by using imagery and proper equipment he could create any illusion. Jasper was nine when his father founded the Magic Circle, an elite organization to protect the family's secrets. At the age of ten, in his top hat and tails, Jasper gave his first Royal Command Performance for the king. Winston Churchill was in the audience. Since then Churchill had made frequent visits to the family theater with its billboard announcing MASKELYNE'S MAGIC MYSTERIES. Photos of Jasper and his father were in the lobby. After his father died in 1926, Jasper carried on topping the bill. Six feet four inches tall, with jet-black hair, a trim mustache, a handsome cleft in his chin, and deep-set dark green eyes, he was a dashing figure, with film star good looks.

In 1935 movie tycoon Alexander Korda built Denham Studios in Buckinghamshire and ran it with a style matching any Hollywood mogul. One of the first films the studio made starred Jasper as a detective using magic to solve crimes.

The war clouds deepened over Europe. First Poland, then Norway and the Low Countries fell to the Nazi blitzkrieg, followed by the French government surrendering and the Chamberlain government resigning in London to be replaced by Churchill. Luftwaffe bombers roared across the Channel, and the first bombs fell on London. Jasper became preoccupied with one thought: Would it be possible to adapt the power of magic to defend Britain?

He shared the thought with the one person he loved and trusted, Evelyn Enid Mary, his wife. She had been his stage assistant since 1924, spending her evenings arriving on stage on a motorcycle, which he made to disappear with her into a Chinese cabinet; she'd suddenly reappear at the back of the auditorium to ride her motorcycle back onto the stage. Over dinner one night Mary had suggested that he should devise an illusion in which Hitler suddenly disappeared. Shortly after war had broken out she had once more driven her motorcycle onto the stage, carrying a stuffed eagle. Jasper had sent the bird flying across the stage, clutching in its talons a dummy of Hitler before dropping it into what appeared to be the English Channel. The audience rose to their feet and cheered.

Next day Jasper received a hand-delivered letter asking him to come to the Ministry of Economic Warfare to meet Professor Frederick Alexander Lindemann, Churchill's advisor on scientific matters. Lindemann wasted no time in saying the prime minister had asked him to see if Jasper could create more "tricks which would be a valuable asset to the war effort."

Dressed in his finest suit, Jasper sat in Lindemann's office and spoke with the certainty he had rehearsed with Mary the previous evening. The couple had discussed his ideas about bringing stage magic to the battlefield. "If I can stand in the focus of powerful footlights and deceive an audience on the other side of the orchestra pit, I can fool German pilots 15,000 feet above us in the air or Hitler's soldiers miles away on land."

Lindemann considered what Jasper told him. To deceive an audience in a theater under prepared conditions would be quite a different trick from fooling the Nazi war machine. What would Maskelyne propose to do?

Lindemann took notes as Jasper spoke. "There are no limits to the effects I can produce. I can create cannons where they don't exist and make ghost ships sail the seas. I can put an entire army into the field when there is not a soldier there."

Lindemann sat back in his desk chair and smiled. "Tell me more."

The illusionist would recall, "I told him autosuggestion is the key to magic. It is not different from the scientific principles of deception when creating military camouflage. What I do is the fulfilment of creating carefully planned expectation. The Nazis will see guns where they don't expect to see guns and tanks where there will be none. It's delusion. Illusion creating delusion."

Lindemann came to a decision. "Right now we need something new to show the Germans that we have a few surprises up our sleeves," he said.

Lindemann handed Jasper a copy of the Official Secrets Act, told him to read and sign it, and said he would be commissioned into the army with a rank of a captain attached to the War Office Camouflage Development and Training Centre at Farnham Castle near Aldershot in Surrey. There he would demonstrate an illusion of his choice to a senior officer at the War Office.

In the following days, Jasper collected his officer's uniform, went to an enlistment center, and swore to defend Crown and country. Afterward he went to the workshop below the theater stage to design the illusion he intended to demonstrate at Farnham Castle. Lindemann had told him that it would be observed by Lord Gort, commander in chief of the army. After spending days designing and testing every part of the illusion, Jasper was satisfied it would convince even the sharpest military eye.

He arrived at the castle in an army truck carrying his equipment and one of his stagehands to help rig the illusion. After walking the castle grounds, he chose a natural depression through which ran a stream. Helped by the stagehand, Jasper carefully positioned the pieces of mirror glass he had cut at various distances from the water so that viewed from a distance the stream appeared to be wider and more like a river.

He and his assistant began to place cutout stage props on the stream bank depicting the Thames running past the East End of London, Big Ben, and the Houses of Parliament. The reflection from the glass gave an impression of buildings lining the river banks. Finally they carried from the truck the model that would be the centerpiece of the illusion and placed it on the water. It was the German pocket battleship *Admiral Graf Spee*. It was operated by a windup mechanism attached to a small clock that allowed its guns to turn and fire puffs of smoke. The effect was of the battleship in action on the Thames in the center of London. The farther from the stream they moved, Jasper and the stagehand saw, the more realistic the illusion became. Jasper reset the mechanism and hurried back to the castle. The stagehand crouched in the depression, ready to retrieve the model and the props.

Jasper joined Lord Gort at his vantage point in the castle as he scanned the grounds with his binoculars and asked what he was looking for. Jasper said he hoped it would be a surprise. Gort grunted and turned back to scanning. Suddenly he stopped. "My word," he whispered.

Jasper would recall, "Lord Gort lowered his glasses and stared at me. 'That's the *Graf Spee* sailing down the Thames. There is no river anywhere near here,' he said. I politely told him there was a stream. He looked at me, shaking his head, and said it was one mighty trick."

Over dinner Lord Gort questioned Jasper as to whether there was anything he could not do. The response was a polite head shake.

Gort poured them another drink and asked Jasper if he could disguise an airfield so the Luftwaffe wouldn't spot it from the air.

That was no problem for Jasper. That evening he was given a set of the surveyor's blueprints of the airfield that had been chosen for the SOE, which was now known as RAF Tempsford.

He spent six weeks there supervising a team of film set builders from Denham Studios. Roof slates were removed from Gibraltar Farm buildings so they would look derelict from the air; rainproof canvas protected the rooms below. Weatherboarding was stripped from sheds; windows were left without glass, with outdoor doors swinging on their hinges. Other buildings were expertly painted to give the impression that their walls were covered with mildew and cobwebs. Nissen huts were given thatched roofs to look like cow barns. Other huts had the appearance of abandoned pig stalls. Hangars and barracks were camouflaged to give them the look of old haylofts from the air. In various parts of the farm, Maskelyne placed pieces of old farm machinery: a plow, a couple of tractors, and a hay cart.

Particular attention was given to the farmhouse. It was to be the airfield's nerve center. While the outside would appear as run-down as the other buildings, the inside would have an operation room linked to the SOE headquarters. The barn behind the house would be the departure waiting room for agents going on missions. It, too, was given a shabby exterior and a pond occupied by a few ducks.

Maskelyne spent considerable time deciding how to conceal the two runways. Finally he ordered that they should be painted black. He then added patches of green and brown paint to resemble clumps of grass on the tarmac.

When finished, the runways looked like hedges of brambles and weeds. To complete the illusion, farm gates were painted on the runways to give the impression of access to the adjoining field where cattle would graze. An old shed was erected close to the illusion to complete the camouflage. At night, when missions would take place, the cows would be herded inside.

The work complete, Gubbins asked the Air Ministry to send a plane to overfly the base. A photo analyst interpreted the aerial pictures as depicting a "not very active farm."

4

Slipping into the Shadows

IN WASHINGTON, DONOVAN HAD set up his Office of the Coordinator of Information, COI, with $450,000 from Roosevelt's secret fund. He had created it after Churchill had told him about the British Treasury fund for MI6 and MI5. "It's their no questions asked money box," the prime minister said.

Having decided his post as COI would require his full attention, Donovan divided his law practice clients between his senior partners, but he took his secretary with him. Eloise Page had managed his office diary, booked his luncheon appointments, and organized his travel plans in her soft southern accent. Five years had passed since she had graduated from the Peabody Conservatory in Baltimore, where she had learned typing and shorthand.

Donovan was her first and only employer. After a short interview and a typing test, which consisted of him dictating a page of a legal document and checking it, he had given her the job. It came with a generous salary, birthday and Christmas bonuses—and learning to cope with his moods and standing up to his Irish temper. Bringing her with him to the Office of the COI as his executive secretary, he told her, "Better salary, more glamour, more interesting work."

Her first task in the COI's temporary office in the Apex Building near the White House was to contact the list of names Donovan told her would be the nucleus of his staff. They included journalists and broadcasters who could gather and analyze information from all over the world. Others were lawyers he had met in the courts of New York and Washington who would summarize the latest government reports. Some names she recognized from their visits to his law office. One was David Bruce, a lawyer who had told her he had been in London and had watched RAF fighters dueling with the Luftwaffe over the cliffs of Dover in August 1940, a curtain-raiser for the London Blitz. Next to his name Donovan had scribbled INTELLIGENCE ANALYSIS. Eventually Bruce would become Donovan's station chief in London.

Edward Buxton, who had served in the Great War with Donovan, was marked down to be an assistant director to organize a unit to interview "friendly foreigners arriving in Washington with useful information."

One name on the list particularly impressed Eloise Page: Marine Captain James Roosevelt, the president's son. He would become Donovan's can-do fixer in Washington. Soon his brusque demands could be heard in government offices from dawn to dusk: "COI needs it *now* not *today*."

In the meantime Donovan had persuaded the navy department to loan him its latest Buick sedan and to install a shortwave radio, which allowed him to make calls while driving. He used it to talk to his staff in what was now COI's new headquarters on E Street NW. The three-story building was fronted by impressive granite columns and had housed the Public Health Service.

Throughout the summer of 1941, Donovan's organization became the talk of Washington. More than one newspaper columnist speculated why he could walk into the White House to see FDR at all hours. The *Washington Star* began to run a comic strip, *The Exciting Adventures of Wild Bill Donovan*, which became breakfast table must-read in Georgetown homes. When Secretary of State Cordell Hull sniffed at the strip, the president told him, "Bill is doing a good job."

....

Donovan had also come to the attention of General Friedrich von Boetticher, the military attaché at the German embassy in Washington. Of average height, blond, heavyset, and genial, Boetticher was fifty-eight years old when the war started, and in Berlin he was seen as one of the most important of the forty-three military, naval, and air attachés serving the Third Reich in thirty countries.

Boetticher had at his command the German consuls in America who eagerly performed the task he set them of obtaining military intelligence. In New York there was Eduard Kurtz, Erich Windels in Philadelphia, Georg Krause-Wichmann in Chicago, Karl Kapp in Cleveland, and Georg Gyssling in Los Angeles. All clipped local newspaper stories on political, cultural, and military affairs. Boetticher would often receive a hundred cuttings in a day. He would compile the information into reports that he would transmit by cable or send in the embassy's diplomatic bag by air, depending on how important he judged the information to be for the Foreign Office in Berlin. At Wilhelmstrasse 76, at desks in the political or commercial branches, these reports were read by diplomats looking to shape the future foreign policy of Germany. Many were passed on to Adolf Hitler, and Boetticher knew that his reports were among those read by the führer.

He not only used the printed sources from consuls about America's military forces but also received information in response to questions he put to government departments. He attended maneuvers and parades and military lectures. The State Department also regarded him as one of the most important military attachés in Washington.

His post gave him a comfortable house, a housekeeper, and a cook to host dinner parties in return for invitations to important social engagements. He became a guest at parties at the White House, State Department, and other government departments. His social calendar had given him contact with General Douglas MacArthur and General George C. Marshal, enabling him to tap into their rich sources of information.

Boetticher had taken up his appointment in 1936, when MacArthur was still the only four-star general, on a salary of $10,000 a year and had the exclusive use of the army's only limousine. Major

Dwight Eisenhower, his aide, received $3,000 and acted as the army's lobbyist in Congress.

In one report to the Foreign Office, Boetticher wrote he had sat next to Professor Robert Goddard, the guest speaker at a dinner, who had explained his rocket experiments and outlined "the first practical reality of a usable rocket" he was close to creating. Boetticher persuaded Goddard to let him have a copy of his speech, in which Goddard had said his rocket would reach an altitude of 2,400 meters and a speed of 1,000 kilometers. Boetticher sent the details to Berlin, adding that the Guggenheim Foundation and the Carnegie Institute financed Goddard's research.

Boetticher described the funding as "Jew money that controls American military policy." In Berlin his report was sent to Luftwaffe Chief Hermann Göring, who would later call them "precious pages" in helping to create the V-1 and V-2 rockets that would rain down on London.

After a Thanksgiving luncheon at the State Department in 1941 he cabled Berlin, "No land and air armaments adequate for an aggressive war policy by the United States are to be expected in the near future. The army and air force still do not have the necessary forces to undertake any important aggressive manoeuvres outside the western hemisphere. By that time England would be occupied or turned into a waste of rubble."

In between his reports Boetticher updated his profiles of important members of the Roosevelt Administration. Treasury Secretary Henry Morgenthau Jr. was described as "A Jew and close adviser to Roosevelt." J. Edgar Hoover, the head of the FBI, was called "Anti-German in his speeches."

Donovan's profile dealt with his life before his visit to London and his appointment as Coordinator of Information. There were also extracts from society gossip columns about his relationship with women—married or unmarried—some of whom he had represented in their divorces. One was the millionaire Helen Astor; another was Marion Davies, the film actress and mistress of William Randolph Hearst. "The newspaper magnate had told columnist Walter Winchel that the FBI is investigating

Donovan for his connection with suspect fascists. Roosevelt has ordered Hoover to send Donovan a letter insisting that the Bureau does not possess any information concerning him." The latest item in the profile was from a Washington gossip column that Donovan was about to take a tour of the Mediterranean that included the Balkans.

Boetticher took the details to the embassy communications room in a nineteenth-century mansion on Massachusetts Avenue. He instructed the duty officer to mark it IMMEDIATE IMPORTANCE and transmit it to Admiral Wilhelm Canaris, the head of the formidable Abwehr, the German secret service, in its headquarters at 72-76 Tirpitz Ufer in Berlin.

Roosevelt had agreed with Churchill's suggestion that Donovan should see the importance of Britain's front line, which extended across North Africa from Gibraltar to Cairo. The friendship between the leaders had deepened since Roosevelt had been returned to office for a third term in the previous November election despite the sustained attacks by the isolationists, who worried that Roosevelt was ready to abandon American neutrality and lead the country to war.

....

Prime Minister Churchill had ordered William Stephenson—the newly appointed head of British security in the United States—to institute adequate security measures against the threat of sabotage to British property in the country and to organize American public opinion in favor of aid to Britain.

The British ambassador in Washington, Lord Lothian, was further instructed to publicize that Britain would fight the war with additional vigor now that the Lend-Lease Act of March 1941 formally committed the United States to support the war effort. Britain was facing a situation in which a great proportion of its war production, supplies, and shipping depended on the United States.

Between them, Stephenson's and Lothian's lobbying in Washington had played a significant part in the agreement in which the United States provided Britain and Canada with fifty badly needed US destroyers. They would fly the Union Jack on Atlantic convoy escort duty in exchange for rights for their bases to be used by the US Navy.

....

Earlier, with the war only weeks old, MI6 chief Menzies had asked Stephenson to meet J. Edgar Hoover, the head of the FBI, to discuss cooperation between the SIS and the Federal Bureau of Investigation in the event of the United States becoming involved in the war. On April 16, 1940, Stephenson cabled Menzies, "Meeting completely successful. Hoover will cooperate fully. Code names established. You will be 'S.M. Scott'; he will be 'H.E. Jones.' Jones sends Scott assurances of goodwill and a desire to assist far beyond confines of officialdom."

Hoover had told Stephenson he should "procure an official position and should become Britain's Passport Control Officer in New York." The post would give him cover to liaise with the FBI to track Nazi sympathizers and enemy companies. He also should develop contact with journalists, newspapers, and wire services and provide them with pro-British stories. Stephenson's office in Rockefeller Center would eventually combine the functions of MI6, MI5, and the SOE, as well as liaising with the FBI.

In their work together, the low-key Canadian Stephenson and the hard-driven Donovan would find they were remarkably similar. Both agreed that the Mediterranean was not only strategically important for Britain but would also become important if America entered the war, which Donovan said "would only be a matter of time." Stephenson cabled Menzies that it was a matter of urgency for Donovan to visit the region.

On January 30, 1941, Stephenson's official position as British director of British Security Coordination, BSC, in the United States, was registered in the State Department. The formality was required for a foreign intelligence officer of a friendly nation to operate in the country.

Before the war, MI6's presence in the Americas had been in three stations: Washington was staffed by an intelligence officer and a secretary, Panama City was responsible for Mexico and Central America, and Montevideo covered South America. They would all come under Stephenson in New York, which would become MI6's most important overseas station in the war. Churchill had instructed him to "create the clenched fist that would provide the knockout blow to the Axis Powers," and gave Stephenson the code name Intrepid.

However, Stephenson's position aroused suspicion about his activities in some quarters. Adolf Berle, the assistant secretary of state, told Congress, "Although Stephenson is ostensibly involved with the protection of British supplies under Lend-Lease, he is developing a full-size secret police and intelligence service with a string of secret agents and a much larger number of informers."

....

Within days British ambassadors and military commanders in the Mediterranean region had all received cables from the Foreign Office to regard Donovan "as fully in our confidence and will be accompanied by a senior British officer, Naval Commander Ian Lancaster Fleming, of Naval Intelligence."

Fleming came from a wealthy London banking family. He was educated at Eton College and the Royal Military Academy at Sandhurst. He spent less than a year there, leaving in 1927 without gaining a commission, after contracting gonorrhea. Behind his correct manner was a rather perverse sexuality, which led to numerous affairs. To prepare Fleming for possible entry into the Foreign Office, his mother sent him to the Tennerhof in Kitzbühel, Austria, a small private school. After improving his language skills there, he studied briefly at Munich University and the University of Geneva.

Failing the Foreign Office entrance examination he joined Reuters news agency and was sent to Moscow as a correspondent. He wrote to the Soviet premier Joseph Stalin asking for an interview and personally received a handwritten apology for "not having the time." It made a story for Reuters.

In October 1933, bowing to family pressure, he went into banking with a position at the financiers Cull & Co. In 1935, he moved to Rowe & Pitman as a stockbroker. Fleming was unsuccessful in both roles.

In 1939 he began an affair with Ann O'Neill, the wife of the third Baron O'Neill; she was also having an affair with Esmond Harmsworth, the heir to Lord Rothermere, owner of the *Daily Mail*. Fleming's affair with O'Neill was a passport to London society where his charm made him a regular guest at dinner parties.

At one he sat next to a man with clipped speech and probing questions. He was Rear Admiral John Godfrey, director of naval intelligence. By the end of the dinner he had invited Fleming to come and see him at the Admiralty. He offered Fleming the post as his personal assistant. With it came a commission into the Royal Navy as a lieutenant. Fleming accepted. In August 1939, in his new uniform, he started work in room 39, which adjoined Godfrey's suite on the Admiralty's third floor.

Navy Intelligence, NI, had direct lines to the prime minister's office, the Foreign Office, Air Ministry, Scotland Yard, MI5 and MI6, and the SOE. Fleming's first brief was to study the files, which contained intelligence from Britain's forty-three seaports, about foreign vessels and their crews. Godfrey called the files "our Scarlet Pimpernels" and told Fleming he was to look for anything that posed a threat to the country. After reading, Fleming would knock on the green baize door of Godfrey's office and report with his favorite remark: "Well, there it is, nothing untoward." Godfrey would smile and more than once invited Fleming to join him for lunch in his club, telling Fleming of those days when he had sailed the seven seas; how he had taken Lawrence of Arabia into Arabia and had worked with the navies of Japan, Greece, France, and Italy during the First World War and later had been given command of the battle cruiser HMS *Repulse* and had taken his ship to evacuate British subjects caught up in the Spanish Civil War. Fleming's diary began to fill with the admiral's recollections.

Within months Fleming had shown his skill at running Godfrey's office and, discovering Godfrey had enemies within government circles, he learned to keep them at bay from the admiral, fielding their calls and responding to their demands with a promise: "I'll see to it. Your matter will be top of the Admiral's agenda." By the outbreak of war Godfrey had promoted him to a commander in the Royal Navy. Fleming became a familiar figure at Whitehall meetings, seated beside Godfrey and anticipating his request for a document from the files he carried in a leather briefcase.

The war was weeks old when Fleming was told to join the morning senior staff conference to discuss ideas that could be offered to MI6, the Joint Intelligence Committee, and the SOE. Godfrey described them as "our three prime customers." Fleming's own older brother, Peter, who had served under Gubbins in Norway, had become an analyst at the SOE's Baker Street headquarters. Ian Fleming's own suggestions had gained praise from Admiral Godfrey, not only for their possibility but for the style and research. Godfrey had appointed him to accompany Donovan on his visit to the Mediterranean, describing him as "the ideal choice as a traveling companion, witty, a gourmet, and [with] an understanding of secret intelligence." He would report directly to Menzies during the tour.

....

In Berlin Boettcher's encoded message to Wilhelm Canaris about Donovan's visit to the Mediterranean and the Balkans had resulted in Abwehr agents in the region being ordered to track his every step. An agent in Cádiz, a fishing port on the Spanish coast of the Strait of Gibraltar, reported Donovan and Fleming had arrived on the Rock and had met with a man who was the MI6 agent in the British overseas territory. From there they traveled to British bases in North Africa and Cairo. Abwehr agents cabled Berlin that their informers had told them Donovan had delivered the same message: the United States was not prepared to let the United Kingdom lose the war.

Increasingly the tour involved meetings with British military authorities, diplomats, and MI6 operatives. The more he learned from them the more determined Donovan became to create an intelligence service like Britain's. Every evening he wrote detailed reports of his meetings and placed them in the leather pouches with the documents he had been given to take back to Washington. The files included reports on the right-wing government of Spain's General Franco and his pro-German activities, which allowed the German navy to use Spanish ports and detect British ships passing through the Suez Canal and the Strait of Gibraltar.

Throughout the summer, reports continued to reach Canaris, the Abwehr chief. The agent in Madrid reported that "Spanish cabinet circles" feared Donovan's visit was the precursor of an invasion should the United States enter the war. Franco had assured his ministers that Spain would continue to receive help from Germany as it had from Germany's elite Condor Legion during the Spanish Civil War. The air fleet had bombed Guernica, the cultural and religious capital of Basque Spain, and reduced it to rubble on April 26, 1937. It was the first blitzkrieg.

The Abwehr spy in Lisbon had a family connection with Portugal's ruling dictator, António Salazar. Salazar's discussion with Donovan had centered on the three Atlantic archipelagos. Portugal's Azores lay a thousand miles west of Lisbon, Cape Verde stood off the bulge of Africa, and Spain's Canary Islands were off the northwestern coast of Africa. Salazar had told Donovan that Franco was allowing U-boats to refuel in the Canaries before continuing to attack Allied merchant ships on their way to England. Salazar had promised Donovan that Portugal would refuse to provide refueling facilities and was sending troops to the Azores to protect its neutrality.

The Abwehr agent's reports were a reminder to Canaris of when he had met Donovan on his visit to Berlin in 1937 as Roosevelt's special representative. He had decided then that Donovan was like the trio of brass monkeys on his desk who symbolized the way he ran the Abwehr: "See all, hear all, say nothing." The trio had been a gift from his wife, Erika, after he had been appointed by Hitler as head of counterintelligence. However, the strain of his duties as Hitler's intelligence chief had whitened his hair and given him a frail look accompanied by an occasional lisp and a speech pattern of answering a question with another. He was now also convinced that Donovan was not only still Roosevelt's spy but was on a mission to prepare for America to enter the war.

What Fleming called "Wild Bill's tour" reached Sofia, the capital of Bulgaria, where Donovan met its king, Boris III. Donovan had been briefed by one of America's few Balkan experts, George H. Earle, a former governor of Pennsylvania and a friend of Roosevelt. Donovan planned to use the information to persuade the king to remain neutral.

But for once, Donovan failed to persuade and closed their meeting with the warning that "any nation which submits to Nazism will receive no sympathy from Washington."

Fleming cabled Menzies that the words marked the end of Donovan's tour.

....

Donovan broke his journey back to the States with a stopover in London to meet David Bruce. He had appointed the tall, articulate Maryland lawyer to run the London end of the COI. Its office was in Grosvenor Square and was listed by the Foreign Office as an annex of the American embassy.

After graduating from Princeton, Bruce had traveled extensively through western and eastern Europe before returning home to Baltimore to pass the Maryland bar and win a seat on the state legislature at the age of just twenty-six. Throughout the 1930s he had sat on the boards of some of America's largest corporations. He was a man at home with the wealthy of Washington and New York, but with a deep fondness for England and Europe. In the summer of 1940, with Britain standing alone among the free states of Europe, he had visited London as a member of the war relief committee of the American Red Cross. He was in London during the Battle of Britain and the Blitz.

On his return to America he had been active in the Fight for Freedom, a group of rich businessmen who lobbied against the isolationists across the Atlantic, and he had spoken on the radio about the resolution of Londoners.

While America's defense built up and Lend-Lease moved the nation closer to the conflict, Bruce also knew it was still hard to persuade the isolationists to stop accusing the internationalists back home of dragging the United States into the war. Their activities had percolated through Donovan's mind as he arrived in England. Bruce sent a car to collect him from the RAF airfield at Hendon and had reserved a suite for Donovan at the Savoy.

Driving into the city, Donovan saw that although the bombing destruction was bad enough, his driver told him there had been no air raids for a week, giving time for some of the debris to be removed since his last visit. Bruce was waiting in a soft armchair in the front hall of the Savoy. He was his usual ebullient self. Donovan smiled when Bruce said he had booked a private dining room overlooking the Thames for lunch. An Anglophile like Donovan, Bruce also had a connoisseur's taste for wine and food.

Donovan explained that as the result of his Middle East visit the intelligence sharing with the British had grown, though there were moments in Cairo when there had been tensions about Britain's reaction to the attitude of American isolationists. More than once Fleming had played his part in calming matters. The result was that Donovan was returning to Washington with an insight into both British political thinking and intelligence in the region. He was convinced that, when the time came for the United States to enter the war, there would be a role for the COI, but not in its current form. He told Bruce he intended to create America's first strategic intelligence service, adding that he even had a name for it: the Office of Strategic Services, or OSS. Bruce had arranged for Donovan to meet Gubbins for dinner that evening.

....

Gubbins suggested that before Donovan fly back to Washington he should first accompany him to visit the SOE paramilitary training schools in Scotland. They spent a day sitting in on lectures and watching agents taking part in unarmed combat and field craft exercises as instructors fired live rounds over their heads.

Some trainees were women, and Gubbins said he would arrange for Donovan to meet Selwyn Jepson and Vera Atkins to learn about the role women would have in the SOE.

When Donovan told them of his plans for women, Jepson said there was still opposition in Whitehall to their doing the same jobs as male secret agents. Atkins asked if there would be similar discrimination in the United States. Donovan said he would overcome it "by recruiting women who came from the same stock which had founded my country."

Gubbins also arranged for Donovan to meet the head of the SOE's French Section, Maurice Buckmaster, who said that women had been his first choice to be trained as couriers and wireless operators. He invited Donovan to come with him on his weekly visit to Wanborough Manor, the section's training school for agents.

Over lunch in the canteen he spoke to some of the other agents. Buckmaster translated his questions, explaining agents were required to speak only French. In between watching them mastering Morse code and learning how to code and decode messages, Donovan saw them learning in the manor workshop how to diagnose and repair faults in their wireless sets. Afterward he went to a classroom to hear a psychologist's lecture on how to handle the stress of their work once they were in France.

On the drive back to London, Buckmaster said that female recruits were achieving excellent results not only in shooting and sabotage but also as potential clandestine radio operators. The next day Donovan flew back to Washington to begin the search for such women.

....

The pilots of RAF 138 Squadron sensed their time at Newmarket racecourse was coming to an end. There had been flights out over the Channel, flying at no more than fifty feet above the water before turning back and giving the correct Morse code signal that would allow them to reenter friendly airspace. By day there was firearms training at the shooting range and lectures on escape and evasion tactics should they be shot down on a mission.

At night they were awakened from their bunks, driven in a closed truck several miles away, and dropped after being told they would be hunted by the local and military police as escaped prisoners from a local army lockup. Their instructors warned they could expect to be roughly treated, a forerunner of what they would face if they crash-landed in occupied Europe.

One morning, returning from an exercise, the pilots found new faces in the officers' mess with their aircraft parked on the airfield. The newcomers told them they were joining the squadron in time to go with them to their new base.

....

For the first time in weeks, William Donovan had taken off a Sunday afternoon on that December 7, 1941. Wrapped in an overcoat he had bought in Savile Row on his visit to London, he sat in the stands in New York's Polo Grounds, one of fifty-five thousand fans who'd come to watch the National Football League matchup between the Giants and the Brooklyn Dodgers.

He had hardly settled in his seat before a voice came over the loudspeakers: "Attention please! Here is an urgent message. Will Colonel William J. Donovan call operator 19 in Washington immediately."

Donovan left his seat and found a phone booth under the bleachers. In moments operator 19 connected him to his assistant, James Roosevelt. "Bill, the Japs have attacked Pearl Harbor. The President wants you back as soon as possible. I've booked you on the 5:15 flight out of La Guardia."

Donovan ignored the reporters waiting at the terminal. He had asked James Roosevelt to call Eloise Page and have her drive his car to the airport to collect him so he could use its radio to communicate on the way to the office. In the meantime, playwright Robert Sherwood and his team in the COI's Foreign Information Service, based on New York's Madison Avenue, would prepare stories to distribute around the world about America's response to the attack.

Page drove him at speed to headquarters on Navy Hill. He used the car radio to give orders. He told Sherwood to contact the radio networks and instruct them to prepare their anchormen to broadcast the stories crafted by Sherwood's staff. Priority to the copy would be given to stations in Los Angeles and San Francisco to broadcast on their shortwave transmitters to Latin America and the Far East. By the time Donovan reached his office he was told that four thousand words of copy had been broadcast. Each story carried the same words that Donovan had provided: "What the Japanese have done doesn't frighten but unifies the United States."

Stephenson had called to say that Churchill had phoned FDR and told him, "We are all in the same boat now." Donovan told Sherwood to use the words in the next stories, which were broadcast to Canada and Europe throughout the night.

As evening fell, he visited every office. He told staff the point of no return had been reached when the Rising Sun, Japan's emblem, had arrived over Pearl Harbor earlier that Sunday and "by God had caught our planes on the ground, crippled our battleship, and killed Americans." Donovan called it a day of infamy.

Radios in the building continued to report the mood in Washington. Cherry trees outside the Japanese embassy had been cut down by super patriots among a crowd watching smoke rising from the building's chimney. The Japanese were burning diplomatic papers. Police cars were patrolling the streets, and officers were calling for calm.

Donovan drove to the White House. He found the president alone in his study behind his desk, its top scattered with cable messages from naval headquarters in Pearl Harbor. The empty chairs that cluttered the room were a reminder of the visitors who had come and gone. His voice thick with the start of a cold, Roosevelt asked Donovan if Hitler could have had prior knowledge of the attack. Donovan said he didn't know but Hitler would almost certainly have been the first to be briefed by Tokyo after the raid.

Roosevelt said, "I'm glad you pushed so hard to have an intelligence agency."

Donovan said he would like to rename the COI. He wanted it called the Office of Strategic Services, or OSS. Roosevelt nodded approval. If he was curious he did not show it. But it would be something to tell Churchill when he arrived in Washington.

While they sat there, Grace Tully, Roosevelt's secretary, brought messages from the navy and Pearl Harbor to the study. Thumping his fist on the desktop at the latest news that 90 percent of the Pacific fleet had been lost, Roosevelt asked Donovan how the American public would react. Donovan was reassuring; Americans would be ready to go to war and not just talk about it. He suggested that the speech Roosevelt would make to Congress at noon the following day to declare war on Japan should start, "What they have done on this Sunday will live in infamy." The president wrote down the words on a pad. Later, they would form one of the most powerful speeches of his presidency.

Returning to his office, Donovan worked until daylight, drinking coffee that Eloise Page regularly brought in. He requested reports from the Research and Analysis section on what foreign radio stations were saying about how vulnerable the United States was to another attack.

James Baxter, the head of R&A, produced several scenarios: The Japanese navy could send its aircraft carriers in pursuit of the remaining American Pacific fleet if it attempted to head back to the mainland. The Japanese could attack the Panama Canal. The attack on Pearl Harbor could "discourage the Russians from joining forces with us."

On December 9, Stephenson alerted Donovan that Germany was about to declare war on the United States. Hours later the American embassies in Berlin and Rome were closed down. Two days later, in a joint statement, Hitler and Mussolini declared war against the United States.

With the Middle East trip still fresh in his mind, Donovan suggested that Roosevelt should contact Portugal's ruler, António Salazar, and persuade him to accept a joint American and British force to protect the nine hundred miles of Azores coastline, which American convoys passed on their way to Britain. Roosevelt decided to put the idea on hold until Churchill arrived. Other proposals from Donovan were circulated to government departments and rejected.

The navy rejected a scheme that Japanese Americans could be selected by the OSS and trained at Camp X in Canada before being sent to the South Pacific to spy and wage guerrilla war against the Japanese. General Douglas MacArthur, no admirer of Donovan, bluntly told him he needed "broadcasts and leaflets to counter Tokyo broadcasts to the Philippines urging its soldiers to desert."

The idea of using Japanese Americans continued to preoccupy Donovan. He sent a memo to Roosevelt that they did not pose a sabotage threat and to intern them, as some newspapers were demanding, would only make enemies of loyal citizens. He said he would like to recruit some to broadcast OSS propaganda aimed at Japan and to decipher Japanese broadcasts. He had asked Sherwood to prepare a draft speech in which Roosevelt would stress the "government has faith in their loyalty and feels no enmity toward the Japanese people, but only for the clique of military leaders in Tokyo who had betrayed Japan."

The draft remained in Donovan's office. Roosevelt had gone ahead and ordered the internment of Japanese Americans.

....

On December 22, wearing a Royal Navy pea jacket and yachting cap, Winston Churchill and his advisors arrived in Washington. They included Averell Harriman, the US ambassador to Britain, Menzies, and Gubbins. Stephenson and Hoover, the FBI chief, had flown up from New York to join Donovan.

The second floor of the White House was code-named Arcadia and became the base for the British party. Churchill had the Rose Suite and the Lincoln Study, where he could confer with his staff. Its walls were covered with maps of Europe his staff had brought with them and which they updated morning, noon, and night with information from London. Menzies, Gubbins, and Stephenson had adjoining bedrooms. Donovan chaired his own meetings with Menzies, Gubbins, and Stephenson to discuss cooperation between the SOE and OSS.

Initially the White House meetings took place in an atmosphere of mutual wariness among the various groups, despite the magnificent rhetoric of Churchill at meals, which convinced Roosevelt that Britain would fight for her life and that a two-way exchange between both countries would help them to win the war.

It was left to Churchill to tell his own advisers, "We are here to bring our ally into the war with us. How wonderful it will be if Hitler can be made to fear when he is going to be next struck by such a powerful force." He looked around the Lincoln Study, his voice firm. "We must cooperate with our hosts as they do with us."

At their meeting next morning, Menzies told Hoover that the MI6 agent in Mexico City had learned that four German ships were preparing to outrun the Royal Navy blockade across the Gulf of Mexico; the US Navy had stopped the ships and escorted them back to harbor, where they would remain "until further notice." The details were transmitted to the Admiralty's Royal Navy intelligence department, NI, and encoded and sent to the patrolling warships in the gulf.

Meantime Hoover, after saying that "South America is FBI territory," revealed that Italians in New York were in the process of smuggling $4 million in cash to finance attacks against British companies in South America. The FBI had stopped the transaction and confiscated the money. In answer to Donovan's smiling question, Hoover said it was "now in the US Treasury and waiting to see if they will claim it. If they do I'll tell you."

It was the start of a growing relationship between the FBI and BCS as they exchanged intelligence about enemy activities in the United States, South America, and the Caribbean. The White House meetings concluded with Donovan and Gubbins finalizing the relationship between the OSS and SOE.

Donovan was frank. He wanted his agents trained to the level he had seen in England and Scotland at OSS training camps in Maryland and Virginia. America's foreign-born and first-generation population—close to forty-five million—would be tapped for those who spoke the languages of occupied Europe, especially German. Donovan would also like the OSS to have its own airfield in Britain. Gubbins said if OSS pilots flew their own planes to England, he would make sure they had their own base. He would also arrange for SOE instructors to work in OSS training camps in the United States and would help to select OSS agents to be trained in Canada.

5

Enigma in the Suitcase

ON SUNDAY, JANUARY 11, 1942, when Churchill had flown back to England, Eleanor Grecay Weis, a trim, soft-spoken twenty-three-year-old who shared a Brooklyn apartment with her school friend, Charlotte Gristed, had spent her morning on her regular task of scanning the *New York Times* want ads for jobs. As usual there were plenty of vacancies, but she wanted something more exciting than working behind a counter at Macy's or serving in a restaurant on Third Avenue, like Gristed. Her own present post as a receptionist for a Polish dentist had lost its appeal, the more so as he complained about New York and spoke of Warsaw as the center of Europe, and in between his patients, told her that he was going back there once he'd saved enough money. But the war had stopped that—just as it had ended her dream of going to France to see Paris and, afterward, London. Gristed had shaken her head and said it wouldn't be safe now to go there because of the war. Besides, New York was getting more exciting with all the émigrés from Europe. Was that why there was no job that would excite her? Weis asked herself.

Earlier that morning she had listened to the radio reporting the departure of the British prime minister back to England and Donovan describing the visit to a radio reporter as "a curtain-raiser to history." Her uncle had served with Donovan in the First World War, and had taken her to see *The Fighting 69th*, the movie about Donovan's regiment in the trenches of Flanders. "A man's man," her uncle had said at the end of the movie.

The film had made a sufficient impact on Weis for her to listen whenever Donovan spoke on the radio or in a newsreel. His deep voice had never lost its Irish brogue. She wondered if what seemed a hint of sadness in his voice came from the death of his daughter, Patricia, in a road accident, driving the convertible he had given her to celebrate her college graduation in 1940. But on that Sunday morning in January, Donovan's tone on the radio in answer to a reporter's question was positive. "Smart people like Churchill can do the job of winning the war with our help."

Encouraged by the words, Weis continued to work her way through the *Times* section advertising jobs. One had caught her eye, for a secretary with administrate skills, ready to work long hours. Applicants were to phone a telephone number and leave their name, details of present work, and a call-back number.

The advertisement had been placed by Allen Dulles, a Wall Street lawyer, the first of a number of attorneys and professional acquaintances Donovan had invited to "come aboard" the OSS.

Dulles was forty-nine years old, smartly dressed, a pipe smoker, and still in a marriage he knew was long over. The son of a Presbyterian clergyman and educated at Princeton, he had traveled around Europe, had served in the State Department, and was on the US delegation to the 1919 Versailles peace conference. Returning to New York, he had become a corporate and international lawyer with an office on Wall Street.

Like Donovan, he had developed connections with lawyers in Europe. They included several in Berlin opposed to the growing threat posed by Hitler's National Socialism and who were founding members of what became known as the Rote Kapelle, the Red Orchestra, a network with links to Moscow.

Those connections attracted Donovan. He knew that Dulles had served in US embassies in Vienna, Paris, and Bern and had spent six months in the Legation in the Swiss city, which was not far from the border with Germany. Donovan was optimistic that Dulles's contacts in Bern would still be there. Switzerland was a neutral country in a hostile desert, but Bern offered an ideal listening post to spy on Germany.

Donovan had appointed Dulles as the head of the OSS office in New York, located on the fifth floor at 630 Fifth Avenue, and told him he would once more be attached to the US Legation in Bern as the OSS station chief. He would have a $1 million initial budget in a bank account lodged in his name and would be free to choose his own staff and initiate his operation.

On that Sunday evening Dulles went to his office and listened to the recordings of the latest applicants for the advertisement in that morning's *Times*. The only one that attracted him was Eleanor Grecay Weis.

....

The requisitioned Victoria Hotel where Selwyn Jepson interviewed women for the SOE was a dingy building on Northumberland Avenue in the heart of London. Its windows were boarded up and, apart from the sandbags around the entrance, there was no sign that the building had any connection with the war. The hotel bar and restaurant had been closed, and the lone man stationed at reception checked each woman's name on a list. After noting the time she arrived, he would take her to the elevator and escort her to the second floor, where Jepson had his office in what had been a bedroom.

The bed had been removed and in its place were a desk and an armchair. Blackout curtains were kept drawn over the window. A ceiling light and a desk lamp lit the room. The walls were without any pictures, but a poster was hung behind the desk to catch the eye of anyone entering the room. It showed a woman seated on a couch in an evening dress. She looked alluring and desirable, as she listened closemouthed to three serviceman gathered around her. The poster was captioned CARELESS TALK COSTS LIVES.

Jepson had sent each woman a brief letter requesting them to come to the hotel to discuss "their role in the war." His letters were written on War Office stationery and sent to their home addresses, which MI5 had provided along with the background checks he had required for potential agents.

A number of the women had come to their interviews dressed in clothes that were both fashionable and respectable. Others came in well-worn dresses he suspected had been in use for some time. Since the start of the war, new clothes were rationed and expensive. Some of the women wore the uniforms of the Auxiliary Territorial Service, ATS, or the Woman's Auxiliary Air Force, WAAF.

Many were Anglo-French, with British fathers who had married French women after the First World War, and included Jews, Roman Catholics, Buddhists, Protestants, and Quakers. Their mixed parentage and a French upbringing had given them knowledge of French customs. The MI5 checks established that most of the women had come to England before the occupation of France. While some had been aware of the French Resistance, most had no hands-on knowledge of its activities.

Jepson structured each interview to last no longer than an hour, during which he explored a woman's personality and motives, doing so in the French language to test her fluency. As she entered his office, he "would see if she had the French look—dark hair, olive skin, and medium height."

There were other qualities Jepson looked for. "Honesty and a sense of purpose and ability to okay instructions and issue orders. Leadership qualities and a total belief in what they were doing was important along with coolness and courage. But courage was not the absence of fear: it was the willingness to carry out actions which required taking a calculated risk while at the same being aware it would also endanger not only her own life but not put other lives in danger."

To more easily learn about the women who sat opposite him in his office, he conducted interviews more as conversations. He sensed that when they entered his office they were filled with expectation. But apart from the wall poster there was nothing about him in his lounge suit to suggest he was in any way involved in the war. It was a presence he deliberately created to explore the qualities he was looking for: character and inner strength and a readiness to live near the edge of death under the Nazi jackboot.

His first questions explored why she had accepted the invitation to the interview. Background checks had shown that Anglo-French women were equally as loyal to Britain as to France. He discussed their own feelings about the German occupation. Would any relatives there be willing to help the Resistance? Jepson intended the questions would establish how far an interviewee would be committed. The majority answered that they were sure their relatives would join the struggle against the German occupation and the Vichy government.

He noticed many of the women came from either middle-class or slightly upper-class backgrounds, and their linguistic skills convinced him they could pass as native French. Jepson knew that if they completed their training they would be assigned to the SOE's French Section, where language skills were essential for couriers and wireless operators.

When he was satisfied a woman had shown both her ability to speak French "like a native" and her British patriotism, he asked his key question: Was she willing to return to France after she had been specially trained for a mission where she would learn to kill and would face death at the hands of the Gestapo if captured?

Jepson had discussed with Vera Atkins how far he should go in dealing with the mistreatment a woman agent could expect if captured. They had agreed that how an agent looked and dressed would be an essential part of their clandestine work as couriers to allow them to operate in a world where German soldiers manned road checkpoints and Gestapo officers traveled on trains to check tickets.

At the end of every interview Jepson asked each woman the same question: Did she really want to be trained? If she said she did, he handed her a copy of the Official Secrets Act and reminded her of the penalties of prosecution and jail she faced if she broke it.

With a handshake at the door he said she would hear shortly whether she had been selected for training.

In the two years that Jepson had been the SOE's recruiting officer, he had interviewed over seventy women. The majority had successfully passed their training. Thirty-nine would be parachuted into France and thirteen dropped into Holland and Belgium.

....

In New York, Dulles interviewed Eleanor Grecay Weis in his office at 630 Fifth Avenue. The blue-uniformed guard in the lobby telephoned Dulles to confirm her arrival, and he had been waiting to greet her with a friendly smile at the door. There was still the maturity and poise in her voice he had detected on the tape in response to his advertisement. She glanced around to see if there was anything about him or his office that offered a clue to what the job could be. He asked her about her work as a dentist's receptionist and said working for him would be different. She asked him in what way? He suspected her experience of job hunting had taught her to ask questions at the outset of an interview.

He said her work would involve the war. The OSS had been created to analyze and correlate all information and data relating to national security. Its most secret work was to wage unorthodox war in support of the armed forces and would include sabotage and subversion to assist the French Resistance fighting the Nazis. She asked another question. What did he want her to do?

Dulles explained she would set up a filing system, handle the switchboard, and log all calls. Other women would be recruited; a number would be émigrés who would work with her. Later they would be transferred to other OSS offices in the city once she was satisfied they showed an English language capability in writing reports on the countries they had emigrated from. She was to bring the reports to him before she filed them. Everything she read must be kept secret. Dulles sensed the proposition appealed to her sense of patriotism and taste for adventure.

On the same floor of the building, William Stephenson ran his British intelligence operation. He wore a suit so shapeless it did not appear to be his own. He had adopted the American penchant for informality and would call the OSS, "Oh, So Secret." In turn Dulles, with whom he had established a close relationship, would call him "Our Friend."

They would exchange messages and documents by pneumatic tubes, which Dulles had installed in their offices. It reminded Weis of how Macy's staff sent sales details to the accounts department.

In her own office outside Dulles's suite, she became used to the sound of messages coming from and going to Stephenson's suite at the far end of the floor. He would regularly stride into her office and, in his soft Canadian accent, tell her it was going to be another long day before opening and closing the door of Dulles's office behind him.

Often the red button on her phone would flash for her to connect Dulles with OSS headquarters in Washington, and she would put the call through to the deep Irish voice she had heard on the radio that Sunday morning saying "smart people can handle any job."

Since then she had seen Donovan as he had walked into Dulles's office. "He had a quiet unassuming manner and I realized that I was working for a man like no other," she would later recall.

....

On his visits to New York, Donovan discussed with Dulles the expansion of the OSS in the city. Research and Analysis had an office at 55 West Fifty-Third Street to catalog and assess photographs that could be used in planning subversive operations. Morale Operations was housed on Times Square, where its staff created "black" propaganda against Germany and Japan.

X-2, the Counterintelligence Branch, had its office on the West Side of Manhattan, where a number of women were engaged in building up backgrounds on personalities, various industries, and ongoing political developments in European countries.

At 610 Fifth Avenue was another OSS office that was simply marked at its entrance as UNITED STATES GOVERNMENT. It was the Biographical Records Division.

It had been formed to obtain intelligence, mostly about Germany, from émigrés arriving in New York, among the last to have Nazi exit visas. The majority were Jews. Among the first staff recruited to work in Biographical Records was Emma Crisler Rado, an attractive, dark-haired, Swiss-born wife of a New York psychologist with a busy practice. He knew Donovan and had recommended that his wife could make a good interviewer.

She had become one of the section's most skilled interviewers, using the methods her husband told her worked with his own patients: "Let the subject talk about himself or herself. It makes them feel good and loosens their tongues. Be a good listener. Don't take notes; it will intimidate interviewees. Tell them that what they are saying was of interest." Using those methods, she had learned a great deal about life in Germany.

Over the weeks, men and women were referred by Emma Rado to Biographical Records to be interviewed for jobs in one of the other OSS offices being set up around New York. The candidates would be taken to a waiting room to be called for an interview. A team of linguists who spoke French, Dutch, Italian, and German were seeking those who not only had knowledge of foreign affairs but were suitable to be selected for the training camps that the OSS had opened in Maryland and Virginia. The sixteen-week courses were run by instructors who had been transferred from the SOE's Camp X in Canada, which had opened on December 6, 1941. They taught how to pick locks, take photographs without being spotted, and piece together small scraps of documents retrieved from trash baskets.

....

Eloise Page, Donovan's secretary, was one of the few in OSS headquarters in Washington who knew where he could be reached in an emergency; she would tell other staff wanting to contact him that "he is where he needs to be." She became known as "Hush-Hush." At the end of her day she would send him a list of callers.

When Donovan went with Stephenson to London to discuss matters connected with their clandestine collaboration, they first headed to Bermuda. There, Page reserved seats 4 and 5 in first class on the Pan Am 314 Clipper flying boat that made the twenty-two-hour journey from Bermuda to Lisbon. From Lisbon, they flew to London. Donovan traveled under the name of Donald Williams and Stephenson as Michael

O'Connell. Page had concluded the seat numbers and aliases were part of the secret lives they both lived.

Part of that secrecy was connected with Bermuda. The island was Britain's oldest overseas territory, with a long tradition of self-government, and had become a key satellite in Stephenson's networks since the U-boat campaign in the Atlantic had intensified. The devastating losses from submarine attacks on convoys—twenty-nine ships sunk in one night with vital supplies—was destroying the lifeline that Roosevelt had promised Churchill at their meeting in Washington.

....

To make their deadly patrols in the Atlantic, U-boats were returning to and going from their bases on the French coast at Brest, Saint-Nazaire, and La Rochelle. By 1941 there were thirty-five short-range submarines and twenty-two newly delivered long-range submarines able to stay at sea for over a week. Château de Pignerolle at Saint-Barthélemy-d'Anjou became their communication center. From there Vice Admiral Karl Dönitz commanded the submarines. With better U-boats equipped with improved torpedoes, his operational plans had increased the number of kills, which had a serious effect on the British economy. On December 11, 1941, following Hitler's declaration of war on the United States, Dönitz launched his Unternehmen Paukenschlag, Operation Drumbeat, to target merchant ships sailing from the east coast of the United States and Canada. The US Navy, unprepared for antisubmarine warfare, depended on the Royal Navy and the Canadian Navy to prevent shipping losses.

Churchill and Roosevelt knew the vital importance of maintaining control of the sea lanes. The prime minister had told the War Cabinet, "It is the dominating fact of the war. Never for a moment must we forget that everything that happens elsewhere on land, or in the air, depends ultimately on winning the Battle of the Atlantic."

The entry of the United States into the war had increased the opportunity for U-boats as now there were many more convoys leaving New York and the East Coast of America for Europe. Often mist reduced visibility to a few hundred yards, making it difficult for ships' lookouts to spot a periscope in the towering waves. The sudden explosion of torpedoes striking, followed by the sinking of a ship and the screams of men drowning in icy water, could be heard in the night. The U-boat crews themselves received news on each convoy via the highly sophisticated cipher machine that every submarine carried. It was called Enigma.

It had a keyboard resembling a typewriter, and the keys were connected in a complex arrangement of wiring to drums inside the machine. If the message included the letter *A*, a drum would change it to a *Z*. *B* would become a *Y*. The permutation of letters could be endless. Only a U-boat commander knew how to decode the message by adjusting the settings of the drums. The Enigma's codes were regarded as unbreakable.

....

The machine was invented after the First World War by Arthur Scherbius, a gifted mathematician in Berlin, who sold it as "a secret writing machine." In the early 1920s banks and other financial institutions around Europe bought copies; the Vatican used it to communicate in Latin with nuncios, the Holy See's diplomats stationed around the world. The American ambassador in Berlin sent a machine to Henry Stimson, the new secretary of state in Washington, and received a curt response: "Gentlemen do not read each other's mail."

The German Navy was the first military branch to adopt Enigma, introducing it into service in 1926. By 1928 the German army had introduced its own version, the Enigma G, updated in 1930. The addition of a plugboard greatly increased its cryptographic strength, and additional complexity was repeatedly added to the military Enigma machines, making decryption more and more difficult. Each rotor could be set to one of twenty-six possible positions. Codebooks were printed in red, water-soluble ink on pink paper, so they could easily be destroyed if a U-boat was endangered and captured.

But in the summer of 1938, the Polish Army cryptology unit had been working to develop its skill of reading Wehrmacht code traffic, and had found reasons to fear that Hitler planned to invade their country.

....

In 1938 the Polish Army had not yet been ready to share its secrets on Enigma with British codebreakers. But a well-placed agent inside Warsaw would help.

Betty Pack's marriage to British diplomat Arthur Pack had suffered a terrible blow when he was transferred to Warsaw. Arthur Pack blamed what he saw as his wife's personal and political indiscretions in Spain. He had no idea that Betty not only was keeping a succession of love affairs from him but also was reporting back to British Naval Intelligence. She had already come to the attention of the SIS, and Arthur's transfer to Warsaw might well have been an excuse to move her to an area of Europe that, in the summer of 1937, was fast becoming an important place to have a cool and effective spy. Betty was twenty-seven when she arrived in Warsaw that September, young and vivacious, with a reputation for fun. Her easy manner with men made her disliked by the conservative diplomats and hostesses with whom she mixed in Warsaw, but it would make her an agent of real importance to the SIS. Her work in the Polish capital would have a real effect on the outcome of the war.

On New Year's Eve 1937, her husband suffered a stroke. Betty nursed him with care, and in February 1938 they visited England, where Arthur would stay to convalesce. Betty returned to Warsaw alone, and within a few weeks her double life of sexual and international intrigue had moved into a new gear.

Living across from the Packs' apartment in the diplomatic quarter of the city was a handsome young diplomat named Edward Kulikowski who worked at the Polish Foreign Office. Over suppers of caviar, picnics by the Vistula, and nights of passion in Kulikowski's small apartment, Pack gently questioned her lover about Poland's foreign policies toward its German neighbor.

One night Kulikowski let slip about a possible Polish agreement with Germany in which Warsaw would receive a small area of Czechoslovakia, known as Teschen, in return for acquiescing to Hitler's planned annexation of the Sudetenland. The next morning Pack relayed the conversation with the British embassy's passport control officer, Jack Shelley, who found the information fascinating and instructed her to immediately find out more. Lieutenant Colonel Shelley was the SIS's senior officer in Poland. From then on Pack received a monthly stipend from the service's funds.

Suspicious that the vulnerable Poles might be seeking to make further deals with Hitler, Shelley asked her to increase her contacts with senior Polish diplomats and politicians. Very quickly, she made what would be a vital contact at the American embassy when she found herself seated at a sumptuous dinner next to Count Michael Lubienski, the Polish foreign minister's senior advisor. As the guests moved from the dining room to the glittering ballroom, Pack, realizing that the count had access to the highest levels of secret documents, gave him her undivided attention. He was similarly transfixed, and next morning a bouquet of roses arrived at her apartment. That night Pack made love to the married count.

As the pair became increasingly inseparable, she began to gently inquire about his work. As she later said, she was always surprised at how easy "close-mouthed patriots give away secrets in bed."

Through her affair with Lubienski, she garnered information about Enigma. The Poles had obtained early commercial versions of Enigma and were by far the most advanced in understanding how it worked. The SIS knew the Germans planned to make Enigma their central method of message transmission and that breaking its cipher would be of utmost importance in a coming conflict. Lubienski's boss, Foreign Minister Józef Beck, was kept up-to-date with all developments on Enigma, and Lubienski himself had sight of these secret reports. Through her passionate relationship with him, Pack was able to pass Shelley confirmation that the Poles had been able to read some Enigma traffic, the details of the Polish cryptanalysis unit, and the fact that the Poles had been able to manufacture some of the machines.

Pack sensed how enormously important it would be for Polish cryptanalysts to be able to intercept secret messages from within the German

High Command to its generals whose troops were beginning to amass close to the Polish border.

She told Shelley that her lover had told her that the Polish crypt-analysts had learned that the Wehrmacht had a machine, called a radio-telegraph, which would encode a typed message to be sent over the airwaves and decoded by a machine at the receiving end.

In his report to London, Shelley wrote, "It means more traffic and codes for your end to break."

From Britain, where plans were developing to create a code-breaking center in a Buckinghamshire mansion called Bletchley Park, came a priority response: "Send more."

Pack's information had reached London months before Polish intelligence officially shared some of its knowledge of Enigma with Britain. While Britain's cryptanalysts were beginning to consider the information sourced on Enigma from Pack and other intelligence routes, Shelley brought her to the attention of Colin Gubbins. Gubbins, in turn, mentioned her to William Stephenson, who quickly realized he had an effective, if unorthodox, agent right at the heart of the unfolding events in Europe. Instructed to stick close to Lubienski, Pack even went to Berlin with him when he made a trip there on official business in September 1938. Lubienski had orders from Warsaw to travel to Nuremburg, where he was to be the Polish representative at the Nazi Party Day rally. Pack kissed him good-bye in Berlin; she had secret orders of her own.

International events were unfolding rapidly, with Hitler demanding the incorporation of the Sudetenland in Czechoslovakia into Germany, while British and French leaders were advising the Czechs to concede to the Nazi demands. The SIS urgently needed information on how far Germany's real plans for Czechoslovakia went. One source was the office of Konrad Henlein, of the Sudeten German Party, whose political dominance in that region was partly behind Britain and France's feeling that Prague should accept its loss. Henlein had met Hitler on September 1 to complete the plans for German accession of the Sudetenland and, by September 14, the day Lubienski sat through the rally in Munich, he had instructed his men to carry out a series of terror attacks. The

SIS instructed a local agent in Prague to burgle Henlein's office and pass documents to Pack to copy. This she did.

On September 29, Germany, Italy, France, and Britain signed the Munich Agreement, designed to trade Sudeten territory for peace. The Czechs were not consulted. German occupation of the area was to be completed by October 10. In the fullness of time, as Pack's previous lover Kulikowski had predicted during those romantic walks by the Vistula, Poland's own claims to Teschen would be honored by Germany when it occupied the rest of Czechoslovakia early in 1939.

As tensions mounted, most British diplomats left Poland. Pack wanted to stay, but Beck had become aware of her affair with Lubienski. She would almost certainly be in danger if the foreign minister began to suspect that his chef de cabinet had been sharing secrets with her. It was time for Betty Pack to move on. It hurt her to leave Lubienski but, as she later wrote, this was "the end of my first secret service mission."

Before she flew out of Warsaw, Jack Shelley told her that "the firm" would be back in touch. In the meantime, Enigma remained a priority in London.

....

In July 1939 Menzies, concerned about the increasing possibility of war, had asked Gubbins if he would use his contacts in Polish intelligence, which he had developed during his mission to Warsaw six months before, to discover more about Enigma. He had arranged for Alastair Denniston, the senior cryptographer at the Government Code and Cypher School in London, to brief Gubbins on Enigma. He told Gubbins his own network of international cryptologists included three codebreakers working with Poland's cryptology unit. They were using "reverse engineering and theoretical mathematics" to break the Enigma's Wehrmacht code.

Gubbins had discussed the situation with his contacts in Polish Intelligence. He was told to reserve rooms for himself and Denniston in Warsaw's Bristol Hotel, long a favorite stopover for English travelers.

Denniston would carry a large leather suitcase, suitably plastered with hotel and ship stickers, which would mark him as a seasoned traveler. Arriving at the hotel they saw in the lobby a suitcase matching Denniston's in a pile of baggage. While Gubbins distracted a porter with his own luggage, Denniston removed the identical suitcase and placed his own in its place before taking it out of the lobby and getting in a waiting taxi. The driver was a Polish intelligence officer who took him to the airport. The suitcase contained a German Wehrmacht Enigma cipher machine that Polish Intelligence had stolen. In hours Denniston was back in London with it. After meeting with his own intelligence contacts, Gubbins caught the next flight to London.

....

On August 22, 1939, Denniston drove forty miles out of the city, with the suitcase holding the Enigma encryption machine, to Bletchley Park, the new home of the Government Code and Cypher School. Its staff were at the peak of their careers as mathematicians, linguists, and university professors who had taught Latin and classics. They were assisted by women who had been drafted in from around the country.

Rozanne Colchester was nineteen when she arrived at Bletchley and found herself working in one of its wooden huts helping to decode messages between Luftwaffe bomber pilots during the London Blitz. She would recall, "We girls worked through the night in smoky, claustrophobic quarters and off-duty we amused ourselves with card games and gossip. We were each reminded that if we talked about our work you could be shot. But it was all terribly exciting."

That excitement increased with the arrival of Denniston and the suitcase. He carried it into hut 8, where day and night a guard was posted. Alan Turing was among the men who inspected the Enigma machine, along with others who would become legends in the code-breaking world of Bletchley: Gordon Welchman, Edward Travis, Hugh Alexander, and, of course, Denniston. A Cambridge University graduate, Joan Clarke, would soon join them in their examination of Enigma.

Her work as deputy head of hut 8 would later be key in cracking the code used by the German navy to communicate with its U-boat fleet.

Two days after Denniston had lifted the cipher machine out of the suitcase, Britain signed a Mutual Assistance Treaty with Poland. On September 1, Germany invaded Poland. Two days later Britain and France declared war on Germany and the Chamberlain government appointed Churchill First Lord of the Admiralty, the precursor to him becoming prime minister and forming a coalition government in May 1940.

On the day Britain declared war on Germany, Denniston told Gubbins he would need the "professor of mathematics type" to work with his codebreakers to decode the Enigma machine. He organized a crossword competition in the *Daily Telegraph*. Winners were discreetly asked if they would like to take part in a "particular type of work as a contribution to the war effort." Responses came from chess champions, crossword solvers, and an academic who lectured on the esoteric subject of papyrology, turning reeds into writing paper in ancient Egypt. It had been one of the clues in the competition. Those selected were sent to Bletchley Park to work with Team Enigma.

Denniston also chose a number of women whose skills in the crossword competition satisfied him they would make good cryptologists. Within Bletchley Park the newcomers became known as the "Boffins and Debutantes." The intelligence they would produce would be classified as "Ultra Secret," higher than the normally highest classification, "Most Secret." Ultra Secret messages were sent to the intelligence chiefs at the War Office, Air Ministry, Admiralty, and the Foreign Office. On Churchill's instructions Gubbins also received copies over the teleprinter installed in his office.

The women would also download information transmitted from British embassies or traffic generated across the British Empire by the telecommunications company Cable & Wireless, Britain's link with the world of business. Since the outbreak of war the company's traffic was read by MI6 for anything of interest to the war effort.

Traffic that was decided to be "only commercially sensitive" was rerouted to the intended recipients, including banks in the City of

London and corporations. Some of the messages were sent to Churchill's war rooms under the pavement of the Whitehall area of Westminster. Those were read by Colonel Henry Bevan, listed on the bunker's staff list as controller of deception. How he decided on the fate of those documents remains unknown to this day.

....

A month after Team Enigma had produced its first encoded messages, Churchill had described the transcripts as his "golden eggs," and ordered they should be delivered daily to him. A dispatch rider brought them in a buff-colored box whose key Churchill kept on his watch chain. On the cover of the locked box Denniston had written, ONLY TO BE OPENED BY THE PRIME MINISTER IN PERSON. Churchill would read them in bed. In his midsixties Churchill slept little, his moods raced like clouds across his baby face, as he reminded his staff of the pace of Hitler's victories: Poland in twenty-six days, Norway in twenty-four days, Denmark in twenty days, Holland in five days, and Luxembourg in twelve hours. Then he would smile and read out the Enigma transcripts at a Cabinet meeting. "Now we know his next move. We are resolved to destroy Hitler and every vestige of his Nazi regime. We will never parley, we will never negotiate. We will never surrender."

In their huts in Bletchley Park, the growing band of eavesdroppers worked through the night deciphering the meaningless letters and figures. Encouraged by Denniston, others tested all the possible settings on the stolen Enigma as they decoded the steady stream of messages.

Within months Team Enigma began to read messages from Hitler's generals to their field commanders, reports on the position of U-boats, requests for men and material.

....

Strategically located a few hundred miles off the coast of the Carolinas, Bermuda had become a base for monitoring U-boats lurking under the sun-glazed surface of the Atlantic. A special liaison unit, SLU, composed of codebreakers from Bletchley, had been posted to the island. It was stationed at the Royal Navy base near the ancient town of Saint George. The unit's members had arrived with their decoding equipment on board Britain's latest and most powerful battleship, *King George V*. The SLU included a number of women cryptologists—in fact, the women outnumbered the men, who were mostly married, middle aged, and absorbed in their work. The women were young, single, and excited at the prospect of serving the war in a sunny climate while unscrambling U-boat radio traffic and plotting their positions. The information was sent to US Army Air Force bases on the East Coast from where USAAF aircraft flew patrols to attack the U-boats. An early success came when two U-boats were located carrying mines to lay in the shipping lanes out of New York. The aircraft spotted them on the surface with their crew manhandling the mines into sea. As the U-boats crash-dove they were sunk.

....

At their regular monthly meetings in London, Stephenson and Donovan had discussed with Gubbins how the Pan Am Clipper flights from Bermuda to neutral Lisbon could be used to the advantage of the SOE and OSS. The plane carried not only mail from other Caribbean islands but also passengers from South America.

Before the war those passengers had included German ambassadors and their staff returning for home leave and Abwehr agents from missions on the continent. All were protected by the diplomatic immunity of their passports. That protection had been withdrawn at the outbreak of war at the request of MI6 after it was discovered that Canaris had planted spies in British companies in Buenos Aires, Santiago, Rio de Janeiro, Montevideo, and elsewhere on the continent.

MI6 spies in Argentina learned that its government had been told by the Japanese ambassador that Japan planned to invade the Falkland Islands, long a British territory in the South Atlantic. The islands would be used as a base for the Axis to launch attacks on British merchant ships carrying supplies for Britain. The ambassador promised the occupation of the Falklands would also ensure the return of Argentina's sovereignty over the islands, and the aircraft carriers from which the attack on Pearl Harbor had been launched would lead the attack.

On hearing the news, Churchill sent seventeen hundred British troops to the Falklands, telling Foreign Minister Anthony Eden, "It will be a serious matter to lose the Falklands to the Japanese." Navy warships were dispatched from Gibraltar to reinforce the Royal Navy base at Port Stanley, the Falklands' capital. In Buenos Aires the British ambassador, Esmond Ovey, had delivered a blunt message from London to the government "not to become involved in a matter which would end their neutrality."

The Japanese threat never materialized.

....

FBI agents stationed in Bermuda checked the mail bags on Pan Am flights for letters with a suspicious address that could be destined for German intelligence. One of the world's experts on secret ink, Stanley Collins, was employed by the FBI to examine confiscated envelopes. At his disposal was a 200-power microscope that could reveal if secret ink had been used to address an envelope and if the handwriting on a letter inside the envelope contained an unusual number of punctuation marks—periods and commas. Collins had discovered they could be microdots containing messages. It was a subtle method used by the Abwehr of sending secrets through the mail. Using a method Collins had developed called "hypermicrophotographic," the microdots could be enlarged and viewed while still inside the envelope. Messages they contained were read before the letters were returned to the mail bags from which they had been removed.

In London, Stephenson, Donovan, and Gubbins had decided how the Pan Am Clipper flight to Lisbon from Bermuda could be used to unmask the clandestine activities in Latin America of citizens working for German intelligence. Their passports identified them as businessmen of various countries flying to Lisbon on business. Often it was to meet with the Reich Ministry for War Production at its offices in Lisbon to sign contracts. Their names were passed to MI5 and FBI officers in Bermuda to be checked against known collaborators. However, there was a limit to what could be done to stop them from using the airline. To go too far could result in a public outcry in their own countries and damage trade with the United States and Britain.

Using his contacts with Pan Am, Donovan arranged for suspected Latin American passengers on the Lisbon flights to be wined and dined in the island's colonial-style Princess Hotel while the flying boat was being fueled. Their baggage was placed in a storage room and would be taken on board when the flight was called.

Gubbins had agreed a dozen SOE women—who had learned how to pick locks, open sealed envelopes, and use a matchbox-size camera—could be sent to Bermuda. Dressed in airline overalls, they were taken to the baggage storage room and began to open the suitcases and trunks. Once open, a case or trunk was carefully searched and envelopes and documents were photographed with their cameras.

The documents were then replaced in the same position from where they had been taken and the baggage locked without leaving a trace of tampering. The rolls of film were taken to Stanley Collins to develop in his laboratory. In an envelope stamped DIPLOMAT MAIL, the negatives Collins had developed were entrusted to the seaplane's pilot. At Lisbon he would hand over the envelope to a member of the British embassy. It would be couriered to London by a Queen's Messenger.

....

On a late spring day in March 1942, seven Special Duties high-winged Lysanders left Newmarket and flew to their new base at Tempsford. They descended between a gap in the hills and passed over small villages to land on the longest of the runways, which Jasper Maskelyne had disguised as hedges on either side of farm tracks. In the distance were Gibraltar Farm and several other farm buildings. All bore the hallmark of the illusionist's skills: moldering thatch on roofs, windows with broken glass, barns with gaps in their roof slates. What had been a worker's cottage had been left with only its gable ends standing.

Wherever the pilots looked as they taxied along the perimeter, the impression was of dereliction everywhere. An old tractor and trailer stood in a field that had been plowed as if ready for sowing. Hay rotted in a loft. Two pig sties stood empty. The only signs of life were ducks on a pond.

Watching them park on their hardstands was a tall young woman in a WAAF uniform. She stood beside a truck with a welcoming smile and said she had come to bring them to their quarters. She pointed out the boxlike Flying Control Tower, standing alone, and the other Nissen huts that housed the necessities of an operational airfield: the equipment store, meteorological section, photographic section, the parachute packers hut, aircraft maintenance where the ground staff worked, the sick bay, the canteen, the officers' mess, and the quarters for the other ranks. Finally she pointed to the derelict-looking farmhouse. "Gibraltar Farm. Everything you will do starts inside there. It's the Ops Block."

With another smile she climbed back behind the wheel to drive them to their quarters.

....

On a sunny afternoon in April 1942, Selwyn Jepson walked across the lobby and past the sandbagged guard post at the entrance to SOE headquarters in Baker Street. His FANY driver waited with his car. In his briefcase were the latest files he had collected from Gubbins's office of the women who had told him he was satisfied they were ready to be sent behind enemy lines.

Between them they would liaise with the French Resistance and recruit and build networks across occupied France, and teach the members of the Resistance how to carry out sabotage operations. The women agents would use their wireless sets to arrange parachute drops of weapons and ammunition and act as couriers, passing messages from one group to another.

They all had their cover stories and had demonstrated their mental and physical fitness, their linguistic ability, and all they had learned about the L-pill, the suicide pill they each could carry. The capsule's skin was insoluble and if swallowed would pass through the body without causing harm. Only when crushed between the teeth would the pill release the potassium cyanide, bringing instant death.

Jepson had sent copies of the files to Vera Atkins to review. She had an encyclopedic knowledge of wartime France, about travel, curfews, food, and fuel rationing and a multitude of other restrictions that would govern the agents' day-to-day lives. Her information had helped to forge documents for their cover stories.

Atkins also used it in the lectures she gave to recruits at the training camps and the finishing school at Beaulieu. At the end of each lecture she would collect from trainees credentials they still had: visiting cards, Metro tickets, family photos, French matches. They would be added to cover stories, giving them more credibility if they were stopped and searched by a German patrol.

After attending her lecture, Jepson saw Atkins had a magnetism that he had seen in only some of the women he had interviewed. On that sunny afternoon he told his driver he would walk to Orchard Court, the apartment block where the SOE had provided Atkins with an apartment on the second floor. It had three bedrooms: one for Atkins, one that had been converted into her office, and one for her butler, Andrew Park, who spoke fluent French, wore a dark suit, and kept the apartment spotless. He used Vera's ration book to do her shopping and prepared afternoon tea for his employer and her visitors.

Jepson used the elevator to the second floor at Orchard Court and walked down the corridor to a door at the end. It was opened by Park, who said that Madam was waiting in her office and led the way down the hall, knocked, and opened a door announcing, "Major Jepson is here, Madam." Jepson had decided Park had the quiet efficiency of Jeeves and only ever heard him call Atkins "Madam" or "Miss Atkins."

She motioned Jepson to sit in an armchair that matched the one behind her desk, on which the files Jepson had sent her were neatly stacked.

Atkins reached for a cigarette in a silver box on the desk and lit it with a lighter beside the box. Both were gifts from Buckmaster after she had been appointed as the French Section Intelligence Officer. Drawing on the cigarette until its ash glowed, she placed it between her first and second finger, stained with nicotine on her right hand, and nodded at the cigarette box as if to offer Jepson one. He shook his head; he had given up smoking months ago. Atkins smiled. It was a running issue between them how long he could abstain. She admired determination.

What followed could well have reminded Jepson of one of the stage plays he had written. Atkins said it was time for tea and stood up and clapped her hands. Almost on cue the door opened and Park entered carrying a butler's tray holding a teapot and two cups, a milk jug, and a plate of jam on toast. With a deferential nod to Atkins he left the room.

6

Agents by Moonlight

IN THE GATHERING DUSK on that April evening in 1942, blackout regulations had once more come into force as Atkins and Jepson continued their discussion about the files of the women agents he had asked her to review.

She went to her office window to draw the black curtains. Below in the road the taxis and buses had their headlights screened and lights in shop windows were being switched off. The first of the air raid wardens were patrolling the streets and shouting, "Lights out!"

Park had reported he had ensured all the drapes in the apartment were drawn, as were those in other apartments. He was Orchard Court's air raid patrol officer. When a siren warning wailed across the city he would go to the lobby with a list of residents and check them off as they hurried to their designated shelter. The exception was Atkins. On the first night of the Blitz she had told Park she would remain in the apartment; she gave him no explanation and he had not asked.

As she turned from the window, Jepson was again struck; there was something about Atkins, not just her tweed suit, neatly styled fair hair, and shoes that set off her ankles. "There was something else, a protective look, as if she had a personal duty of care for the young women being selected to go behind enemy lines," he would recall.

Settled behind her desk, Atkins lit another cigarette and turned back to the files. Each was stamped STUDENT REPORT. A passport-size photo was pinned to the cover on which was written the woman's date of birth and nationality. Each file contained reports from instructors and psychologists on every stage of the women's training, which had been designed to push them to the limit of endurance.

At Arisaig on the west coast of Inverness, Scotland, they had each undergone a grueling twenty-four-hour trek through the mountains to learn how to live off the land and how to plan an attack by using small ravines as cover. They had been taught to throw themselves off swings and slides and keep their legs together to practice parachute landings without breaking a limb.

All students had been given demolition training and had been shown how to use plastic explosives to derail trains. The combat course had taught them how to use the knife each had been given, and how to adopt a crouch position when using a revolver and to shoot twice at a target in quick succession.

Beaulieu was the climax of their training. On arrival Lieutenant Colonel S. H. C. Wooldridge, the commandant, had invited them to dinner in the staff mess and introduced them to their instructors and domestic staff, and had set out to make them feel at home. They would each have their own bedroom in one of the estate houses, but they should observe the government notice in bathrooms to use only five inches of water for a bath to save fuel. Meals would be plentiful, and tea and coffee would always be available. Alcohol, on the other hand, would only be served in the bar in the main house. The curriculum would cover all they had learned at other training camps but was intended to refresh them at this final stage of their training.

The commandant told them they would all have cover stories that had been created to enable them to survive in France. They would be taken to London to the SOE clothing section to select the clothes they would wear in France. These had either been produced in France or made to look as if they were. They would start to wear the garments so the items would look well worn and not arouse the suspicion of the police or Gestapo in France.

....

The instructors came from various backgrounds. One had been a Scotland Yard Murder Squad detective. Another a radio operator on a ship. A gamekeeper at Balmoral, the Royal estate in Scotland, had taught the students that hill climbing at night strengthened their legs while they searched for the perfect field for receiving parachute drops. Another instructor showed them how to hold a flashlight to send a recognition signal in Morse code to the aircraft approaching with supplies. Students had been taught how to prepare a landing strip for aircraft that would deliver and collect agents.

The instructors included Harold Philby. The son of the great Arabist, Sir Harry St. John Philby, friend and adviser to King Ibn Saʻūd of Saudi Arabia, he was born at Ambala in India's Punjab. Despite his crippling stutter his lectures made him a popular member of the Beaulieu staff. Nicknamed "Kim" after the boy in Rudyard Kipling's novel *Kim*, he had the captivating charm of his father and had won a scholarship to Trinity College, Cambridge. Fluent in German, French, and Spanish, he had graduated with a degree in economics.

In February 1937 he had become a foreign correspondent for the *London Times* in the Spanish Civil War. His reports from the pro-Franco forces were noted by Stewart Menzies at MI6. The *Times* editor was asked to switch Philby to cover the Republican side. On Christmas Eve that year, the car he was in with three other correspondents was hit by a shell. The other reporters were killed. Philby suffered a head wound.

In July 1939 he returned to the *Times* office in London and became the paper's correspondent with the British Expeditionary Force until the Dunkirk evacuation. In July 1940 Philby joined MI6 as a counterintelligence officer. Months later, on the strength of his knowledge and experience in Spain and France, he joined the SOE as an instructor.

....

Philby's arrival in the SOE followed after Atkins heard him lecture on sabotage and subversion. She told Gubbins that the training curriculum should include his lectures.

Philby had been given a cottage on the Beaulieu estate where he would prepare his lectures for students. He would start with their cover story. It not only had to be memorized but also required that the students think not in English but in the regional dialect from where they would be operating. Above all they must be familiar with their papers—work passes, travel documents, and identity papers that had been forged for their cover story.

At the end of his lecture Philby would choose students to test on their cover story. He would often remind students to make a will and write a letter to a loved one, which would be kept by the SOE and, in the event of their death, sent to their next of kin.

....

At Beaulieu, Army Captain John Taylor gave a lecture he called "Surviving." He began in a soft voice: "Being in the field sounds glamorous, but is also very lonely. You are cut off from your family, from your friends, from your country. You will have a cover story which you must live by as you set out to undermine the morale of the enemy and raise the morale of those you will be working with, the Resistance."

As he spoke he moved among the students, watching their reaction, knowing they were waiting for the gruesome things that he had to tell them. "Over the past weeks you will have learned from other lectures all aspects of the underground life you will lead. What I am going to tell you does not guarantee your safety. Your motto must be 'Kill—or be killed.' But remember that while the chance to be caught is small, the mistake of thinking the enemy is asleep is a mistake not to make."

"If they catch you they will try to be friendly, saying they are not barbarians, but that they want to obtain from you all you know, names, networks, and targets. If you are caught you need to hope it is by only one soldier not even a Gestapo officer. Then you need to insert your finger into the corner of his mouth and turn it in his mouth against his cheek. You will find it tears the skin easily and rips open his mouth. At the same time kick him in his testicles. As he crumbles under the pain, use your knife and insert it behind his ear. He will be dead. But remember: Never relax your cautions."

....

Judgments on students were recorded in their files in neatly penned comments by their course instructors. They were intended to provide guidance when selecting agents for missions.

"Student shows she can work alone and has leadership qualities." Another observed, "She had a reserved personality but has determination." One student was described as "excellent with shooting with a pistol, coding and decoding messages."

The head of the training school at Thame Park in Oxfordshire, where wireless operators were taught, wrote of one student, "When she came here her transmission speed was slow, owing to her fingers being swollen by chilblain. Six weeks later with help from our doctor her speed has improved every day and she leaves here as one of our best operators."

A graduate's report from Arisaig, the SOE training school in the wilds of Scotland, noted, "This student can run very fast during combat training and has become an expert in using her knees and elbows, and to chop with the side of her hand, use finger jabs to the eyes or the throat, and perform holds to snap a wrist."

One female agent had passed all her courses in transposing Morse into cipher at a rate of over twenty-five words a minute and had developed a "fist," or style, that would identify her as the sender. She had also been taught how to create a "Sked," a schedule of times and days when she should send messages, and to keep them to no more than ten minutes for each. Another had passed all her courses in clandestine communications and how to create a dead letterbox and live an illegal existence in enemy territory. Her pass-out report marked her as A-Plus.

The psychologist reports were analytical. "This student is rather fastidious in her attitude but can be exacting in taste." Another was "prone to self reproach and traces of perfection, but never indecisive. Makes good contact with others."

There were comments on student responses at classroom lectures on subjects such as map reading; making a cast of a key by using a bar of soap; silently breaking a window; recognizing the uniforms of the Gestapo, SS, SD; and using a shop window's reflection to see if one was being watched from behind.

....

Gubbins knew that as speculation grew on both sides of the Channel that an Allied invasion of the European mainland was inevitable, it was critical for the SOE to provide the Resistance with agents who had been trained to form and lead groups of patriots from all quarters of the population. Some were opponents of Marshal Philippe Pétain, who had said, "It is better to become a Nazi province than to collaborate with a corpse across the Channel." Others were encouraged by Charles de Gaulle's broadcasts from London. He had regularly broadcast that Pétain was senile and betraying his country and that its people should have the confidence to stand against the Nazis. Many were Communists who, after Hitler had invaded Russia, had joined Resistance groups. In France, all men, unless they were classified as "essential war workers," were often drafted to Germany as forced laborers.

Gubbins had discussed with Buckmaster how the SOE could best use women to create and equip a secret force to work with the Resistance. Networks would be formed and based across France. Each would have an organizer, a courier, and a wireless operator. The organizer would be responsible for recruiting local Resistance groups and selecting targets. The couriers would be a link between other Resistance groups. The wireless operator would keep London informed on suitable drop zones for parachuting in agents, ammunition, and equipment.

Operating a radio would be one of the most dangerous jobs for an agent. Radios needed to be transported and would be hard to explain if an agent were stopped and searched by a patrol. Soon the Germans were using sophisticated detection equipment installed in trucks to pinpoint radio transmissions. SOE operators had to transmit and receive on same "skeds," which meant they had to stay on the air for long periods. Every wireless operator lived in constant fear that they would hear the slam of a truck's door outside where they were tapping out the Morse code.

Yvonne Cormeau would recall, "I'm very nervous but patient; you need that for radio work. You need the patience to do the coding and the decoding. You need the resourcefulness to be able to decide whether to go on if you think somebody's listening in or to cut off and ask for another 'sked.' I must admit to butterflies floating in my tummy all the time. You had to have your eyes in the back of your head as well as in the front."

In February 1942 Churchill informed the War Cabinet he approved the use of women behind enemy lines. They would be enlisted into the FANY as a cover for their role in the SOE.

Gubbins told Buckmaster that the work of couriers and wireless operators would be performed by women. They would arouse less suspicion; they had been trained to memorize messages or conceal them in the hems of their skirts or in underwear. Women could travel on trains to visit relatives or ride bicycles to go shopping with messages hidden beneath groceries. Buckmaster had promoted Vera Atkins to become F Section's senior intelligence officer, with prime responsibility for selecting women for their missions.

He had sent Atkins a memo, which she passed across the desk for Jepson to read. "Female agents must always look ordinary and in no way conspicuous. When she goes over she will have learned to pass as a French woman."

....

The all-clear siren had sounded across London on that April night as Atkins continued to discuss with Jepson the women whose files she had reviewed. She had used two judgments when reading them. Was the woman capable of carrying out a special mission? Could she remain behind enemy lines for an indefinite period?

Atkins picked up a file with a photo on the cover of Yvonne Rudellat. Jepson recognized her from her interview six months earlier. Her dark hair had strands hanging over her broad forehead, and her eyes and cheekbones were striking features in her oval face. Her smile was relaxed as if she accepted one of the observations in her file that she was "unworldly with an innocence and anxiety to please." That quality would be "a valuable asset," an instructor had written.

Born in Lille, France, Rudellat's father had been a horse trader for the French Army in the First World War. Her mother was already a widow when she had sent Yvonne to England to find work during the Depression. She already spoke English and had become a salesgirl in Selfridges, the department store in Oxford Street. From there she had taken a job as a hotel receptionist and had met and married a waiter at the hotel. The marriage had ended in divorce.

When the war started she had met Buckmaster when he came for dinner at the hotel and spoke to her in French. She told him she "wanted to do something to help France." He had given her an address and told her to write there with any photos she had of France and include her own details.

It was one of the letters that had landed on Jepson's desk. The result was an interview, which had led to his recommendation she should be sent for training. In his own report after the interview he had described her as "someone who outshines several of those I have seen so far."

Yvonne had been two of the women on a course at Wanborough Manor learning how to shoot and make explosives. At night when it was completely moonlit she was taught to hide in the shadows. On other nights she was sent into a forest with a revolver in her hand to shoot as fast as she could at targets that popped up. One day she had been sent to a railway tunnel and told to study what damage could be done and to decide which kind of explosive devices should be used, where they should be positioned, and the time fuse needed. Her report was read out to her class as an example of excellence. She was sent to the Western Highlands of Scotland and finally to Beaulieu, where she was given the code name Jacqueline.

Atkins told Jepson she was going to recommend Rudellat as a courier and wireless operator for the network Buckmaster was planning to establish in Paris and the surrounding region. It would have the code name Physician, chosen from the notebook of fifty names he kept to select networks for F Section. Beginning with Acolyte there was Wrestler, Hermit, Juggler, Tinker, Bricklayer, Clergyman, Freelance, and Ventriloquist. He had told Atkins that the names "reflected moments in my own life."

Atkins picked up another folder with a photo of a face with a dark complexion and stamped with the name Andrée Borrel. She wore her cap at a jaunty angle with a neatly knotted khaki tie, drill jacket, and khaki shirt, the FANY uniform she had worn during training.

Born on November 18, 1919, in a working-class Paris suburb, Borrel had left school at fourteen to work in a bakery to support the household budget. Her parents were both left-wing idealists. When Borrel was seventeen they sent her to a cousin in Bilbao, Spain, to help the anti-Franco rebels in the Spanish Civil War. She had returned to Paris at the outbreak of war, and the family had moved from Paris to Toulon in the south.

Jepson told Atkins that when he had interviewed Borrel she had produced a document confirming she had been trained as a nurse's aid with the Association des Dames Française, the ADF. Following her training she had nursed wounded French Army soldiers in Beaucaire Hospital in Nîmes during their retreat from the advancing Wehrmacht.

She had been nursing on that summer day, June 17, 1940, when Marshal Pétain had told the nation France had been defeated and now that he had been appointed prime minister, he would seek an armistice with Germany. Borrel, not willing to accept the defeat of her country, joined the French Resistance and, together with her lover Maurice Dufour, helped RAF pilots who had been shot down over France to escape through the Pyrenees into Spain from where they were returned to England. Together the couple ran one of the last safe houses before the Pyrenees, near Perpignan. After the escape line was betrayed in 1941, they had to escape themselves. She had found a job in the British embassy in Lisbon as a French linguist and persuaded the ambassador to support her application to go to London. On arrival she had been sent to the Patriotic School that the SOE had set up to choose agents to be interviewed by Jepson and Atkins.

Her SOE report showed that instructors at various stages of her training had described her as having "current knowledge of French conditions, knows the reality of war; tough and committed; always enjoys nothing better than the use of weapons and explosives; says stabbing through the ear with a pencil is a good way to kill a German when he sleeps."

While Atkins lit another cigarette, she told Jepson that now that Churchill had decided that women agents would combine the roles of wireless operator and courier, Borrel was ideal for the Physician network, which was being set up to replace Autogyro, a Paris-based network that had been penetrated by the Gestapo earlier in the year.

....

As F Section's new intelligence officer, Atkins had read the SOE file on Francis Suttill, the agent Buckmaster had chosen to run Physician. Born to a British father and French mother, he had been educated at Stonyhurst College in Lancashire and studied law at the University of Lille in France. In 1931 he moved to London to continue his studies and eventually became a barrister. Buckmaster had met him in the French Club in Mayfair, where he was a member. Buckmaster used the club to find recruits. Buckmaster had decided that Suttill had "a clear intellectual vision and logical perspicacity," and asked Suttill if he would join the SOE and after training would be prepared to return to France as a link between F Section and the Resistance.

Atkins told Jepson that Suttill's file described him as "outstanding in all he does."

Borrel would have a cover story that would give her a key role in the Physician network. She would be the assistant to an agricultural salesman traveling through the departments of central France marketing equipment to farms. Her role would cause no comments in the farming community, where women generally did all the bargaining. She would recruit resisters and identify railway lines that could be sabotaged and places where arms could be dropped.

She had been given the code name Denise. Her identity card listed her as the sister of her employer, Francis Suttill. His code name was Prosper, the fifth-century theologian who preached predestination.

Atkins picked up Borrel's file, looked at her photo again, and said: "When I first saw her, I knew she had something special to offer."

....

It was late evening when Atkins and Jepson continued discussing the remaining files of female agents. Lise de Baissac was born in Mauritius. Vera Leigh was born in Leeds, England, but had been adopted by an American racehorse trainer with stables near Paris. Diana Rowden had been born in London and raised on the Italian Riviera, where her mother had a villa and a yacht named *Sans Peur* ("Without Fear"). Yolande Beekman was Dutch with a Swiss father. Maureen Patricia "Paddy" O'Sullivan was born in Dublin, the daughter of a French mother who had died of Spanish flu; her father was the editor of the *Freeman Journal,* an Irish republican newspaper. Denise Bloch was the daughter of a Jewish family in Lyon, France. Violette Szabo was a French national. She had met and married a French Foreign Legion officer who was killed in action. She had written to the War Office saying she wanted to enlist so that she could "avenge my husband's death." Each had received a letter inviting them to be interviewed by Jepson.

All had faced a final test near the end of their course at Beaulieu. In the early hours of the morning, an agent would be manhandled to a cellar by two men in Gestapo uniforms. Waiting there were more men in Gestapo uniforms, standing around a table. The agent was shoved to stand at the table. In the corner of the cellar a powerful spotlight would focus on her face. From around the table questions came in harsh German voices, picking apart her cover story, which she had memorized during the course. Any unlikely answer was treated with a slap in the face and threats of torture. The questions came faster, leaving her little time to think. She was told she could have an easy way out if she would tell what she knew. This seemed to go on for hours.

Suddenly the spotlight switched off and the black-out curtain across the window was opened, allowing daylight to flood in. The Gestapo men took off their caps and smiled. They were instructors. One was Kim Philby. Often he told the agent that she had passed the test but should avoid the mistakes made during the interrogation. "The test was designed to save your life in occupied France," he would say.

....

After the excitement of Poland, Betty Pack found herself back in Chile with her husband, Arthur, who, after recovering from his illness, had been posted to run the embassy's commercial section. The Foreign Office felt his old patch in South America would be a good place for him to complete his convalescence and hopefully rebuild his marriage. Betty Pack was listed as what the SIS called a Contact and Source in Place, a CSP.

Initially she passed the time playing with their daughter, Denise, and writing reports on Chile's German community and on the many prominent Chileans who were supportive of the Nazi cause. These were passed to London with the ambassador's dispatches. With Arthur busy in his own role, Betty wrote a series of anti-Nazi articles under the pseudonym Elizabeth Thomas for *La Nación* and the *South Pacific Mail*. During a visit to New York to see her mother, she met and had an affair with an Irish American officer in US Naval Intelligence, Paul Fairly. She told him she felt very removed from the war in Europe and wanted to get involved. On her return to Chile she told Arthur he could use evidence of her adultery to obtain a divorce. He said there would be no divorce until after the war but agreed they would be free to live their own lives. Betty left him and their daughter, who was now five, to return to New York.

An SIS agent was waiting for her when she arrived. John Pepper was a tall, good-looking Englishman who had been recruited by William Stephenson to work for the British Security Coordination. Pepper had been in the United States since June 1940, working on BSC's objectives of persuading Americans to join the war and identify those inside America who may be pro-German.

Pepper quickly formally recruited Pack and told her that BSC would give her money to rent an apartment in Washington on O Street, where she would mix with the cream of the city's diplomatic and political society and write a weekly report on their attitudes, which she would deliver to a BSC contact in a prearranged meeting at the Ritz-Carlton Hotel on Madison Avenue in New York. She was given the codename Cynthia.

Her first mission may well have been a test of her skills; if it was, she passed with flying colors. She was asked to uncover a female agent from a neutral country who was on her way to Britain to make pacifist propaganda for the Nazis. Pack followed the woman, noting her movements and contacts, and the agent was arrested in Bermuda while making her way to Europe onboard a Spanish steamer.

Pack carried out a number of low-grade intelligence-gathering missions until, during the spring of 1941, a man arrived at her apartment and introduced himself as Mr. Williams from the New York office. Pepper had never mentioned him and so Pack was immediately suspicious. She was aware that the FBI had taken an interest in her work, although she did not know that it already had a rapidly expanding file on her social life. Mr. Williams, a small, wiry man who she guessed was in his early forties, knew all about her and her family, as well as about Chile and Poland. He told her "the chief" was very pleased with her. Intrigued, Pack asked Mr. Williams if he knew the chief. "I think I know him well," said Mr. Williams, with a smile. "He is a terrible chap."

It was not until she met with Pepper again that she learned her visitor had been none other than William Stephenson himself, Britain's spymaster in the United States.

Stephenson's visit had been to size her up for a new and extremely difficult job. It had its seed in a memo Churchill had sent to the SIS outlining his concern with the volume and quality of information received from both the occupied and unoccupied areas of France. "So far as the Vichy Government is concerned, it is not creditable that we have so little information," Churchill wrote, and asked if SIS agents in the United States could be put to better use. Could Pack be the answer?

Since the fall of France the southern area of the country had been governed by a council of ministers, based in the town of Vichy. The Nazis permitted it to retain some diplomatic representation abroad and, as the United States had not yet entered the war against Hitler, Vichy France had a mission in Washington. For the British, standing alone against the tide of Nazi victory, the decisions of the Vichy leaders, Marshal Pétain and Premier Pierre Laval, could be vital.

Churchill was particularly concerned about whether Pétain would hand over the French Mediterranean fleet to the Germans, and about the 300 million dollars worth of gold reserves that the French were holding in Martinique in the West Indies. Stephenson had decided the Embassy of the Republic of France in Washington might be a soft target from which to discover this information. Pack was told to find out everything she could about the people who staffed the embassy, and to ascertain if any of them were suitable for helping her to find out deeper secrets.

Using her maiden name, Elizabeth Thorpe, Betty posed as a journalist and arranged an interview with the ambassador, Gaston Henry-Haye. Her meeting with him also brought her into contact with his press attaché, Charles Brousse. Brousse was a charming and good-looking forty-nine-year-old from Perpignan, who had been married three times. He was attracted to Pack immediately and they arranged to meet again. Pack discovered that he disliked the British but was far from pro-Nazi.

Over a period of months their affair developed with Pack reporting back everything that Brousse told her and even copying the entire contents of his address book. Brousse talked about his hatred of Laval and his fears for his family holdings in southern France, where he was co-owner of a major newspaper group. With his wealth tied up in these assets, he had little cash to spend. He had fallen in love with Pack while trying hard to keep the relationship from his American-born wife, Catherine. The strain was taking its toll. By the end of July, Pack had persuaded Brousse of the importance of providing small bits of information, and he began providing daily intelligence reports, which she sent to the BSC in New York.

Pack worked hard to keep Brousse motivated as a subagent, using Vichy support for Japan in the Pacific to persuade him to pass her in-clear copies of all cipher telegrams dispatched and received by the embassy. When the Japanese attacked Pearl Harbor on December 7, she won him over completely to the Allied side. From then on, Vichy cables obtained by Pack arrived on Roosevelt's desk within hours of their transmission.

Soon Pack would have a new contact in the OSS itself, and her relationship with Brousse would be key to an upcoming operation that would help protect thousands of American lives.

....

In March 1942 Betty Pack, SIS agent Cynthia, received an urgent call from her BSC handler, John Pepper, and rushed to meet him at the Ritz-Carlton Hotel in New York. He told her London wanted the Vichy French naval ciphers and asked if she could get them. The request startled her, but the urgency in Pepper's voice told her the only answer would be that she could.

The mission meant so much to London because of Churchill's urgent need to find out what Laval planned to do with the French fleet. Defensive action by the French fleet under Vichy orders would endanger an invasion of North Africa and could cost thousands of American lives—Americans would provide the vast majority of the invasion force. The French naval ciphers were now a target for the OSS as well as the SOE. The two services quickly decided to pool resources.

Since Churchill had returned from visiting Stalin, the Soviet leader had continued to press the prime minister to open a second front to ease the pressure German forces were putting on the Soviet troops. Roosevelt's military commanders had favored a landing in occupied Europe "as soon as possible." Britain's military leaders had convinced Churchill that such an invasion at that stage of the war could end in disaster. In the arguments between London and Washington it was finally agreed that an attack on French North Africa would drive out

Axis powers from the region, improve Britain's naval control of the Mediterranean, and prepare the way for an invasion of southern Europe, which would satisfy Stalin. Roosevelt had reluctantly agreed. It would be called Operation Torch.

Knowing what the Vichy French would do would require intelligence gathering. The secret code books in the Vichy government embassy in Washington were the key to unlocking their actions. Obtaining them fell to Pepper as Stephenson's assistant in New York, and he enlisted the help of Betty Pack, "a spy with no morals," as he later described her.

Pepper told Pack she would now have a new permanent liaison with the OSS, a Mr. Hunter. His real name was Colonel Ellery C. Huntingdon, a former Wall Street attorney with a confident, paternal manner and a soft Tennessee accent. Through Huntingdon, Pack's new American chain of command led to James R. Murphy, head of the OSS branch of counterespionage, and then to Bill Donovan, who was Huntingdon's squash partner as well as his boss.

Pack moved into an apartment in the Wardman Park Hotel in Washington, where Brousse and his wife were staying. It was close to the Vichy embassy. She quickly shared the details of her mission with Brousse, who told her getting to the naval ciphers was impossible. Only the chief cipher officer, a man named Benoit, could get into the locked code room, and the room containing the cipher book was always locked when not in use. Brousse had no access to the rooms, and a watchman guarded the embassy premises. Benoit, Pack discovered, was nearing retirement and was confused about his loyalties to Vichy. She approached him, but he refused to help. When Benoit retired, she assumed a false name and approached his replacement, a young aristocrat known to be anti-Nazi. But he too refused to cooperate.

Now her mind turned to burglary. She had walked near the embassy a number of times and had worked out that the safe in which the ciphers were kept was in a room on the ground floor. It had a window overlooking a small stretch of lawn that was shaded by trees. Pack went to New York, where she told Pepper and Huntingdon that she could enter the window via a ladder placed against the wall. She could pass the cipher books out to an accomplice who could photograph them and return them. On a dark night, it would be easy, she told them. The plan seemed crude but simple enough to work. It fell in line with what the OSS was calling "black bag" jobs, targeting diplomats and pilfering code books, and Huntingdon also knew that accessing the codes had been made even more urgent by events in France; Marshal Pétain had been replaced as head of the Vichy government by pro-Nazi Pierre Laval, whose stated aim was a "reconciliation between France and Germany."

Huntingdon said Pack's room at the Wardman Park Hotel would become the base for planning, and he had it swept for listening devices by an OSS operative, who turned up unannounced in the disguise of a pest control worker.

Over the following days Huntingdon, Brousse, and Pack spent hours going over a floor plan of the embassy and honing the plan. Huntingdon rented another room in the hotel for an OSS security team; they brought camera equipment to the apartment to rehearse copying the ciphers and made sure an OSS safecracker would be available for the night of the burglary. A former jailbird, he would receive $1,000 for the job. Brousse checked out the window in the code room to see how easily it could be opened. Pack began to "stroll home" at the same time each night and call a friendly hello to the night watchman. She was looking to establish a reason for being in the area on the night of the burglary, but her actions helped Brousse form an amendment to the plan. Brousse decided to confide in the guard that Pack was his lover and that they had nowhere to meet. He easily persuaded the man that they could spend some evenings together in Brousse's office in the embassy. Each night as they left they gave the guard a cheery *merci* for allowing them some time alone. They would not need to burgle the embassy after all; copying the documents would be an inside job.

Late in the evening of June 19, 1942, Brousse and Pack arrived at the embassy with two bottles of champagne and something to celebrate. It was the anniversary of the day they had met, they told the friendly guard, and invited him to join them in a drink. The couple then headed happily to a ground-floor room where they had been spending each evening. After a while Brousse checked on the guard and found him fast asleep. The champagne had contained a dose of Nembutal, which would keep him asleep for six hours. His dog had been drugged too. Everything was going according to plan.

Brousse went to the front door and let in the safecracker. He unlocked the naval attaché's office door and began work on the safe. Before he started, Pack made a note of the original settings so the dial could be returned to its place. The safecracker started work at one in the morning, but by the time he opened the safe it was almost four. There was not time to get the books to Wardman Park, have them copied, and returned before the arrival of the embassy's early morning cleaning staff. A dejected Pack held the two code books for a moment before returning them to the safe.

Two nights later they tried again, but this time the safecracker was unavailable and Pack had to try to open the safe herself. She had a note of the combination, but the door would not open. The ciphers again remained beyond their reach. Pack was brought to New York, where the safecracker told her what had happened. She had the correct combination but had failed to wait for the tumblers to fall into place before moving the dial again. It was a trick of the trade she could never have known.

Pack made her third attempt on the safe on June 23. The plan remained the same, but it was decided that it would be impossible to persuade the guard to take a spiked drink again. This time he and his dog would be awake during the break-in, but Pack's gall, cunning, and beauty saved the mission.

Shortly after midnight the two lovers entered the embassy and went to their usual spot on a settee in a salon near the code room. There was no sign of the guard or the dog, and as they sat together they felt uneasy. Suddenly Pack stood up and stripped, throwing her clothes around the room. She urged Brousse do the same, telling him they had to look like lovers if the guard came to investigate. A short while later there was a noise in the corridor and the door opened. The night watchman's flashlight settled on Pack, naked except for high heels and a pearl necklace. There was a gasp and an apology, and the guard disappeared.

With a relieved giggle, Pack pulled on her slip and picked the lock on the naval attaché's door. Then she rushed to the window and signaled with a flashlight. With the guard awake, the plan this time was to bring the safecracker in through the window. He climbed the wooden ladder and picked the lock of the code room. Now familiar with the combination, he quickly unlocked the safe, and Brousse and Pack handed the books—each the size of a large family Bible—to an OSS agent on the ladder outside.

It took more than two hours for the codes to be copied. Unable to dress for fear of the guard returning, Pack and Brousse smoked incessantly, their fear of getting caught building with each passing minute. It was obvious to them that if they were discovered in the act of copying the books the scandal would cause an international incident. An OSS officer, Donald Downes, had earlier cautioned Donovan that "entering a foreign embassy clandestinely and borrowing code books is full of great risk for everyone concerned."

At about 4:40 AM the safecracker returned and the books were put back in the safe. The pair tidied up after themselves, wiped the furniture and safe for fingerprints, and left by the front door.

When they got to the Wardman Park Hotel, they were taken to another room requisitioned by the OSS that had obviously only recently been filled with frantic activity. Cameras, lights, and tripods were positioned in different places, and photographic copies of the codes lay drying on every piece of furniture.

Standing among them with a large smile on his face was Colonel Huntingdon. Following the operation he would become head of the OSS's special operations department and become a key figure in the plans to invade North Africa. Betty Pack's success in obtaining the Vichy naval ciphers helped unlock Vichy communications around the world for the OSS.

On November 8, 1942, the military forces of the United States and the United Kingdom launched an amphibious operation against French North Africa, in particular the French territories of Algeria and Morocco. Torch's impact on the course of Anglo-American strategy during the remainder of the war would be enormous. It would be seen as the most important strategic decision that Allied leaders, including Stalin, made. It would enable the Allies to hold back D-day until the United States could complete the mobilization of its immense industrial and manpower resources for the titanic ground battles of 1944.

Betty Pack remained on the books of the Secret Intelligence Service, to become known as "the spy who slept her way to obtain information." The BSC report for 1943/4 lists her salary as $250 per month.

7

Donovan's Decision

IN WASHINGTON, DONOVAN'S SKILLS in persuasion and manipulation drove the OSS with the same acuity that he used in his days as lawyer, when he had insisted that every statement had to be proven. Now, in partnership with British intelligence, he went about building America's first strategic intelligence service with a worldwide reach. His blue eyes gave every idea a close look, and his calm aura instilled confidence in anyone he wanted to persuade to do his bidding. William Stephenson would recall how Donovan would shake a person's hand and say, "I am counting on you."

By the end of 1941, the OSS had recruited almost six hundred people who had been told he was depending on them: women clerks, secretaries, administrative assistants, planning staff, and liaison officers. All had signed an oath of secrecy, a document shorter but just as important as Britain's Official Secrets Act.

They included those Donovan called "our best and brightest" or "our league of gentlemen." Some were members of a group committed to Anglo-American solidarity and met once a month at the New York mansion of Vincent Astor, the scion of a well-known and wealthy British family. Among them were Junius Morgan, a Wall Street banker; the author Stephen Vincent Benét; Rhode Island governor William H. Vanderbilt; and historian Arthur Schlesinger. With connections around the world, they shared their knowledge and insights with each other.

As the Second World War began with the fall of Poland, and the soprano voice of Kate Smith sang on every radio network her hit "God Bless America," members of the group continued to meet in Vincent Astor's mansion. With international business interests and seemingly infinite social connections, these men ran their lives by the bang of the stock exchange gavel that announced the morning's start of trading on Wall Street. At the end of the day they would talk about Dow Jones stocks and their standing in other markets in the world. Among them was John Lord O'Brian, who had been Donovan's law partner, who suggested that his colleagues would benefit from hearing about the OSS.

....

On a summer evening Donovan's driver, James Freeman, drove him to Vincent Astor's mansion in New York. A footman opened the door and took Donovan to the ballroom where he would speak.

After the audience settled into their rows of chairs on the dance floor, he stood before a lectern and opened his notes. His eyes swept the room as if to remember the faces. When he spoke his voice was deep, soft, patrician, with more than a touch of the Boston-Irish accent. His eyes flashed as he said Pearl Harbor had denied the isolationists their need to continue to attack him as a committed internationalist and accused him of dragging America into the war. He told them he had won the support of Churchill and King George. "For them the point of no return has been reached. Hitler and Nazism must be conquered, and they will remain at battle stations until Britain defeats them. They will not allow isolationism to separate us from helping them. That is why the OSS has been created."

He explained how it was structured and talked about the British intelligence departments that had inspired it.

Britain's SOE has not only men but women who are married and have children, yet are being trained to operate behind enemy lines. Their training is the same as that for its men. OSS also has no restriction on gender. But we want more volunteers. Some will be trained to obtain information as spies. They would be parachuted behind enemy lines or slipped ashore by a small boat to work with local Resistance fighters. I have one rule. I hire on the spot anyone who shows true ability. I'll soon find out otherwise. Working in secret intelligence demands the upmost commitment.

Donovan stepped back from the lectern and said he would be ready to receive applications from those who were ready to join the OSS. As he walked toward the door, hands reached out to shake his. Applause followed him out of the ballroom.

When news of Donovan's speech reached the US intelligence community—the State Department, army, navy, and FBI—General George Marshall, the chief of staff, wrote to Secretary of State Henry Stimson, "It is not clear what Colonel Donovan will do next."

After the next cabinet meeting, President Roosevelt told his spokesman, Stephen Early, to brief his newspaper contacts that the OSS would conduct a range of operations: espionage, counterespionage, guerrilla warfare, psychological warfare, and marine operations bearing on national security.

....

Donovan arranged his day to begin at 6:00 AM, when he arrived in his office to read the overnight cables on his desk in the high-ceiling corner office on the first floor of OSS headquarters. Its tall windows provided a view of the Potomac River. His room number, 109, was his code number and was stamped on all his documents. Maps hung on the wall were marked SECRET and were updated daily to show the position of the war in Europe. There were two telephones on his desk: one linked him to the White House and the other was for incoming calls.

Before he arrived, the night duty officer, one of several Dartmouth College graduates working in the top-secret communications branch, had neatly stacked the overnight call-back messages on his desk.

Most of the messages were to do with the urgent need to recruit. Donovan had cast his net widely, asking close friends, clients of his law firm, and professors at elite colleges and military academies to recommend interviewees. Some were rejected after they admitted that while they were physically and mentally fit, they did not want to be posted to Europe to take part in a war many said they did not understand. Donovan called them "East Coast Faggots." It cost him friends when he said he was also looking for safecrackers and men whose prison records showed they had a background of burgling.

Donovan had discussed with Stephenson how MI6 selected its agents. He explained the service had a team of psychologists to interview candidates who had either applied or had been recommended. The interviewer looked for signs a candidate was motivated by the essence of what MI6 wanted. Those who passed were sent to the training school on the south coast of England. Stephenson said, "The last thing MI6 needs are self-deluded heroes."

Donovan contacted Dr. Henry Murray, a psychologist he had used in prewar law cases involving clients like Mary Pickford and many other Hollywood names who needed his services in contract disputes with studios. Murray, whose gray hair was carefully brushed back from a high forehead, chain-smoked, had a dark sense of humor, and collected antique porcelain objects from Europe.

Donovan chose a restaurant for their lunch where the food was served on century-old plates. He told Murray what Stephenson had said. Almost as if he were giving evidence in court, Murray responded with a statement. Smiling, showing all his teeth, he told Donovan: "From the medical standpoint Stephenson is right about deluded candidates. They are often driven by the thought of being part of a secret world. Careful questioning can reveal their personalities and whether they could work with their own intelligence. The ideal recruit will be honest, devious, audacious, quick, and always cool-headed."

Donovan asked Murray if he was prepared to become the chief psychologist for the OSS.

"I thought you'd never ask," came the response. A retainer fee was agreed, and Murray would have a consultant room in headquarters and have the status of a medical officer with a rank equal to an army major.

There were now over forty-six million foreign-born citizens in the country and a growing number of refugees from Europe, of whom, Murray said, he would expect a number would be suitable for clandestine work and could be trusted to keep secrets.

....

Allen Dulles, among the first key men Donovan recruited, used his office, room 3661, on the fifth floor of the OSS's Fifth Avenue location, to interview émigrés and refugees who came from all parts of Nazi-occupied Europe. He continued to build up a staff of experts on German and European affairs. They included Baron Wolfgang zu Putlitz, a former Nazi diplomat who had worked in the Foreign Ministry in Berlin and had fled to New York on the eve of the war, and Gottfried Treviranus, a Prussian who had once served in the Reichstag.

Among others Dulles recruited were men and women from a wide range of occupations who gave an insight into who made up Hitler's Germany, from the top rank of Nazi Party leaders to SS and Gestapo personalities and experts in the fields of economics, anthropology, and racial ideology. His interviewees told him of the extent of the German Resistance, which included Protestant Christians, Catholic priests, politicians, academics, and artists. Many had been imprisoned and executed; others had gone underground.

Dulles's files contained documents, materials, press cuttings, and transcripts of interviewees' life histories that had revealed the connection between the aesthetic and the barbaric, the homicide and the criminality of the Third Reich.

The files also included information from left-wingers who had escaped capture and moved to New York and had ended up in Dulles's office with information. Inevitably they had also come to the unfavorable attention of the FBI, and J. Edgar Hoover had complained to the president that Dulles "is hiring a bunch of Bolsheviks." President Roosevelt had discussed with Donovan Hoover's claim, which Donovan dismissed as another instance of the FBI director's obsession about suspects with Communist leanings.

The international career of Allen Dulles—a future director of the Central Intelligence Agency (CIA)—began on that summer day in 1942, when he told Donovan that Bern, the Swiss capital where he had once served as a State Department diplomat, had become a spy haven through which important information passed, to and from Nazi-occupied countries and Berlin. The news confirmed Donovan's own belief that the most effective center from which the OSS would operate would be a neutral country like Switzerland on the enemy's doorstep. Switzerland had continued to protect its neutrality since the outbreak of World War II. Knowing how close the country had come to becoming occupied since the quick collapse of France, which would have made it a stepping stone to supply the German armies in North Africa and Italy, the Swiss government had passed a law against any act of favoring the interests of belligerents.

A special force, the Fremdenpolizei, the foreign police, had been formed to monitor all foreign embassy staff, and the Swiss counterintelligence service was equipped with the latest surveillance equipment to spy on suspects.

Donovan decided Bern was where Dulles, graying and bespectacled with the disarming charm of a country lawyer, would use his instincts to operate at the back door to the Reich. There was one hurdle to overcome: his official post. The State Department had finally agreed he would have the title of legal assistant to the American minister, Leland Harrison. The Swiss newspapers published Dulles's photograph under the caption, "Personal representation of President Roosevelt posted to Bern."

....

Dulles's final days in New York before going to Bern as the OSS station chief in Switzerland had been filled with the minutiae of spycraft. He had been given his own code number, 116; Donovan would be 108, and David Bruce, the London station chief would be 105. All cables from Bern station were to carry the prefix "Victor," and all incoming messages would bear the word "Burns."

He had hosted a farewell party for his staff and introduced them to his replacement. The next day, he flew to Lisbon to take a train across Spain and Vichy France to Geneva, and he reached Bern five days after leaving New York. He arrived in time to hear of the successful Allied landings, Operation Torch, in North Africa.

Dulles's first cable to Donovan included his contact with the World Council of Churches organization in Geneva from which he had received the first reports of Hitler's extermination of the Jews, including details of the volume of murders and locations of the death camps. Dulles also made contact with the Italian-Socialist Resistance fighting the SS in the North Alps of Italy and his connections with the Italian political and military hierarchy in Rome, which, in July 1943, had deposed Mussolini.

Every morning Dulles culled reports from Swiss newspaper correspondents in Berlin. Himmler, commander of the Home Army, was raising fifty new divisions—the Volksgrenadiere—to defend the Reich, which was being firebombed by the RAF and USAAF.

Another report contained news that a Wehrmacht force, called Brandenburger, was being posted to the Swiss Alps. Was it in readiness to cross the border into Switzerland? Dulles sent the story to David Bruce in London, knowing it could be of interest to the intelligence planners preparing a prelude for Operation Overlord, the invasion of occupied Europe. Updating pulsating gossip was a part of Dulles's work.

....

Shortly after Dulles arrived in Bern his secretary showed a very tall woman in her midtwenties into his office. Her clothes were shabby but, despite the exhausted look on her face, she had the air of someone with a privileged background.

Without speaking he looked her over, studying the notes he had been handed by his team. "You claim to be an American?" he said.

"I am," came the reply.

"I'm Allen Dulles," he said. "In charge of everyone claiming to be an American."

"My name is Elizabeth Devereaux Rochester," she said proudly, allowing her Manhattan accent and a little of the haughtiness she had inherited from her English mother to come through. She could be herself now, after more than a year of passing herself as a Frenchwoman.

Rochester was twenty-six years old, tall, with a slim, long-legged athlete's figure. She had been educated at an English public school and had been traveling in France when the Germans invaded. She spoke French with a confident tone. Her mother would be proud of the way she spoke and fit in to French life.

Like her mother, Rochester had grey eyes that she knew men found attractive; in Paris they called her *très joli* and *sympathique* with dark hair cascading to her shoulders and a jaw suggesting she did not suffer fools or pointless argument.

Her eyes had become forbidding at the sight of Paris buildings bedecked with swastikas and German soldiers marching in the streets to the sound of martial music. Their uniforms were everywhere, while in the background guttural, rasping voices shouted over loudspeakers. The sounds of occupation.

Her own father had been a soldier in the First World War and served in France. Her parents' marriage broke up on his return from Europe. Elizabeth had been four when her parents divorced, and then her mother met and married Myron Reynolds, a rich American businessman; he had tacked his own surname on to Elizabeth's. When she started school she had insisted her mother register her by her own father's middle and surname, Devereaux Rochester.

The Reynolds family lived in a spacious apartment on Fifth Avenue, staffed by a cook, a maid, and a governess who taught French to Elizabeth. When she reached her teens her mother sent her as a boarder to Roedean, a private school in Sussex, England, overlooking the English Channel. She was one of several American pupils. After graduating with honors in French and history, her stepfather paid for her to travel around Europe while she decided her future. Vienna, Budapest, and Munich had all been on her itinerary by the time she arrived in Athens on September 4, 1939. Rochester had gone to the American embassy to register her name as an American passport holder and found the building to be bedlam, with American citizens waving their passports and seeking consular help to return home.

Three days earlier, Germany had invaded Poland and sparked World War II. Fifty-two Wehrmacht divisions, 1.5 million men, led the blitz-krieg, an aerial and ground tactical attack that swiftly destroyed the Polish defense.

Rochester cabled her mother and said she was going to head for Paris and stay there for a while to see what developed. Her stepfather wired her money and told her she should buy a car in case she had to drive to the coast and catch a ferry to England.

As she boarded a ship for Marseilles, the radio revealed the news that the previous day a British passenger liner *Athenia* had been sunk west of Scotland en route to Canada. No warning had been given by the U-boat commander. Of the 1,400 passengers, 118 were drowned, 28 of them Americans.

In the first week of war the belligerents had all stated they would observe the Geneva Convention and not use gas, as they had done in the Great War. In France, the population was ordered to collect their gas masks from the depots distributing them. Rochester carried hers in its canvas bag wherever she went. In her purse she had her American passport and French identity card, which she was required by law to carry.

Regular visits to the American embassy kept her updated on the war. When the United States had declared its neutrality on September 5, Canada had announced it was at war with Germany. Two days later Hitler broadcast that the German navy would not attack neutral ships, "especially those of the United States."

....

As the months passed, Rochester continued to look for work. In her diary she wrote, "I continue to hammer on doors. I climb stairs and knock on doors. No one seems to want an American to help La Belle France. There are lots of Frenchmen and women ready to do this. They see me as an American in a French war against Germany with America looking on."

Finally a clerk at the embassy told her that the American Hospital was looking for ambulance drivers. They needed to speak French and know their way around not only the city but the countryside beyond.

She went to the hospital for an interview. Its director was an elderly woman from Boston in a nurse's uniform. She took Rochester to one of the ambulances and told her that if she passed her driving test she would be assigned to it. For an hour the nurse sat beside Rochester as she drove them through the streets. The job was hers.

There were eleven ambulances, each with two drivers, one of whom would serve as a paramedic. She had learned first aid at Roedean and in weeks was assigned to bring back the wounded in her ambulance from the badly mauled French army making its last stand on the banks of the Loire.

She was dressing wounds in the back of the ambulance when an old, broken voice came over the radio informing the people they had lost the war; Marshal Philippe Pétain announced the armistice. Within days the hospital was emptied of its lightly wounded soldiers, and some of the more seriously injured were driven south in trucks, along with doctors and nurses. Rochester found herself alone with her ambulance and its equipment.

The hospital director said she could use her ambulance to take food to French prisoners of war held in a compound in a Paris suburb. In between she could take one of the few doctors remaining for house calls now that the hospital emergency room had closed down. Their visits turned out to be to Jews.

The Milice, French men and women working with the Gestapo, were combing the Jewish quarter in the city to bring families to a holding camp in a suburb near the Gare du Nord, from where the trains left for the concentration camps in Germany and Poland.

She drove the doctor to a Jewish family, a mother and her sick children. A stranger introduced himself as the district Resistance leader. He thanked them for coming but said he would soon have to move the family as he feared they could be betrayed. He explained he had a relative, a farmer, outside the city. Could Rochester drive them there?

She immediately agreed and soon learned the Resistance was helping Jews to get out of the country and into Switzerland. Rochester and her ambulance became its transport.

America was still neutral, and the Paris embassy regularly reminded those Americans still in the city that the State Department wanted its citizens to remain that way.

After another trip that had brought another Jewish family to safety, she stopped at a field on her way back. There were freshly dug graves with French helmets stuck on rough crosses, each with a number. She knelt in prayer as she had done in chapel at Roedean. Nearby she found a box filled with Croix de Guerre decorations. She brought the box back to the apartment and gave them to the Resistance leader. He said he would keep the ribbons to give to the relatives of the fallen.

Rochester also began to escort RAF pilots who had been shot down over France and hidden by the Resistance in the countryside.

Some were destined to be picked up from north Brittany beaches by Royal Navy high-speed motor gunboats or a submarine lying offshore in the Atlantic swell. More than once she found that a village priest would supply more than pastoral care. On one occasion a clergyman dressed two airmen in priest robes and gave her a nun's habit and wimple to wear as she drove them to the next stage of the escape line. Before long she was making dangerous drives to the South of France and into the Pyrenees for the pilots to be escorted by British officials from the Madrid embassy. They were ultimately returned from Gibraltar to England.

In late 1942 Rochester had only narrowly escaped being interned as an enemy alien. She buried her American passport and fled to the South of France, before heading for the Swiss frontier.

She and a group of refugees paid a *passeur* to take them to an unguarded stretch of the border where they laid coats and blankets over the thick bundles of barbed wire and pulled themselves over.

....

Dulles listened to her story and noted how eager she was to return to France. He decided to use Rochester as a courier. She returned to

France with messages for Resistance groups and to help refugees escape the police roundups, *rafles*, in southern France. On one occasion she smuggled three airmen across the border into Switzerland.

The Frenchmen she worked with complained about a lack of arms. She understood their desire to fight back hard against the Nazis; a trip to Berlin in her teens had turned her violently against all that Hitler stood for.

A Resistance leader in the Haute-Savoie urged her to travel to London to explain what they needed. She could plead their case, have armaments dropped. She agreed that her next mission would take her not back to Switzerland but to London as an envoy for the Resistance.

....

That summer Donovan had also established a permanent OSS headquarters in London. The five-story office block was at 70-72 Grosvenor Street in the center of Mayfair. But the cost of converting it into America's first overseas spy organization had once more caused Harold Smith, Roosevelt's budget chief, to blink furiously behind his wire-frame glasses.

Donovan had already spent several million dollars refurbishing his Washington headquarters, including salaries for over seven hundred staff and purchasing real estate in Maryland and Virginia to be converted into training schools. For OSS London, another million dollars was spent to purchase furniture, safes with special combination locks, and a range of equipment listed on invoices as "communication materials."

On the first floor was Secret Intelligence (SI) and Special Operations (SO) together with Research and Analysis (R&A) including cryptographers and cartographers. On the second floor was Counter Intelligence (X-2) and Sabotage. The third floor was Communications and Propaganda. The fourth floor housed a small unit that worked with Charles de Gaulle's Free French intelligence section in London. On the same floor were the Country Units, each assigned to collect geographic, economic, political, and military intelligence to support OSS missions into occupied Europe. All the departments had their quota of women.

In a memo Donovan circulated to his heads of departments, he wrote, "Our women are the invisible apron strings of our organization which will touch every theater of war. They are not just there to file reports, encode and decode messages, and keep the records. Much of what they do is essential for the success and security of our operations."

Donovan brought a new idea each time he visited OSS London. One was to create a unit—the Labor Branch—that would identify potential agents from newly arrived immigrants in Britain who could be trained for missions. Arthur Goldberg would head it. Donovan had set up a clothing depot where agents would be fitted with clothes worn in the country where they were being sent. He decided to change how the OSS referred to agents. The men would be "Joes." The women would be known as "Janes."

....

Life in France for the general population, as well as for agents and *résistants*, was sharply affected by Operation Torch. Three days after the landing, the Germans responded by occupying the area previously controlled by the Vichy government. While the Vichy state officially continued to exist, there were now Wehrmacht soldiers in the streets and Gestapo men in the shadows.

In addition, after Torch, the threat of invasion always seemed near for the men and women of the occupying forces. The Milice and those French police officers who had sided with the Germans became ever more desperate and vicious, knowing that the Resistance had warned them that there would be no quarter given or mercy offered once the invasion had led to liberation.

Soon after the Gestapo arrived in Marseille it began to hear reports from informers about a female Resistance leader who ran an escape line for British prisoners of war, distributed subversive literature, and organized Resistance throughout Provence. The Gestapo opened a file on this elusive figure, whom they nicknamed the "White Mouse."

Thirty-year-old Nancy Wake might have been running rings around them like a little white mouse, but she was anything but mouse-like in character. Wake was bawdy, adventurous, and known for her infectious high spirits. She drank, smoked, and partied.

Wake had been born in New Zealand to a journalist father, who deserted the family when she was a small child, and a strictly religious mother, against whom she quickly rebelled. At eighteen she lied about her age and obtained a passport. She traveled by ship to New York, where she spent her time drinking in speakeasies, and then used the last of her money to buy a ticket for England. In London she decided to study journalism and got a job as an overseas correspondent for the *Chicago Tribune*. She was posted to Paris, from where she was told she might be sent on assignment throughout Europe and the Middle East.

As well as enjoying the Paris café lifestyle, Wake traveled to Austria and Germany, witnessing the rise of the Nazis and the persecution of the Jews. "It was in Vienna that I formed my opinion of the Nazis," she said. "I resolved there and then that if I ever had the chance I would do anything, however big or small, stupid or dangerous, to try and make things more difficult for their rotten party."

Wake's work and social life helped her develop excellent French—although she had little time for "all that bloody feminine/masculine stuff, all the *le* this and *la* that"—and brought her into contact with a wealthy industrialist named Henri Fiocca, who had fallen for her when he saw her dancing a tango with a boyfriend in a nightclub.

In November 1939 she and Fiocca were married. Wake resigned from her job and settled in Marseille, where the couple bought a penthouse apartment with a balcony with a view across the red rooftops of the old city and down to the deep blue waters of the Mediterranean.

Fiocca was called up to the French Army soon after and, when the Germans invaded France, Wake borrowed a truck from one of his factories and drove north. Converting the truck into a makeshift ambulance, Wake joined a voluntary ambulance corps and headed to the Belgian border. As she drove she was swamped by the thousands of refugees fleeing the German advance from the opposite direction. Wake's knowledge of first aid was rudimentary, but she had purchased a good selection of medical supplies and was able to carry injured soldiers away from the front line.

After the French surrendered, Wake returned to Marseille and was joined soon after by her husband. The couple remained wealthy and continued to live a privileged life in the "free zone." But Wake wanted more.

She realized that her husband's wealth and status gave her opportunities to travel and fund various illegal activities. She discovered that British officers had been interned by the Vichy government inside the seventeenth-century Fort Saint-Jean, which stood at the entrance to the Old Port of Marseille, and she began to supply the prisoners with radios, cigarettes, and food. Then, teaming up with an escaped Scottish officer named Ian Garrow, she helped develop an escape line for some of the men. Fiocca's factory and an Alpine holiday home were used as safe houses.

Garrow was arrested and Wake pledged to free him. When he was moved to Meauzac concentration camp, near Bergerac on the Dordogne River, Wake contacted a former prisoner there who said there was one guard who was open to bribery.

Wake rented a room in the little town of Meauzac and began visiting Garrow every day, telling the authorities she was his first cousin. After a couple of weeks the corruptible guard—seeing her devotion to her "cousin"—approached her in a bistro and wondered if she would like to do a deal. The price was half a million francs. Fiocca had already said he would pay.

A couple of days later Garrow was given a guard's uniform and was allowed to join a line of guards as they walked out of camp. Wake organized his escape to Spain.

By the time of Garrow's escape the Germans had moved into southern France. One day Wake stopped to buy cigarettes in a corner bistro near her home and was told by the owner that he thought she was being followed. She was not surprised. She and Fiocca had begun to suspect that the strange clicking sound on their phone indicated that it had been tapped, and they had discovered a man going through their mailbox.

She did not want to leave Fiocca but he insisted. He sent her away to a safe house in Toulouse. Soon after she followed Garrow across the Pyrenees and into Spain.

....

On July 18, 1942, William Phillips, a distinguished Foreign Service officer who had held several State Department postings in prewar Europe, was chosen by Donovan to oversee the settling-in of the London station. Sitting beside him on the Pan Am flying boat flight to London was a slim, attractive young woman, Evangeline Bell. A graduate from Radcliffe College, she had also been educated in Paris, Stockholm, and Rome. She had followed Donovan's advice and packed in her luggage linen bed sheets—"not available in London," he had said—and warm clothes.

Bell would be responsible for the OSS women assigned to the station. The first consignment would arrive onboard the *Queen Mary*, along with fifteen thousand American troops—a full division. Before they sailed for England, the women had gone to an army commissary at the dock and collected their prepacked box containing pajamas, toilet paper, soap, toothpaste, and candy bars. They were told these items would not be available with their ration books, which would be issued to them in England. They were each issued an American passport identifying them as a member of the OSS, which they must carry at all times.

Among the women was Lillian Traugott, a trim twenty-three-year-old Swede. She would be the only OSS woman agent assigned to work with Communist groups in Scandinavia. Her mission was to use the training she had received at Camp X in Canada to prepare agents to go to Germany and provide important intelligence that she would transmit to London. Sue Hannifin, a New Yorker, had been assigned to work in X-2 counterintelligence. The unit included Grace Tully and Aline Griffith, a striking runway model from Pearl River, New York. The three women would later run an OSS network from Madrid that provided significant information for the preparation of D-day.

On arrival in England the women earmarked as agents were sent to what Donovan called his "finishing school" north of London to be readied for their missions. They would later join OSS stations in Algiers and Rome.

....

After a five-day voyage across the Atlantic, the OSS women disembarked at Southampton in their Women's Army Corps uniforms and had the first sight of bomb damage as they were taken by train to Paddington Station in London. They arrived as the all-clear siren sounded across the city.

Priscilla Symington, whose father worked in the State Department, recalled she was "impressed by the buoyant good mood of the station porters as they stacked our luggage in waiting trucks, and Red Cross women offered us tea and coffee."

Waiting on the platform was Evangeline Bell, who had arrived earlier and had helped to set up OSS London. On her clipboard she checked off their names, next to which she had written the department to which they would be assigned. They included secretaries, filing clerks, interpreters, and translators.

From the list provided by Eleanor Grecay Weis in New York, in charge of vetting recruits for London, Bell had selected a number of them to work with her in the Document Branch of Counterintelligence. The department provided identification documents and suitable clothing from the countries where agents would work in Europe. Their lives would depend on the cover stories she would produce with the help of her staff.

Donovan described Evangeline Bell as "intelligent, beautiful, mysterious, and ethereal." The daughter of an American career diplomat, who was posted to Peking, she and her nanny used to take walks along the Great Wall of China. She was still a child when her father died and her mother married the British diplomat Sir James Dodd in 1927.

Already word perfect in French, she went to Radcliffe in 1937. Her history teacher, Arthur Schlesinger, saw her as "charmingly seductive and quietly amusing; she knows what she wants." In 1942 she met Donovan and was recruited into the OSS to work in London. She was given the demanding responsibility of ensuring there were no inconsistencies in the forged documents that retouch artists, photographers, and printers produced.

When finally checking the documents, Bell would pore over the French permits embossed on them. A permit was needed to own a bicycle, to possess a food ration book, or to purchase a rail ticket. Sometimes an engraving plate would be made for a hospital certificate to be attached to a cover story to explain why its holder was not at work. A forged letter from a friend would feature condolences for a death in a family and details of a funeral, and so could explain why someone needed to travel to a particular area.

She made regular visits to the clothes unit in the headquarters attic to complete cover stories. For an agent posing as a French farmer she would select patched blue work clothes, heavy hand-knit socks, and a beret. She checked that buttons had been sewn with parallel threading, not the usual British cross-stitch style. Teams of women did the sewing. Others crumpled French notes in small denominations, the way many workers carried their money.

....

At headquarters the OSS accommodation officer, Lieutenant Jane Tanner, handed out billets to the newly arrived recruits, using a wall map of Mayfair to point out the townhouses and saying they were all within walking distance from their workplaces. She issued bicycles for those who wanted them and informed agents they would be responsible for their own bikes, adding that having one stolen was part of day-to-day living. One recruit would recall she was billeted in an apartment behind Marble Arch, overlooking Hyde Park. It had a housekeeper who shopped and cooked for her and two colleagues.

Tanner told the women there was an OSS mess in the basement, as well as several restaurants in the area. "The British call them cafés, but don't serve what we call coffee."

Their work day would officially end at 6:00 PM, and they would have to wash their clothes and often bathe in cold water. They would live by army regulations, which included keeping their billets spotless and submitting to spot inspections. During an air raid they must wear their helmets in their offices.

Lieutenant Tanner ended with a warning. "You can expect when you go out at night you will attract wolf-calls and whistles, not so much from the British but our GIs. They will tell you that you were [sent] overseas to sleep with our men."

David Bruce, the new OSS London chief, completed their briefing by stressing the importance of the relationship between the OSS, SOE, MI5, and MI6. Each had a liaison officer with the OSS.

"It will be vital from the beginning that you develop a good working relationship with all of them, if you are to have an effective role in helping win the war. You must derive the fullest benefit from what you have already been taught. You will be working under air raids on London that its citizens have come to live with. You will have night duty on the top of your headquarters to watch out for any fires that could threaten the building. The view will show you that the great church of St. Paul's is still standing, its dome radiating defiance to the Luftwaffe. You will find that your sisters in SOE will welcome you as warmly as you should welcome them," Bruce said.

....

When Elizabeth Devereaux Rochester arrived in England, she went straight to the War Office to plead for weapons for the Resistance fighters she knew across France. Officials heard her plea and listened to her own story.

A WAAF, dressed in air force blue and a cap, drove Rochester in a staff car through the dimly lit streets to a building near Baker Street. There she was handed over to a man in an army officer's uniform. He explained this was a reception center, speaking English with a French accent. He led her to a kitchen, where a cold supper waited. The officer sat opposite her as she ate, explaining as she had recently arrived from France, she would spend the night here. He led her upstairs to a small bedroom.

After breakfast the officer brought her down a corridor to a door, knocked, and motioned Rochester to enter. Perched on a corner of a desk was a tall, slim man with a narrow face and fair hair. He came forward, smiling, shook her hand, and introduced himself in French. It was Maurice Buckmaster, the head of SOE's F Section. He led Rochester to one of two armchairs facing the desk. On a table between the chairs was a tray with two cups and a coffee pot. He poured and handed one to Rochester.

Continuing to speak French, he explained that she had come highly recommended by a Resistance chief in Paris. He then began to inquire about her background, pausing to listen carefully as she described some of her adventures as an ambulance driver. He told her that her fluent French was good as it would be essential to speak and dress like a Frenchwoman. While she had shown exceptional skills in getting Jews and pilots out of France by pitting her wits against the Gestapo and the Milice, there would be nothing glamorous in what she would be taught, and a close watch would be kept on her during training, as it was with all agents. In her case, her American habits would be corrected, even how she used a knife and fork. There would be weekly reports about her progress, including if she still used the occasional American colloquialism.

Buckmaster told her she could still change her mind. But she said she wanted to help her friends in France. He went to his desk and handed her a copy of the Official Secrets Act. He waited while she read it, and explained that if she signed the document it would be binding her not to reveal anything she learned. She signed the paper where he indicated.

Rochester sensed the satisfaction in Buckmaster's voice as he continued to describe the training she would undergo. Her body would be conditioned to withstand fatigue. There would be ten-mile walks, swimming in cold lakes, bicycling for thirty miles. In between she would learn how to avoid making herself conspicuous as a silhouette against the skyline, move silently through undergrowth, and use the natural background of rough country to travel unobserved from one point to another. She would learn to climb crags and cliffs and practice rifle,

Sten gun, and Bren gun shooting. She would live the life of the Maquis, the Resistance in France.

Her instructors would also teach her to be a wireless operator and courier. She would learn to pass messages in a crowded place without being spotted, and to transmit and receive them without alerting the enemy. There would be secret codes to memorize and still more exercises to take part in. She would be sent for training exercises, such as penetrating a dock or a guarded factory. The chance of being arrested by police would be high, and her response if caught would indicate to her instructors her ability to resist interrogation.

Buckmaster finally told Rochester her clandestine experience working with the Resistance escape line in France had given her some direct knowledge of what would be required in the SOE.

He slowly nodded and smiled. He told her he had seen many men and women volunteers and was convinced she was among the best of them. He picked up the desk phone to summon a FANY officer to the room. Buckmaster told her to take Rochester to the clothes store and outfit her as a FANY. She would wear the uniform throughout her training.

....

During periods when the moon was full, the Tempsford pilots had started to fly every night. Those on pickup missions often returned to base with gifts of wine or perfume thrust into the cockpit by grateful Resistance fighters.

A Lysander was sent to pick up the pregnant wife of a Resistance leader who had been caught by the Gestapo and was awaiting execution. His one request to Baker Street was that his baby should be born in England. The child was delivered shortly after the mother arrived at Tempsford.

Another pilot was sent to collect a wireless operator who had been hidden by an undertaker in his mortuary. He had placed the agent in a coffin and driven his hearse to the pickup point.

A Resistance fighter asked the SOE for a replacement wooden leg after he lost his own stump while escaping from a German patrol. It was air-dropped to him.

Vera Atkins worked so incessantly with the departing agents that her mother, who knew nothing of her daughter's secret role, wondered where she was at night. One morning, as Atkins arrived home from Tempsford for breakfast, her mother—who lived with her but knew little of her secret life—commented, "Well, I hope at the end of all this he makes an honest woman of you, dear."

....

Increasingly in the moonlit nights of the war, Resistance fighters took up their positions in preselected fields in France. They included farm workers, shopkeepers, often the local pharmacist, and the church grave-digger. They made their way to the field by separate routes, breaking the 6:00 PM curfew enforced by the police patrols and German checkpoints. Some came on foot, others by bicycle. Usually they had young women with them who acted as lookouts around the field.

The local Resistance leader, *Chef de terrain*, often brought a secret agent with him to the field, a man or a woman being flown back to England after a mission, or a French political figure who was a comrade in arms of General de Gaulle, who had requested that the SOE pick him up as he had important intelligence secrets of value to the war effort.

In the dark of night or in slanting rain, the fighters in the field gathered protectively around the passengers while the women positioned in the hedgerows waited for the sound of an approaching engine. If it came from the nearest road it could be a German patrol. But if the sound came from the air it signified the message the *Chef de terrain* had received over the BBC coded transmission on the 9:00 nightly French news was arriving on its "deliver and collect mission."

The *Chef* pointed his flashlight at the sky at the sound of the Lysander descending toward the field and flashed a coded signal that the broadcast had included. The pilot responded with a flash from his landing light. From the hedgerows came silence; there was no signal of a patrol from the women.

The fighters formed a makeshift runway with flashlights they switched on as the Lysander descended over a hedgerow where some of the women crouched, watching the wheels flick up grass in their wake as the plane landed on its rubber tires, taxied between the flashlights, turned, and stopped, its engine idling while facing into the wind.

The cockpit canopy slid open and a figure in civilian clothes climbed down the fixed ladder on the fuselage to the ground. The *Chef de terrain* ran forward, picked up the suitcase that had been thrown from the cockpit, and motioned for the passengers for England to climb the ladder. In moments the cockpit canopy closed and the aircraft was airborne on its dangerous flight over occupied France back to England.

Long before the Lysander touched down at Tempsford, the *Chef* and the new arrival had reached the safety of the hideout he had chosen for the passengers. The other fighters had gone home. Later the *Chef* tuned in to the next BBC transmission to listen for word of the next operation to transport agents to and from France to support the activities of the French Resistance.

....

The Air Liaison Section on the fourth floor of the SOE headquarters in Baker Street had been alerted that another "Joe" was ready. The section planned the clandestine flights of 138 and 161 squadrons. Operations took place between the eight nights of the full moon every month.

Vera Atkins drove to an SOE safe house in a north London suburb and was let in by a FANY housekeeper. She led Atkins into a lounge, where Elizabeth Devereaux Rochester waited, and served them tea and cake. Atkins told Rochester her departure for France would be soon and reminded her that what she would be doing was never easy, and she must never forget her own life depended on her training. Finally, shaking Rochester's hand, Atkins left the house.

Two days later a Rolls-Royce pulled up outside the safe house. The driver was a young woman in a FANY uniform. Smiling at Rochester's surprise she said, "The car used to belong to a big-wig in a bank who donated it to the war effort as his petrol ration made it not possible to keep on the road." The car drove farther and farther away from London, and gardens gave way to fields as the traffic thinned out. It was late afternoon when the Rolls-Royce was stopped by a soldier at the tall iron gates set in high stone walls with the words GAYNES HALL carved above. He checked his clipboard, peered at Rochester, and opened the gates, motioning for the FANY driver to continue up the drive to a large mansion, its three-story yellow brick walls set in twenty acres of parkland.

For centuries the estate had been the home of the Duberly family, one of the wealthiest landowners in the area, until it was requisitioned by the government when RAF Tempsford airfield was built four miles away. The family was moved out, along with their collection of Chippendale chairs and other antiques. Gaynes Hall was assigned to the SOE and became Station 62, a staging post for agents that had the atmosphere of a country club. There were tennis and netball courts, a hockey field, and walks through the grounds.

Waiting at the steps before the front door was an elderly man in a black frock coat and bow tie. He stepped forward to open the car door and welcomed Rochester with a smile. She asked if this was a hotel. He explained it had thirteen en suite bedrooms, a ballroom, a dining room, a game room, and a library. And that the kitchen was the best in the county of Bedfordshire.

Standing in the doorway, he invited Rochester to look at the countryside. "It is a land that the Romans occupied over 1,000 years ago. When they left the Danes came. Then in the high summer of the year 916 the English rid the land of the upstart Danes. That big battle took place on the very ground you now stand on."

He led her into the hall. "Our motto is that nothing can be too good for our special guests. One of them, of course, is you."

A tall officer in an RAF uniform joined them and introduced himself as Michael, her conducting officer, who would take her to the airfield when the time came. In the meantime she should relax and enjoy the facilities. She could play cards and table tennis with some of the staff, listen to music, or read a book from the library. He asked if she was hungry.

She said that dinner would be fine. Michael told her that the chef was on loan from the Savoy Hotel in London. He turned to the elderly man and asked him to tell the chef to serve fresh eggs. The chef served Rochester two fried eggs. It became a ritual: from then on, every agent who stayed at Gaynes Hall was served two fried eggs before a mission.

....

The Operational Room in Gibraltar Farm had become the focus of the mission to fly Rochester into occupied France. Her pilot would be John-nie Affleck, who was making his first flight with an agent in a Hudson.

That October afternoon he sat and studied the mission briefing folder. One Michelin map showed the route to the drop zone, DZ, and another marked German flak defenses close to the flight path. The details had been supplied by the RAF Reconnaissance Unit after one of its high-flying aircraft had also taken photos of the DZ and the surrounding area.

He turned to the next item in the briefing folder. The air move-ment officer had provided the Morse letters for the response signal he should give to allow him to reenter UK air space. Finally there was a sealed escape kit for an emergency landing. It contained a wad of French money, a map of France printed on silk, a compass, a fishing hook and line, and a tube of concentrated food tablets.

Near Tempsford was a field that had been allotted to the pilots to practice landing on grass. The night before, Affleck had made a number of what he called "circle and bumps" landings. He reckoned it did no harm to practice. His colleagues in the Moon Squadrons had warned him that landing in a field in enemy-occupied territory could test the nerves.

Rochester was flying to France with her new network leader Richard Heslop, a wireless operator named Owen Johnson, and a Resistance leader.

It was close to midnight when the Rolls-Royce, driven by the same FANY who had brought her to Gaynes Hall, stopped outside the barn beside Gibraltar Farm at RAF Tempsford. Michael, the conducting officer, stepped out of the car with Rochester's suitcase and led her into a room. Waiting was a WAAF beside a table with cups and a tea pot. "I suppose you are glad not to be jumping," Michael said, as he rubbed his hands together to keep off the cold.

"You'd get chilblains," Johnson joked. They all laughed but there was nervousness in the air.

Out on the dark tarmac, Michael had held Rochester's rucksack as she clambered up into the Hudson. "Have a good flight," he said. "And remember we will all be thinking of you."

The aircraft was loaded with crates of equipment, and Rochester looked for somewhere to tuck her long legs.

"Are you comfortable, miss?" asked the dispatcher.

"No," she said.

They flew with escort planes as far as the French coast and then ducked below the flak over France.

Rochester stretched her cold legs and squeezed into the gun turret. The gunner shuffled aside to let her see the blue, black, and silver clouds that seemed to circle the moon.

"There may be a Jerry on the prowl," the gunner said after a while. "You better go now."

....

Slim, with dark hair and a sophisticated dress style, which Buckmaster later described as "typically Parisian," Jacqueline Nearne had been a twenty-six-year-old former convent girl with an English father and a French mother when she received a letter from Selwyn Jepson in June 1942.

Jepson said that her name had been passed to him as that of someone "possessing qualifications which may be of value in a phase of the war effort." Nearne, who had spent much of her life in France, was intrigued by the letter and wondered whether it had anything to do with a young army cadet she had recently befriended. Out of work and keen to help in any way she could, she went to meet Jepson.

After the end of his usual interview about her life, he asked her how she would feel about returning to France. He advised her to think about it and smiled when she told him, as she was leaving, that she had a younger sister, Eileen, who might be interested in going too.

A month later, after accepting Jacqueline into the SOE, Jepson interviewed Eileen. He found her to be intelligent and sincere, but he was concerned if the twenty-one-year-old would cope with the strains of a clandestine life. He said she could become a decoder in England. She accepted but made clear she would continue to press to become an agent.

Jacqueline was one of the first agents to be trained as part of a group made up entirely of women. Her fellow students were Odette Sansom, Lise de Baissac, and Mary Herbert. The group was sent directly to the finishing course at Beaulieu.

The nature of the group's training, which missed out on some of the preliminary stages and a paramilitary course in Scotland, may be indicative of the SOE's inexperience at training groups of women. Within Baker Street there had been an early fear that captured female agents might not face the same hardships as their male counterparts. It was a misconception that Gubbins quickly corrected in a memo on recruitment and training.

While enduring parachute training, which she hated, Nearne became close friends with de Baissac, who was thirty-seven and whose brother, Claude, was already an SOE agent. Born in Mauritius—then under British rule—she had lived in France from the age of fourteen. Like Nearne, she spoke fluent French and was intensely loyal to Britain.

The four women parted company after their time at the finishing school in the New Forest. De Baissac was the first into action, parachuting into the countryside to the north of Bordeaux. She dropped from a Whitley, seconds after Andrée Borrel, the agent whose file had so impressed Vera Atkins.

De Baissac's mission was to establish a safe house in Poitiers where subsequent agents could be settled and to set up a new network, Artist. Borrel traveled to Paris to work for Francis Suttill's Physician network as a courier. Both would become involved in the extended network, Prosper, which would spread across large parts of the occupied zone between autumn 1942 and summer 1943.

Mary Herbert and Odette Sansom landed by felucca on the south coast of France on October 30, 1942. Herbert headed to Bordeaux to act as a courier for Claude de Baissac, with whom she would have a relationship and a child, to whom she gave birth while living her double life. Sansom traveled to Cannes and would also become involved in a relationship with an agent, Peter Churchill.

Nearne was given a cover story as Josette Norville, a sales represen-tative for a pharmaceutical company, and would work with Maurice Southgate, an Englishman born in Paris. He and Nearne would create a network, code-named Stationer, which would operate across almost half the area of France, from Châteauroux in central France to Tarbes, sixty miles from the Spanish border.

After a number of aborted attempts to get into France, Nearne and Southgate dropped from a Halifax of 161 Squadron into fields in the Auvergne on January 25, 1943.

Landing blind without a reception committee, they hurried to hide their parachutes and began to walk. Tired and slightly disorientated, they eventually saw a peasant woman cycling toward them and agreed to ask her if they were on the correct road for the small town of Bri-oude. What followed was a stark and sudden warning as to how easily things could go wrong.

Southgate stopped the lady and spoke to her. She looked bewildered: Southgate had asked the question *in English*. Nearne turned pale and hissed "*Speak French!*" before jumping in to ask the question in the right language. The woman smiled weakly and nodded, before moving on down the road. They realized by her slightly jumpy manner that she had thought they were Germans. Southgate, considered "one of the greats" by Vera Atkins, had made a simple but potentially fatal mistake within hours of arriving in France. His blood ran cold.

They headed to the railway station and caught a train for Clermont-Ferrand. Nearne avoided the attentions of a German soldier who shared a railway carriage with her by burying her face in a French newspaper.

....

One female SOE agent had already been living an undercover life for six months by the time Jacqueline Nearne arrived. She was Yvonne Rudellat, the French-born divorcée who had met Buckmaster when he visited the hotel she worked in and had told him she "wanted to do something to help France."

Rudellat had landed by felucca on France's Riviera coast under the moonlight on July 30, 1942. Vivacious and charming, Rudellat was one of the oldest female agents and, at forty-five, she was not only a mother but a grandmother.

However, her air of vulnerability was deceptive, and she was calm as she boarded a train and headed to Lyon, where she had collected forged papers from Virginia Hall. She now had to cross the demarcation line, which split the country in two. Crossing the line required an Ausweis, an official permit, but many *résistants* chose to smuggle themselves across. Only two months before, an agent, Henry Labit, had tried to cross by train. While being searched at the crossing checkpoint a spare, blank set of forged papers fell out of his pocket. The two German guards took him off the train and opened his suitcase, which contained his radio set. Labit took out a revolver and shot them both. Chased and surrounded by a large number of troops, he took out his cyanide pill and crunched it. He was dead in seconds.

Yvonne Rudellat decided not to risk her false papers at the checkpoint. Instead she snuggled down into the coal bunker of a steam train and crossed safely, eventually reaching Paris and then Tours, where she was to be a courier. Through August and September she worked with a local Resistance leader, Pierre Culioli, to pinpoint landing grounds and carry wirelesses and explosives, traveling mainly by bicycle.

After the arrival of Prosper—Francis Suttill's code name in the field—Rudellat and Culioli met parachuted agents joining his network, including Andrée Borrel and Lise de Baissac.

One day she came to her rented room to find that someone had left a mass of incriminating evidence, including a radio set and code books, on her bed. Unsure if her landlord had seen them, Rudellat decided to move. She and Culioli went to a district of the Loire Valley known as the Sologne to create a subnetwork.

There, between November 1942 and the summer of 1943, they carried out a series of sabotage operations that caused chaos for the Germans over a 250-mile area between Caen in the north and Romorantin in the Sologne. Working with local Resistance groups, but sometimes alone, they destroyed trains, railway bridges, and a food store, as well as welcoming and supporting new SOE agents into the area.

On June 21, 1943, she and Culioli were driving in their Citroën toward the railway station at Beaugency. Using a car was often dangerous in occupied France, drawing unwanted attention. On this occasion there was an additional risk: in the back they were carrying two Canadians, a wireless operator and a courier, who had just arrived from England. As they passed through Dhuizon, about twenty minutes from their destination, they were stopped at a roadblock where the German on guard had some questions about the Canadians' papers. Both were ordered to leave the car and walk to the town hall.

Rudellat and Culioli waited in the car, the engine still running. They looked at each other anxiously, knowing that any French official at the town hall would know immediately that the Canadians, whose French was heavily accented, were foreigners. After a few moments, a German at the roadblock ordered them to switch off the engine and walk to the town hall. Culioli hit the accelerator hard and the Citroën leaped forward, careering down the road. Three German cars set off in pursuit.

Determined to shake them off, they ran into another roadblock, where the Germans had laid a barricade across the road. Machine gun bullets peppered the car, and one hit Rudellat in the head. She fell across Culioli and, believing his friend dead, he accelerated the car into a wall, hoping to kill himself as well.

Instead, the car rebounded off the wall and spun back into the road. Culioli managed to fire on the advancing Germans but was shot in the leg and forced to give up. He was sent to a military hospital, given minimal care, and then taken to Paris for interrogation.

Rudellat was dragged from the car, still alive. She was treated sympathetically at a civil hospital, where it was decided it was safer to leave the bullet in her skull than to operate. Despite the German guard on her door, the nuns nursing her managed to sedate her unnecessarily every time interrogators arrived to question her. Eventually, though, the Germans saw through the ruse and Rudellat was transferred to Frèsnes prison in Paris, the Gestapo having been unable to get any information from her.

8

The Russians Arrive

SINCE JUNE 1940, WHEN the British Expeditionary Force had been evacuated back to England, Bill Donovan had followed events in Europe. King Leopold had ordered the Belgian Army to surrender. Queen Wilhelmina of the Netherlands and her government went into exile in London, followed by the Grand Duchess of Luxembourg and the members of Belgium's government. Along with Poland's government-in-exile, all were diplomatically recognized by Churchill's coalition government.

A number of their citizens who had arrived in London had been recruited into the SOE. French Air Force pilots who had escaped to England were recruited and trained and attached to the French Section of the SOE. Together with Polish pilots, they would later carry out missions deep into occupied Europe.

Polish pilots had arrived in England during the winter of 1939–40. When Poland had been overrun they had flown west to find a base from where they could carry on the fight against the Luftwaffe. Cut off from their families suffering cruelly under the Nazi occupation, they found a welcome in Britain.

Under an agreement on January 4, 1941, with the Polish government-in-exile, Britain agreed it would take twenty-three hundred Polish pilots to be trained in RAF operational methods, including use of the radio-based detection systems linking ground control with aircraft, which was a key part of Britain's defense system. Frontline RAF pilots from thirty-four squadrons would teach the Polish pilots using about four hundred aircraft, including Spitfires, Hurricanes, Defiants, and Blenheims.

The Battle of Britain had begun in the late summer, and the first Polish pilots had flown in British squadrons. They soon had claimed over thirty enemy aircraft shot down, and their British comrades were quick to give them credit for reaching RAF tactical standards. Most of the Polish victories were scored in Hurricanes. The kills were not reported in the press, for fear of causing reprisals against their families in Poland.

In the meantime, while the air battle was being decisively and brilliantly won in three hectic months, other Polish pilots, themselves already trained bomber pilots in the Polish Air Force, were being trained by Bomber Command. Increasingly, as men joined the service from around the British Empire, the production of heavy bombers increased—including the Lancaster. There were complex instruction manuals to be learned in a few days and questions to answer in class from instructors who often spoke only English. However, as their training progressed, the Poles were attached to RAF bomber crews to observe their work and bombing tactics.

Navigators learned how to set a course by celestial navigation, using a clear sky to fix their position. Those pilots who had gone for conversion training from the bombers they had flown in Poland, had spent hours in link trainers before being allowed to take control of a new bomber. Wireless operators, sitting huddled in darkness behind the flight deck, took radio bearings. Gunners waited behind their guns, having spent hours at drogue-target shooting, before being assigned to a crew.

On February 23, 1942, Sir Arthur Harris became commander in chief of Bomber Command, which by then included four fully operational Polish squadrons. Along with the RAF roundels on their aircraft wings, each had the Polish Air Force standard painted on the fuselage: a red and white checkerboard pattern, often with the words of the national motto, "God, Honor, Country," added in Polish.

For strategic reasons and prestige, Berlin was a high-priority target following the Luftwaffe's merciless bombing of London and Warsaw.

Two of the Polish squadrons—304 and 305—were chosen for the first mass bombing raid on Berlin, a distant and well-defended target. Within weeks all four squadrons were attacking targets at Mannheim, Cologne, Bremen, and the ports of Brest and Le Havre.

After debriefings they gathered in their mess halls around its fire-place, remembered their time in Poland, and discussed their missions. Their conversations were peppered with words like "flak," "tracer trails," and "dazzling searchlights."

By 1942 the Polish squadrons in Bomber Command had flown between them 15,365 hours on 18,000 missions and dropped 1,795 tons of bombs.

When the underground movement in Warsaw asked for an airdrop of equipment, volunteers from the Polish squadrons were selected for Special Duties operations. From the rush of volunteers, three air crews were selected. The operational crews were withdrawn from bombing operations and posted to RAF Tempsford to join 138 Special Duties Squadron.

....

Bill Donovan flew to London to discuss the formation of an OSS air wing to work with the SOE. It would be a major operation to supply Resistance movements in France and elsewhere in occupied Europe. The operation would be code-named Carpetbaggers, a word dating from the American Civil War. The name had been chosen by the Joint Chiefs of Staff in Washington who had ordered that the OSS—which until then had only supplemented SOE operations—should now have a full role "in the Organization and Conduct of Guerrilla warfare." A copy of the document was given to Donovan to take with him to London to hand to the two key commanders in the joint OSS-SOE operation.

Group Captain Edward Fielden was the commanding officer at Tempsford when it became a secret airfield. He had been King George VII's personal pilot and had arrived at Tempsford in the Royal Family's own aircraft, with Churchill's order to be ready to fly the queen and her two daughters, Princesses Elizabeth and Margaret, to Canada in the event of a German invasion. The aircraft, a Handley Page, remained in one of the airfield's disguised hangars, "Fuelled and ready to go," Fielden later told the king and queen when they visited the airfield during the war.

Fielden had brought with him some of the pilots of the Royal Flight, airmen whose previous work had been to transport the Royal Family on their various duties. All had logged at least four thousand flying hours, five hundred of which were night flying. Their qualifications made them suitable for the Moon Squadrons—138 Squadron and 161 Squadron.

Pilot Officer Lewis Hodges recalled "there was a tremendous spirit which penetrated into squadrons. We had Lysanders and Halifaxes to fly. I joined the Halifax flight that did most of the parachute operations, dropping containers and agents. Our lives were governed by the phases of the moon. We needed moonlight to map-read; we needed moonlight to find our way to the dropping zones for parachuting and to the small fields that served as landing grounds; and we needed moonlight to be able to see the ground clearly enough to make a safe landing. We needed moonlight as we carried agents to and from the Continent on their intelligence and sabotage tasks."

....

At 3:00 on the morning of June 22, 1941, German armies and the Luftwaffe had swept across the Russian border on a two-thousand-mile front. Operation Barbarossa had become the defining event of the Second World War. Winston Churchill, who less than twenty years before had expressed the need for "a crusade" to reverse the Bolshevik Revolution, had decided that the Kremlin must fight on against the Nazis.

On August 12, 1942, with his chief of staff and Menzies, the prime minister flew to Moscow to explain why the Western Allies could not invade Europe that year, and to assure Stalin that Britain would continue to send convoys of Merchant Navy ships with armaments to support the Red Army.

Churchill suspected Stalin was unlikely to forget his words about "a crusade" or that Britain after World War I had sent fifteen thousand troops to Russia or that Gubbins had spent five months with those

1. Andrée Borrel, a Paris-born courier who carried out acts of sabotage. (Courtesy: Eileen Dwyer)

2. Mary Herbert helped organise sabotage attacks on the docks at Bordeaux and carried on working as an agent after becoming pregnant. (Courtesy: Paul Monaghan)

3. Virginia Hall spied for both SOE and OSS in Occupied France, despite having only one leg.

4. Yolande Beekman hid in a freezing cold attic to send wireless messages to London requesting arms and supplies for the Resistance. (Courtesy: specialforcesroh.com)

5. Yvonne Rudellat spied for SOE despite being a grandmother. She crossed the demarcation line in France by hiding in the coal bunker of a steam train. (Courtesy: Eileen Dwyer)

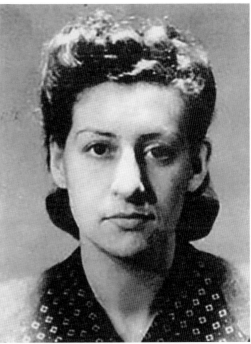

6. Denise Bloch worked with former racing driver Robert Benoist to sabotage German communications lines in the run-up to D-Day.

7. Vera Atkins, an intelligence officer in SOE's French section, who helped prepare agents for work behind occupied lines.

8. Nancy Wake was almost thrown out of SOE but returned to lead a deadly attack on a Gestapo headquarters.

9. Eileen Nearne sent dozens of messages to London from her hideout in Paris until a German detector van tracked down her signals.

10. Violette Szabo was arrested on her second mission to France after being caught up in the search for an assassinated SS officer.

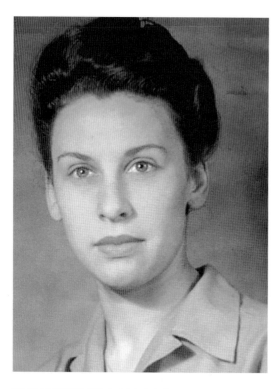

11. Anne-Marie Walters, a courier who escaped her hill-top headquarters as German soldiers closed in. (Courtesy: Le bataillon de guérrilla de l'Armagnac 158 R.I., Jacques Potet, 1997)

12. Elizabeth Devereaux Rochester was honoured by the Maquis with the nickname *La Grande* because of her height and bearing. She led sabotage missions in the mountains of eastern France. (Courtesy: Forum Le Monde en Guerre)

13. Christine Granville planned and led a daring mission to rescue a fellow SOE agent. (Courtesy: SpyMuseum.com)

14. Lise de Baissac worked largely alone in the town of Poitiers and helped agents as they arrived in France.

15. Francine Agazarian worked undercover in France at the same time as her husband, Jack. (Courtesy: specialforcesroh.com)

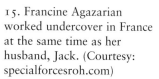

16. Jacqueline Nearne posed as a sales rep and helped create an intelligence network which operated across almost half the area of France. (Courtesy: specialforcesroh.com)

17. Jacqueline Nearne's fake identity card. (Courtesy: specialforcesroh.com)

18. Odette Sansom felt broken hearted leaving her children in London but headed to France by boat in October 1942. (Courtesy: specialforcesroh.com)

19. Pearl Witherington began as a courier but became one of the great leaders of Resistance activity. (Courtesy: specialforcesroh.com)

Above: 20. An aerial view
of Camp X, an SOE training
camp in Canada, from 1943.
One-man submarines and
underwater demolition devices
were tested in the lake near the
camp. (Courtesy: Inside Camp
X, Lynn-Philip Hodgson)

Right: 21. William "Bill"
Fairbairn, a former Shanghai
police officer who taught
female agents the art of
unarmed combat. (Courtesy:
Robert Stuart/Inside Camp X,
Lynn-Philip Hodgson)

22. Selwyn Jepson,
a thriller writer who
became SOE's recruiting
officer.

23. Colin Gubbins learned
about guerrilla warfare
in Russia and Ireland,
and brought what he had
learned to SOE.

24. RAF Tempsford in 1943. (Courtesy: Carpetbagger Aviation Museum, Harrington)

25. Gibraltar Farm, RAF Tempsford, in 1943. (Courtesy: Carpetbagger Aviation Museum, Harrington)

26. A Lysander Mk 3 with underbelly fuel tank, prepared to take an agent into Occupied Europe from RAF Tempsford in 1943. (Courtesy: Carpetbagger Aviation Museum, Harrington)

27. A Halifax from 138 Squadron at RAF Tempsford in 1943. (Courtesy: Carpetbagger Aviation Museum, Harrington)

28. An SOE radio set photographed at RAF Tempsford in 1943. (Courtesy: Carpetbagger Aviation Museum, Harrington)

29. William "Wild Bill" Donovan, head of the OSS.

30. Natzweiler-Struthof, the only Nazi-run concentration camp in France. (Courtesy: Wikimedia.org)

31. Bergen-Belsen Concentration Camp in northern Germany. (Courtesy: wikimapia.org)

troops in North Russia in 1919 as one of their commanders fighting Bolsheviks, and had returned to England with "a hatred for Communism and all it stood for." For those reasons, Churchill had decided not to take Gubbins with him to Moscow.

The two leaders met for the first time beneath the portraits of Stalin and Lenin in the Kremlin. Stalin wore a lilac-colored tunic with his trousers tucked into his boots. Churchill's military secretary, Colonel Ian Jacob, noted in his diary that Stalin was "Cold, crude, and calculating. Making friends with him seemed the equal of making friends with a python."

Stalin asked through his interpreter, "Why is Britain so afraid to attack Germany?" The bristling prime minister replied: "We are making plans to deal with Hitler—and show him when we land in France we will stay and drive him out."

Jacob's diary caught the atmosphere. "Churchill did not say when or where the operation would be, but it would draw off the Nazi strength from Russia. Stalin asked, 'So there will be a Second Front?'" Churchill "burst into a speech that sounded like he was back in the House of Commons." Stalin held out his hand and declared he did not understand the words, "but by God I like your spirit, Mr. Churchill."

The following day was taken up in an exchange of memorandum between the leaders in written rather than spoken words between their delegations. Suddenly, Churchill told Stalin about the SOE.

Stalin turned to Lavrenti Beria, who had been introduced to Churchill as the head of the NKVD, Soviet intelligence. He had sat at the meetings beside Menzies, so far not saying a word until Stalin ordered his spy chief to find out all he could from Menzies about the SOE.

Like Churchill, Stalin had a deep interest in intelligence and espionage, and in December 1938 had appointed Beria to head the NKVD and develop the service so that Stalin's enemies could be discovered and often executed, if they were a threat to him.

Some Russians had fled from Moscow into Germany, France, Spain, and other nations, and became supporters of fascism, which they saw as a higher cause. Tracked down by the NKVD, some were killed. Others were told that if they became informers about their new countries, one day they would be able to renew their Party membership and return home.

Churchill told Menzies to explain to Beria the roles of MI6 and the SOE. By the end of the evening, Beria and Menzies had each drafted an agreement in Russian and English. Both copies carried the same heading: *MI6—SOE—NKVD*. Menzies and Beria signed and exchanged their copies. The agreement called for an exchange of both countries' secret intelligence about Germany and that both the SOE and NKVD would do everything to work to fight the Hitler regime. Britain would supply Russia with arms. The final clause stated that the SOE would agree to share its training methods with NKVD agents.

The document was taken to Stalin and Churchill. Both signed it. That night it was presented to Vyacheslav Molotov, Russia's foreign minister. He signed both copies and said in English, "It is the future."

....

On February 11, 1942, the British Merchant Navy freighter *Arcos* once more arrived back in Aberdeen's harbor in the north of Scotland. Since October 1941, the ship had been in one of the convoys carrying arms to Murmansk to supply the Red Army. The Soviet Union lacked modern aircraft and tanks as well as a range of other equipment. In winter the ships were coated with ice and the sea was treacherous; they were also vulnerable to air attacks from the Luftwaffe bases in northern Norway as well as torpedo attacks from U-boats. A quarter of one convoy, which was code-named PQ-13, was sunk.

Churchill, determined to honor his promise to Stalin to maintain supplies, ordered the Admiralty to send another convoy, PQ-6. Six of its thirty-six ships were sunk. The next convoy, P-17, the largest sent to the Soviet Union, turned into one of the greatest Royal Navy disasters of the war. Faulty intelligence—later laid at the door of Naval Intelligence—claimed that three German battleships, *Tirpitz*, *Admiral Hipper*, and *Admiral Scheer*, were lying in wait for the convoy. The First Sea Lord, Admiral Sir Dudley Pound, ordered the convoy to scatter when it was once well into its voyage. Within hours the Luftwaffe and

U-boats struck. Out of thirty-nine freighters, twenty-four ships were sunk. The loss was nearly one hundred thousand tons of arms, tanks, aircraft, and vehicles. In Berlin, Hitler ordered church bells to ring to celebrate the sinkings.

In Britain the first group of NKVD agents started to arrive aboard surviving convoy freighters that had returned from Murmansk. Initially they all would be trained in an SOE school in Scotland. Ten of them were women. One of them was onboard *Arcos*.

....

Gubbins had sent one of his senior officers, Major David Stacey, a former stockbroker who spoke Russian and Polish, to bring her to the SOE training center at Lochailort in the Highlands. Handing her a sandwich pack and a flask of coffee, he told her it would be a long drive. She told him her name was Francine Fromont.

In her midtwenties, she was petite and muscular and spoke passable English. When asked where she had learned it she told him, with pride in her voice, at the NKVD training school. He decided she was not only good-looking but perhaps a "hard type." Under the terms of the SOE-NKVD agreement, her instructors would not be told the purpose of any mission she, or any other NKVD agents, were being trained for. As Stacey saw it, "We gave them board and lodging, tuition and cover stories, but never once asked them about being Communists."

Fromont's cover name would be Annette Fauberge. Stacey already knew the cover names of the other NKVD agents at the training center.

Szyfra Lypszyc was Polish, twenty-six years old, and attractive. She had been a member of the International Brigades in the Spanish Civil War and had fled to Moscow after Franco's victory. Recruited by the NKVD, she had been given the name Anna Semenovna Ouspenskaya. Having failed her parachute course, once her training at Lochailort was complete she would be sent to Beaulieu to await being escorted to the River Dart in the west of England, where a high-speed Royal Navy torpedo boat would be waiting to take her across the Channel to Brittany. She would carry a suicide pill in her lipstick tube and would make her way to Paris to work with the French Resistance and carry out acts of sabotage the way she had been instructed.

Else Noffke was a German-born journalist in her twenties who had left Berlin and gone to Moscow when Hitler seized power in 1933. For five years she eked out a living writing articles on the Communist way of life. In 1938 she had met Lavrenti Beria, who was recruiting agents to be trained by the NKVD. He offered her a chance to go to its training school on the outskirts of the city. She found herself the first woman in the class. Her language skills, English and French as well as German and Russian, and her ability to integrate with her classmates had resulted in her being selected for training with the SOE.

Her voyage to Scotland had been more demanding than the instructors at the Moscow training school. She sailed from Murmansk on a ship that had brought Hurricane fighter planes for the Soviet air force, and had been struck by a Luftwaffe attack.

On its way back to Britain bearing its scars, her ship was one of three freighters sunk by a U-boat. Noffke was among twenty-five on board who abandoned ship and were rescued by one of the convoy's escorting destroyers. She had left behind on board her documents that identified her as an NKVD agent. When the ship reached Scapa Flow in Scotland she was closely questioned by an MI6 intelligence officer, and then brought to one of its safe houses at Loughton, Essex. There she was photographed and given a new wardrobe of clothes and documents that had been created by the SOE. Moscow confirmed that she had been selected by the NKVD for SOE training. Weeks later Else Noffke arrived at the training center at Lochailort and was given the cover name Elene Nekitina. She would be trained to return to Germany as a spy and saboteur. Weekly reports on her training described her as clever, calm, a natural leader, and "despite her Communist beliefs, not much taken with talking about political convictions."

Daily, Noffke sat in a classroom and listened to an instructor teaching her how to use an incendiary bomb, time pencils, pressure switches, and gelignite. She learned that the object of any lecture was how to destroy targets quickly. She began to develop a philosophy of irregular war that her instructors saw chimed with her own beliefs.

Noffke, like other NKVD agents, especially the women, was sent down to England from Lochailort for short training courses on forgery, microphotography, picking locks, safecracking, and industrial sabotage. The courses had not been taught at the NKVD's training school in Moscow. The SOE instructors were often ex-burglars, felons, sometimes released from prison by the Home Office, to teach how to successfully commit crimes for which they had been imprisoned.

All fully trained NKVD agents were finally sent to Beaulieu, the SOE's Finishing School in the New Forest, to have a final assessment before they would be sent into Nazi-occupied territory where the NKVD had already established the foundation of its empire of espionage. Its network of informers stretched from Switzerland to Mexico and beyond. Nevertheless, missions that required sending Russian agents from England into occupied France needed clearance from de Gaulle. The Nazis had allowed half of France to be freely administrated from the town of Vichy by the French premier, Pierre Laval, while the Germans ruled the remainder of France from Paris. Since France's humiliating Armistice on June 22, 1940, Vichy was known as the unoccupied zone.

The feisty French general told Gubbins that Vichy "has its quantity of left-wing Communists, some of whom are working with the Germans and could betray your training methods."

Gubbins seriously considered the possibility and discussed it with Menzies. Both agreed that no NKVD agent should risk entering the unoccupied zone.

. . . .

It was late afternoon on that winter February day when Major Stacey arrived with Francine Fromont at the SOE training center. The rain had turned into mist while they drove through the hills past the occasional hunting lodge, and Stacey had remained alert to avoid the deer that darted across the road. She told him the animals reminded her of the time she had hunted in the steppes.

In the distance stood the Victorian-Gothic castle of the training center. Stacey stopped at a checkpoint, returned the guard's salute, and drove on to the castle. Carrying Fromont's baggage, he led the way into the castle, saying, "We call it the Big House."

Standing in the hall was a group of students near the staircase, staring at the landing at the top. Among them Fromont recognized some of her NKVD colleagues. Two men in battledress and webbing belts were looking down at the students.

Stacey whispered to her that they were instructors about to start a lesson. To her they looked older than many of her NKVD instructors in Moscow. They were William Fairbairn and Eric Sykes, the school's experts in fast shooting and silent killing, who worked as a team and had created the double-edged fighting knife. Suddenly they removed their spectacles, stepped to the edge of the staircase, and proceeded to fall down the stairs together and ended at the bottom in battle-crouch position, each with a gun in one hand and a fighting knife in the other.

Replacing their spectacles, in the voices of the double act they were, the instructors promised they would show the agents how to fall down the stairs and be ready to attack.

Sykes motioned for Stacey to bring Fromont forward to be introduced to him and Fairbairn. He told her there were twenty-two points in the human body where lethal blows could be delivered and pointed them out with his finger, adding she would be given a special dummy to practice on. Sykes handed her a knife and said she could keep it. Fairbairn handed her his gun and told the students that action is "faster than reaction" as he swiftly disarmed her by one movement.

Stacey led the students in applause.

....

A cloudless evening in May 1942 would soon see the rise of the moon, which for another week would provide enough light to enable Tempsford to go about its work. Already the first aircraft engines began to turn, their propellers cutting fitfully through the air, and the ground crew retreated from the swirling dust. WAAFs positioned their bomb-trains—a small tractor pulling a series of trailers carrying the bombs—under the aircraft doors of the Polish pathfinder squadron. As well as high explosives, the squadron also carried marker bombs that exploded with pretty colors—red, yellow, and green—to light the way for the main bomber force. The prettiest was called the "Pink Knickers." Their bomb case was stuffed with rubber, phosphorus, and benzene, a combination that ignited on impact with a flash of fire visible to the bomb-aimers in their aircraft.

The WAAFs waited until the bombs were winched up into the bomb bays and positioned so that when the bomb-aimers pressed the button bombs would release in sequence without unbalancing the airplane's center of gravity. More than one WAAF wrote some suitable anti-Nazi message on the bomb casing before she drove her bomb-train clear of an aircraft's belly.

In the base chapel—identified by the sign OPEN TO ALL FAITHS—the Catholic priest finished saying Mass for his congregation of Poles. Afterward a WAAF ladled out soup with an engaging smile. She worked in the kitchen and had taught herself to speak Polish.

That evening in the briefing room used by the three Polish squadrons posted to Tempsford, Squadron Leader Kurylowicz—tall, blue-eyed, thirty years old with the build of the middle-weight amateur boxing champion in the Polish Air Force—studied the map he had prepared and pinned on the route board, and the meteorological reports he had received about the weather over the North Sea.

The Operation Office had sanctioned sufficient fuel for the Halifax's extra fuel tanks. Flying Control had provided the take-off time and the Morse signals needed to clear British airspace and return to base. Kurylowicz had been told that if there were any changes he would be telephoned. There had been no calls.

The ground crew report said the Halifax had been fully serviced since the last mission, from the formers in the aircraft's nose to the tail section. The hinges on the trapdoor inside the fuselage through which agents were dropped had been oiled and tested. The extra fuel tanks were checked to be full. The aircraft's tires had been inspected.

The chemical toilet had been flushed. The map rack in the navigator's compartment and the wireless operator's cabin had been checked; the equipment was in working order. The static line to which the agent's parachute would be attached was finger-checked from its anchor in the fuselage to above the trapdoor. The bomb-bay doors had been opened and closed. The crew chief had signed off with the assurance, "Skipper, she is now in as good mettle as the day you first flew her."

Kurylowicz laughed, "OK, another round of drinks for the ground crew in the Mess." It was a saying among pilots that their ground crew regarded planes as if they belonged to them; beers after a service was their expectation and always honored.

His own crew returned from dinner in the NAAFI and sat on chairs before the stage where he stood by the route board. Some smoked; others had their notebooks open ready to take notes to later jog their memories. All studied the map.

The red blotches indicated German flak positions around the cities of Rotterdam, Amsterdam, and The Hague. All had been heavily defended when their Halifax had flown on bombing raids there. The white tape on the map showed a familiar route, known as Route One. They had flown it several times to drop supplies to the Polish Home Army around Warsaw. Each flight had been a round trip of two thousand miles. With its range of twenty-seven hundred miles, even with its extra fuel tanks, the Halifax had little fuel left by the time they had returned to Tempsford.

Kurylowicz turned to the map, using his pointer to follow the mission to its destination. North to Scotland, across the North Sea, over Denmark, across the Baltic as far as the coast just northeast of Kolobrzeg, then southward over Poland, inland to the Tatra Mountains on the border with Czechoslovakia. Kurylowicz tapped an area on the slopes: the drop zone.

Containers would be loaded in the bomb bays, each one to carry ten kilos of supplies for Czech partisans and the Polish Armie Krajowa, its Resistance, fighting the Germans in the mountains. They had asked for snowshoes, skis, and sleds to replace those they had lost in battles.

Rifles and ammunition, along with medical equipment for doctors who had joined the Resistance, would be dropped, as would food in the form of concentrated blocks of sugar, tea, coffee, and dried milk. Cartons of Polish cigarettes and matches replicating those available on the streets of Warsaw would fill some containers. Each one would contain a message of goodwill from the Czech and Polish governments-in-exile in London congratulating the Resistance on the fight they were waging.

The Halifax had been given a take-off slot at 11:30 that night. Kurylowicz told the crew they would be carrying an extra passenger: a female secret agent. He reminded them that they could offer her a cigarette but no attempt should be made to engage her in personal conversation. It was a Standing Order issued by the SOE, not to be ignored. She would have a sleeping bag on the fuselage floor close to the trapdoor. Kurylowicz told one of the crew he would be her dispatcher.

....

Dark-haired and energetic, the agent had a code name of Maria and a cover story that had been created from her background. She had distant cousins in the Tatra Mountains. When her parents had died she had gone to live with a relative in Bucharest. She had escaped the Nazis with a group of Polish families from a Black Sea port and arrived in France. From Marseilles she had made her way to England. The nineteen-year-old had found work in London. There was a need for French speakers, and her employer took notice of her background. He recommended her to the War Office, and she had been called for an interview with Jepson. Her knowledge of the Tatra Mountains had resulted in her being sent to the training center at Lochailort. With its mountains, lochs, and rugged terrain, the Highlands had the same landscape as the Tatra Mountains.

She had learned how to instruct Resistance fighters to launch attacks against the German SS who occupied the mountains in her homeland. She had been taught to plant road spikes that would stop SS convoys so that the waiting Resistance fighters could machine-gun the vehicles. "They must kill every one of the lice worms," the instructor had said. She had been told the importance of working with the local population while making sure they never betrayed her to the Germans. A betrayer was to be summarily executed.

On her twenty-third birthday she had been sent to Beaulieu and briefed on her mission. Two days later she was waiting in the departure lounge in Gibraltar Farm at Tempsford to board the Halifax.

....

By 11:00 PM, Squadron Leader Kurylowicz had completed his usual walk around the parked black-matte aircraft on the hard standing while its crew had clambered on board. Joining them, he took his seat in the cockpit beside the copilot and together they ran through the take-off checks. The dispatcher was by the closed trapdoor with the sleeping bag.

Shortly before Kurylowicz called Flying Control to report he was ready for take-off, a car drove up and Maria emerged in a jumpsuit and jump boots, carrying her helmet. The car driver helped to push her up through the belly hatch, and the dispatcher reached down to bring her aboard. The driver handed up her two suitcases before the dispatcher closed the hatch.

When the car drove away the aircraft engines came to life, and Kurylowicz pushed forward the throttle and the Halifax moved off the hardstand. He released the brakes and began to roll down the runway, then lifted off, banked, and settled into the first leg of the journey to deliver the containers and the secret agent.

Maria settled in the sleeping bag, using her suitcase as a pillow. It contained the winter-weight clothes she had worn for a few days so that they would not raise suspicion by looking new. Her helmet lay beside her on top of the suitcase containing her wireless transmitter.

After take-off the dispatcher brought her a mug of coffee and said he would be back to get her ready when they reached the drop zone. He returned to his station as a gunner.

Maria finally opened the small paper-wrapped box she had been given in the departure lounge at Gibraltar Farm. The WAAF had said it was a gift from Colonel Buckmaster with the best wishes of all the SOE. It was a gold powder compact. He gave these gifts to every female agent; men received gold cigarette boxes or cufflinks before their missions. They were intended to be reminders that he was thinking of them while they were behind enemy lines.

....

In the cockpit the two pilots guided the Halifax along its given route at twenty thousand feet, in air negative sixty degrees Fahrenheit. From time to time the other crew members reported there was not another airplane in sight as they stared out into the night. The navigator continued to calculate their position on his plotting chart, linking their progress with pencil dots to record how much farther it would be before they arrived over the drop zone. The radio officer heard nothing to alert the skipper. The sound of the Halifax high-performance engines coming through the fuselage was reassuring.

Dawn was breaking in the remaining glitter of moonlight when the navigator called out that they were coming up to the drop zone. The dispatcher returned to Maria, helped her to her feet, and fastened the straps on her parachute over the jumpsuit and attached them to the static line hooked to the rear fuselage. As he lifted the trapdoor, bitter cold air blew into the fuselage.

Ten minutes to go before the container drop, Kurylowicz began the descent of the aircraft. The bomb-aimer peered down through the bombsight, a finger poised over the button that would release the containers. There was a crackling sound as the bomb doors opened. He called out his instructions to the pilot.

"Left" was always said twice. "Steady" was a way of telling the pilot he only needed one touch on his rudder pedal. In minutes came the call that all containers had been dropped.

The Halifax rose as if relieved of the weight it had carried. The pilot eased the aircraft down to nine hundred feet and switched on the light that would turn from red to green over the trapdoor. Red for prepare to jump. Green to jump. The copilot continued to peer out the window at the ground and shouted that he could see the light from below, flashing the Morse signal.

The dispatcher checked that Maria's parachute was secure on the static line. He gently moved her so that her feet dangled in the airflow coming into the fuselage. He kept his eyes on the red light. It suddenly changed to green. The dispatcher pushed between her shoulders. Hands crossed across her chest, she jumped into the darkness. The static line pulled at her parachute as she cleared the Halifax tail wheel, opening her canopy, and she began to fall through the sky into the dawn. The dispatcher closed the trapdoor.

In the cockpit the two pilots looked at each other and agreed it was time to go home. On the ground below, the light from the drop zone had gone out. The bomb-aimer checked through the clear-view panel into the bomb bay that it was empty and its doors locked.

The Halifax began the long flight back to Tempsford.

....

After they received their end-of-training reports in Scotland, the NKVD agents were escorted by an SOE conducting officer to travel to Sandy, Bedfordshire, ready to be sent on their first mission into occupied Europe. They were told that they were being taken to Gaynes Hall, Station 61, the starting point of their journeys. An hour later the Rolls-Royce limousines with blacked-out windows and FANY drivers arrived at the three-story brick mansion.

Just like these luxury cars—obtained from people who could no longer afford to run them—Gaynes Hall had found itself in unfamiliar hands for the duration of the war. It had been requisitioned by the SOE because of its size, seclusion, and, most significantly, its proximity to Tempsford. The airfield was less than half an hour's drive away.

The agents were assigned bedrooms and given medical examinations. The hall was staffed with FANYs who had been specially chosen to be hostesses and housekeepers.

Once the agents were settled in, the conducting officer briefed them that the hall stood in twenty-four acres of land, which they were invited to explore, though the perimeter was heavily guarded. At meals they would dine together; a chef with knowledge of Russian cooking would prepare the food. In the evenings they would do their physical exercises. Afterward there was a range of options for them: table-tennis with the FANYs, the piano in the ballroom for anyone with musical skill, and an assortment of card games, some of which were Russian. While there was no room service, the kitchen was open all night to serve them. House-keepers provided laundry service. The library had been well stocked with books in Russian from Foyle's, the London book depository.

The conducting officer ended his briefing by reminding them they had all signed the Official Secrets Act and must never tell anyone they were Soviet agents.

Over the next days the Russians enjoyed the hall's facilities and grounds, and the building echoed with their voices.

Meanwhile, in the office at the back of the hall, an SOE team continued to communicate with the Baker Street Air Movement Office and the Operations Room in Gibraltar Farm at Tempsford. Routes to drop zones were chosen, weather reports prepared, air crew selected, take-offs listed, and Morse signals sent. Finally, the Order of Departure of Agents, the ODA, was settled. The conducting officer would deliver each agent to the departure lounge at Gibraltar Farm.

....

Francine Fromont arrived at Gaynes Hall on March 3, 1942. Like all agents of the SOE-NKVD pact, she was treated as an officer student and was fed and lodged separately from the others so as to avoid them discovering that Britain was training Soviet agents. Fromont was even more tight-lipped about her history than her comrades. Only an SOE document showed she had given birth to a baby boy just before the war had begun.

She was top of the departure list, and her child may well have been on her mind as she and her two male companions waited one evening for their flight. They were taken to a dressing hut and given a meal of braised ham and vegetables. A WAAF then ensured they were not wear-ing anything that would give them away in France, and double-checked the contents of their suitcases. They were then transferred by car to another building, where their parachutes were harnessed, before being driven to the runway where a Whitley of 138 Squadron was waiting.

Their Czech pilot, Pilot Officer Anderle, gave them a nod and waved them on board. As he opened the throttle and the aircraft rose into the darkness, Fromont exchanged glances with her companions. Daniel Georges had been a political commissar during the Spanish Civil War and was the brother of the French Resistance leader Pierre Georges, known as Colonel Fabien, who had carried out the killing of a German officer at the Barbès-Rochechouart Métro station in Paris in August 1941. The other man was a prominent French Communist, Raymond Guyot, who had been elected to the French National Assembly in 1937 before fleeing to Moscow in 1940.

The Whitley crossed the French coast at Port-en-Bessin and rose to sixty-five hundred feet above the mountains of central France. Using the lights of Agde on the edge of the lake at Thau on the Mediterranean coast as a guide, Anderle swung north again and found the drop zone near Montpellier.

Their missions were to be political leaders for the French Communist Resistance. Fromont would be Guyot's wireless operator. Between them they would organize the French Communist Resistance in southern France. They set about their task with fervor, and with the help of the 6,000 French francs and US$1,050 they carried with them. Guyot became a significant Resistance leader in the area around Lyon.

Fromont's luck ran out after more than a year in the field when, in July 1943, the Germans tracked down her radio transmissions and she was arrested.

....

The German-born journalist Else Noffke followed the same routine from Tempsford. The SOE again knew little about her overall mission but noted, "Towns in which she was interested were Cologne and Berlin and, amongst other things, she asked to be provided with a wedding ring and a crucifix. For most of the men with whom she came into contact, she appeared to exude an ineffable sex appeal, a characteristic which was certainly not based on any misconception of belonging to the weaker sex."

Noffke and her colleague, Georg Tietze, had suffered a series of delays to their mission. They had been due to fly out before Christmas of 1942 until the SOE pointed out that the five Reichsmarks notes they had been issued by Moscow had long been withdrawn from circulation.

Eventually they were ready to go, and Noffke amused the FANY officer preparing her for the flight by insisting on wearing the entire contents of her wardrobe, layer upon layer.

The flight into southern Germany took several hours, and Noffke was slightly airsick, but both she and Tietze were successfully dropped about ten miles northwest of Freiburg, close to the border with Switzerland.

Nothing more was heard from them for more than five months, until the report of a Polish Austrian informer in Switzerland arrived in Baker Street. He reported a conversation he had overheard between German soldiers on a Munich-bound train in which they had mentioned two "English" parachutists, dropped near Kaiserstuhl in early 1943, who had been captured by police in late June. One had been a woman, and she had been arrested at Freiburg.

In fact, the mission had been blown before it had begun and, immediately after their arrival, the two Soviet agents had quickly become the subjects of a massive manhunt.

The Gestapo had been reading Moscow directives since turning an agent, Heinrich Koenen. The unsuspecting NKVD had told Koenen to prepare for the arrival of the two agents so the Gestapo knew the time and location of the drop, and had laid a trap. However, Noffke and Tietze became separated on landing and, although the Germans found a parachute with their wireless set and a suitcase full of clothes, the agents seized the chance to escape.

....

That same night that Else Noffke had flown from Tempsford, another aircraft had delivered Emilie Boretzky and her comrade Hermann

Köhler, both Austrian Communists, into the open countryside near Eisenstadt, about fifty miles south of Vienna.

Described by the SOE as a "somewhat nervous type," Boretzky had originally arrived in Britain with Noffke but lacked her German-born colleague's poise and confidence. She was, however, the SOE noted, a very good wireless operator, and it was in this role that the thirty-two-year-old was to work with Köhler. His mission was to infiltrate a number of factories in the area, but the Gestapo's control over Moscow radio messages ensured that they knew a drop was going to take place.

Köhler was caught after a bottle of cognac he had stored in a pocket of his jumpsuit broke on landing, allowing bloodhounds to pick up his trail. Boretzky was arrested trying to find a building from which to transmit in Vienna. To the Germans' delight she was carrying the latest British wireless set, a thirty-pound, state-of-the-art device with a fifteen-hundred-mile range, which far exceeded the Soviets' own models. Boretzky and Köhler were threatened with execution and chose to cooperate with the Gestapo.

The Gestapo was now fully aware of the SOE-NKVD collaboration, and Boretzky agreed to pretend she had not been captured and to use her own radio to deceive her Moscow handlers, a betrayal that would lead to the arrest of other agents.

Either she or Köhler was also believed to have revealed the address of an elderly couple who were their NKVD contacts in Freiburg.

....

Else Noffke had instructions for what to do if the mission turned sour. In Freiburg she tracked down another NKVD contact, Hans Müller, who coded a message to his sister in Basel stating that Noffke was safe but had lost her radio set. On landing she had been unable to rescue it from a field as the Germans had closed in. The English-born Soviet spy Allan Foote, part of the "Red Orchestra" of agents, contacted Moscow, who then contacted Koenen to prepare for the arrival of a new wireless set for Noffke. However, with Koenen's wireless under Gestapo control, the Germans closed in.

Deciding the couple in Freiburg could lead to other agents, the Gestapo chose not to arrest them but to keep their house under surveillance.

In April 1943 Gestapo officers arrived at the house in Freiburg and a young woman answered the door. It was Noffke. The moment she saw them, she swallowed her cyanide capsule. The Germans rushed her to the hospital to have her stomach pumped.

Noffke was confronted with notes and documents relating to Koenen and quickly realized it was impossible for her to deny her role as a spy. She confessed, hoping for more lenient treatment, and said that she was an NKVD agent who had been told to stay in Germany even if American soldiers eventually fought their way into the country.

The failure of the mission became absolute when the Freiburg Gestapo lured Müller's sister Anna, a key Soviet agent in Switzerland, over the border and arrested her. She was saved from death by her Swiss passport. Her brother and his wife were executed.

Under interrogation, Boretzky and Köhler had told the Germans everything about their training, right down to their farewell drinks at Gaynes Hall and the departure lounge at Gibraltar Farm.

In the summer of 1942, the duty intruder controller in the RAF Operations Room in London reported that a solitary Luftwaffe reconnaissance aircraft had followed the railway line past Tempsford and had fled home. Tempsford went to high alert for weeks, but no Luftwaffe attack came.

....

A third female NKVD agent had also fallen into Nazi hands. Polish-born Szyfra Lypszyc, a former member of the French Communist Party and veteran of the Spanish Civil War, had been deemed physically unfit for parachute training.

On the night of January 10–11, 1942, Lypszyc was transported from the Devonshire coast by boat and landed at a secluded bay in Brittany. Despite the SOE's doubts about her, Lypszyc successfully reached Paris, made contact with two other Soviet agents, and began to report back on German troop movements. She went on to take part in a number of acts of sabotage that led to a crackdown by German police. She and a number of agents in the Paris network were arrested and executed.

By the spring of 1944, the Red Army had made such territorial gains from the Germans that their airplanes could drop agents into any theater of the European war without British help. In all, there were nineteen missions under the SOE-NKVD pact, although not all got as far as actually delivering agents behind enemy lines. It had been, in general, an unhappy arrangement.

The SOE felt that the Russian NKVD agents had been poorly trained before they arrived in Britain. Because of their extra training by the SOE, there were delays in procuring RAF aircraft to transport them, which had angered Moscow. Even before the full extent of the failure of the MI6-SOE-NKVD pact was known, the SIS had described British intelligence's own performance in the operations as "disastrous."

Some of the missions had led to success, most notably the work Raymond Guyot had carried out in the south of France, and Lypszyc, Fromont, and Noffke had undoubtedly displayed great courage. But most of the missions, thanks to the Gestapo radio deception, ended in capture and death.

The German technique of using a captured radio to make a blown agent appear free and active would spell disaster for other Allied female agents, too.

9

Betrayed!

MADELEINE DAMERMENT'S RETURN TO France had been delayed for weeks due to bad weather. The twenty-six-year-old with the round babyish cheeks and dark curly hair had received a briefer period of training than many other SOE agents, most likely because of her previous experience.

She had grown up in the Pas-de-Calais, where her father was head postmaster of Lille. After the German occupation her whole family was drawn into the Resistance, and she quickly became involved with the "Pat" evasion line, which ferried escaped prisoners of war and downed airmen through France and out through Marseille. Damerment had been credited with helping seventy-five British and American airmen by the time, late in 1942, the Gestapo closed in and she herself used the escape line to leave France. She quickly found herself being recruited by F Section and, on the night of February 28, 1944, she boarded a bomber to be dropped into northern France. She was code-named Solange.

Brave and intelligent, Damerment had a difficult task ahead. She and three others were being dropped east of Chartres, into an area known to be insecure, to find out what was happening to local networks and to establish a new safe network—a *réseau*—which would be key to the eventual invasion of France.

With her were France Antelme and a radio operator, Lionel Lee. All three dropped safely into the French countryside and began to gather up their parachutes. They could see figures coming across the field and guessed they were the reception committee from Phono, one of a number of subcircuits of the huge Prosper circuit, which centerd around Paris. Too late, they realized they were not. The shadowy figures were Gestapo men who had been waiting for their arrival. Damerment's mission was over before it had begun.

A few weeks later, F Section received a message from another agent, whose code name was Madeleine. It stated that Antelme had been injured in the drop but all were safe. Madeleine was Noor Inayat Khan who, as a Russian-born princess of Indian and British descent, had one of the most exotic backgrounds of any SOE agent.

But it was not Khan at the controls of her radio transmitter that night. She had been captured in October 1943, a full four months before. The SOE's networks in France were in shambles, but London did not know it. Or rather, it had refused to believe it.

In fact, the exceptionally courageous Khan had put a warning into the very first message she had sent under duress, a key phrase that signaled to code master Leo Marks that she had been captured. Marks told Buckmaster, but he refused to believe that his agent had been caught. Khan tried to alert London again in her next message, leaving out one of two regular security checks; the warning was dismissed as an oversight on behalf of Khan.

From then on there had been no more warnings: a Gestapo officer, Dr. Josef Goetz, had taken over her radio, allowing the Germans to arrange for Damerment, Antelme, and Lee to be delivered right into their hands.

After the three agents were arrested, the SOE was given a further opportunity to realize its networks were in danger. Like Khan, Lionel Lee was forced to send a message to London, and again the brave operator left out a security check in an effort to alert the SOE. Once more, the warning was ignored, until an uneasy SOE operations officer requested that the messages be reexamined. Finally, the missing security checks were noted and the SOE agreed to believe that Khan, Damerment, Antelme, and Lee were in German hands.

The web of deception that had unfolded over the previous twelve months had been simple in its execution but intricate in its effect on the agent network. It was the story not only of a double agent's coldhearted deceit but also of missed opportunities for the SOE to see when its plans for a large and powerful network were imploding.

....

Agents in the field had in fact tried to raise the alarm about the Prosper circuit more than a year earlier.

Courier Andrée Borrel, a working-class Frenchwoman with a nose for action and adventure, had arrived in France with Lise de Baissac in September 1942. Her role was to work for the circuit's leader, Francis Suttill, whose own code name, Prosper, gave the network its name. Borrel used her intimate knowledge of Paris to not only carry messages but conduct acts of sabotage. Her skill and bravery encouraged Suttill to make her his second in command.

Posing as a brother and sister selling agricultural products, they made a formidable partnership. Constantly on the move, they recruited new agents, found farmers willing to receive air drops on their land, and sought out barns and buildings where arms and munitions could be stored.

The development of the Prosper network and its subcircuits meant that by the end of 1942 there was a substantial and well-organized agent network across the occupied zone of France. It had grown quickly, expanding out of Suttill's Physician network. It had excellent support from the local French who, like the agents themselves, generally believed that the Allied invasion would come during 1943. By the end of May 1943, the Prosper network had received 240 containers of arms and munitions.

However, such networks could not be secure indefinitely, and with expansion came new faces and greater security problems. As more and more agents were sent in, very often their French language skills were no better than the average schoolchild's, and couriers had to travel even longer distances and take greater risks to link between agents and deliver messages and supplies.

Francine Agazarian, a twenty-nine-year-old secretary from Narbonne with film-star good looks, had landed with her husband by Lysander on March 17, 1943, and was immediately carrying messages and explosives around Paris and into villages in the countryside. Very early on she found herself on a busy train traveling from Poitiers to Paris. "I sat on my small suitcase in the corridor, a uniformed German standing close against me. . . . Tied to my waist, under my clothes, was a wide black cloth belt containing bank notes for 'Prosper,' a number of blank identity cards and a number of ration cards; while tucked into the sleeves of my coat were crystals for 'Prosper' radio transmitters. The crystals had been skilfully secured to my sleeves by Vera Atkins herself before my departure from Orchard Court. My .32 revolver and ammunition were in my suitcase. The ludicrousness of the situation somehow eliminated any thought of danger."

On June 21, 1943, Borrel, Suttill, and another member of the network met at an outdoor café near the Gare d'Austerlitz to wait for the arrival of four agents, including Yvonne Rudellat, who had spent almost a year working as an agent in the Loire Valley. The four never showed up.

Two days later Borrel and fellow agent Gilbert Norman met at his apartment near the Bois de Boulogne and worked into the night coding messages. Shortly after midnight there was a knock at the door and a shout, "*Ouvrez! Police allemande!*" A few hours later the Germans picked up Suttill. All three were taken to 84 Avenue Foch, the much-feared headquarters of the Sicherheitsdienst (SD)—the intelligence agency of the SS and a sister organization to the Gestapo—where Borrel showed fearless contempt for her captors and "a silence so disdainful that the Germans did not attempt to break it."

Soon after, Gilbert Norman sent a message to London. He appeared to be working as usual. But in his message, Norman—considered to be one of the most adept and reliable of radio operators—had omitted one of his security checks. Buckmaster was alerted.

What Buckmaster did next not only was foolish but also signed Norman's death warrant. He sent a message to Norman reprimanding him for forgetting the check. He not only ignored the warning but also alerted the Germans to the fact that Norman had tried to deceive them.

....

While Andrée Borrel had been required to spend every day on the move, in an almost continual whirl of activity, Lise de Baissac, who had landed in France with her, had to carry out a very different role.

Small in stature and reserved in character, de Baissac had impressed her instructors from the very start. "Intelligent, extremely conscientious, reliable, and sound in every way," one stated. "Is quite imperturbable and would remain cool in any situation," another reported.

Her mission was to remain quiet and underground in the university town of Poitiers, just north of the demarcation line. Here, she lived alone in a two-room apartment and provided a contact point for new agents. She found them shelter and contacts and made sure their identity papers were up to date.

Her life was largely a solitary one; her only regular contacts were an auctioneer and his family, who had Resistance links. She had no wireless operator or courier and traveled alone on her bicycle to meet people from other networks.

She had to be careful when approaching people she had known before the war to see if they wished to join her Resistance network, Artist. Sometimes people were interested; often they were not. Once, she saw a friend in a restaurant and invited him to work with her. "Definitely not," he told her. "I have eight children to look after, four of my own and four of my brother's who's dead. I can't put them at risk." He never joined; she never asked him again.

The agents de Baissac worked with came and went, many going on to the north and east of her to the ever-expanding Prosper network. The only SOE friendship she would allow herself was with Mary Herbert, her brother Claude's courier from the Scientist network, who brought her messages. Occasionally, de Baissac would go to a favorite café of

Claude's in Bordeaux to wait for him. She saw that Claude and Mary had become close and had started a love affair.

In February 1943 de Baissac met the newly arrived air liaison agent, Henri Déricourt, who said he liked many of the landing grounds she had selected and that he would use them. She found Déricourt efficient and courteous, even charming. She had no idea the sequence of events he was about to put into play.

By the end of May she had arranged the arrival of thirteen agents, including Francine Agazarian. With no radio of her own, she had had to use Prosper wireless operators to communicate with London. Both she and Claude, who visited Paris regularly, now had strong links to the Prosper network. In 1943 that was a dangerous relationship for any agent in France.

....

Born in Amiens, France, on April 28, 1912, Odette Sansom was the daughter of a First World War hero, Gaston Brailly, who was killed in Verdun in 1918. Her childhood had been filled with illness, including meningitis, which made her blind for a year. By her teens her parents were both dead and she was sent to a convent to be educated. At seventeen she had refused the offer to be trained as a nun and left the convent. Two years later she had met and married an Englishman, Roy Sansom, who was running a boardinghouse in Boulogne. In 1939 he had brought her and their two daughters to England. He had joined the army, and she had gone to live with her mother-in-law near Bath in Somerset to await the birth of her third child. In 1941 she had responded to requests by the War Office for people to send photographs of France. Her photographs encouraged the War Office to see her as a potential recruit to the SOE. She was interviewed by Jepson, and she became a member of an SOE women's course in May 1942.

She developed a fearsome reputation during training for an almost defiant strength of character. "Her main weakness is a complete unwillingness to admit that she could ever be wrong," noted one instructor.

Buckmaster added with some admiration, "She did it her way and that was it."

Sansom was motivated by patriotism but reluctant to volunteer for operations because of her children. "I left England with a broken heart and I knew that nothing else that could happen to me would ever be that painful; it never was," she recalled.

In the final stage of training, on her parachute course, she was injured and was ruled out of being parachuted into France—the SOE would have to deliver her some other way. Sansom arrived in France around the same time as Andrée Borrel, Yvonne Rudellat, and Lise de Baissac. She landed on the Mediterranean coast east of Marseille on October 31, 1942, only days before the Germans sent their troops south into the unoccupied zone. She landed with Mary Herbert, George Starr, who would develop a key *réseau* to the southwest, and a radio operator named Marcus Bloom.

Sansom had been supposed to work in Auxerre but instead was reassigned to a *réseau* run by a dynamic young man named Peter Churchill, who was working hard to bring under control the large but unorganized Resistance group Carte, named after its leader André Girard's code name. Sansom became Churchill's courier and, eventually, his lover. They worked closely with a wireless operator named Adam Rabinovitz, code-named Arnaud.

The Riviera was a difficult place to work. Cannes was a playground, with a burgeoning black market. Marseille was a center for police activity, where there were regular roundups, *rafles*, to find people for forced labor. A transient population of people had fled from other areas of the country; Sansom felt many were too "ostentatious and flamboyant" for undercover work. Some *résistants* were too proud of their clandestine role, as if wearing a label to say they were members of the Resistance. "I felt fear," Sansom said. "I felt that anything could happen any time."

Sansom's uneasiness was well founded; things started to quickly go wrong. André Girard fell out with his deputy, Frager, so they got little done. Churchill then backed Frager, causing a rift with Girard. A *résistant* named André Marsac fell asleep on a train between Marseille and Paris and lost the suitcase he was carrying. Inside was a list of Carte members and contacts.

Finally, in January 1943, shortly after the Germans razed much of the old quarter of Marseille to the ground, claiming it was full of criminals, Peter Churchill's network was blown.

The key figures managed to get away. Churchill, Sansom, and Rabinovitz headed to the Haute-Savoie and the beautiful countryside around Lake Annecy. They made the waterside village of Saint-Jorioz their base and hooked up with a strong existing Resistance force. Among them was a man named Roger Bardet who, it was said, had escaped from a camp in Germany. Sansom did not like him at all.

In March, Churchill and Frager were picked up by a Lysander and flown to England to seek guidance on the split between Girard and the Carte group. By the time Churchill returned both he and Sansom were in the jaws of a trap.

....

Many of the female agents who had arrived in France during late 1942 and early 1943 had been arrested by that summer. The massive expansion of networks, seen most vividly in Prosper, was about to implode in a sordid, intricate web of betrayal and double-dealing. Henri Déricourt—the SOE's air liaison agent—was at its heart.

Having arrived in France in January 1943, he had made contact with an old acquaintance, Karl Bömelburg, a high-ranking SD officer in Paris. Déricourt now became a double agent, listed by the SD as agent number 48.

Déricourt's betrayal had devastating consequences. Through his role as organizer of SOE flights into France he met leaders, couriers, and wireless operators. They included Andrée Borrel and Lise de Baissac. Déricourt reported to the SD on agents' arrivals and where they went. Each time he reported back to Bömelburg there were further, more detailed, requests for information.

The Nazis were certain that the Allies were planning to land in France some time during the summer of 1943. In April, at a secret meeting in an apartment in Paris, Bömelburg told Déricourt he wanted *advanced* warnings of agent drops and pickups so that his men could observe them. This enabled the SD to watch a network develop, trapping new couriers and *résistants* as they joined. An operation near Amboise involving two Lysanders was watched by SD agents.

Meanwhile, Déricourt met and spent some time with Prosper, Francis Suttill. If the agent network was like a spider's web, there was now a predator hiding at its very center.

....

Despite the SD's apparent control of the situation through the double agent Déricourt, the Abwehr made the first key arrest. The German army's intelligence department, which had an enmity-filled rivalry with the SD, had been holding the list of names André Marsac had lost in the suitcase on the train. That spring the Abwehr moved to arrest Marsac and find out who and what he knew. It had come to believe that the long list of Carte names were actually those of members of the massive Prosper network, which both the Abwehr and the SD were keen to crack.

The Abwehr team was led by an innocuous-looking man in his early forties. With a longish nose and sly brown eyes, Hugo Bleicher's corkscrew mind now came into play. He visited Marsac in Frèsnes prison and introduced himself as Lieutenant Colonel Henri, an officer representing an anti-Nazi group of German officers who wanted to make contact with Allied High Command. His story convinced Marsac, who wrote a letter of recommendation for the colonel and sent him south to Saint-Jorioz.

In April, Bleicher made contact with Sansom and repeated the same story. He wanted a flight to London to discuss terms for peace with Britain. He told her he had arrested Marsac to save him from the Gestapo. Sansom was suspicious and afraid. To make matters worse, Roger Bardet, whom she deeply disliked, met the colonel too. Bardet suggested he visit Frèsnes to see Marsac and to confirm the German's story.

This he did, urging Sansom to schedule a Lysander pickup for Colonel Henri.

Sansom stalled, saying she could not get a plane until April 18. Bardet became angry and left. Sansom could not have known it, but Bardet was by now a key informer for the Abwehr. He was Bleicher's man.

The SOE in Baker Street advised Sansom to cut all contact with the man calling himself "Colonel Henri." Sansom rushed around Annecy telling members of the Resistance that they were in danger and should go into hiding, but she did not immediately do the same herself.

Peter Churchill returned from London, and they both made preparations to go underground. They were too late. Bardet had told the Abwehr that Churchill was back.

On the night of April 16, 1943, Bleicher and his men arrested them both. The network's radio operator, Rabinovitz, escaped.

....

A week later, Bleicher struck again, arresting two sisters whose apartment in Avenue de Suffren in Paris was a meeting point for the Prosper network.

The arrests led nowhere immediately, and it was once again the SD, through Déricourt, that regained the upper hand in the Wehrmacht counterintelligence crackdown. In his role, Déricourt handled the SOE "airmail"—reports too long to transmit by radio that were instead written down to be couriered on Lysanders making agent pickups. Déricourt brought this "airmail" to the SD to be copied before it was taken on to a landing zone. This gave the Germans a detailed picture of the Resistance—its strengths, weaknesses, and locations where agents were in need of arms or support. The SD also continued to track the arrival of agents.

Vera Leigh, a forty-year-old dress designer who landed with three others on May 13, 1943, at a field in the Cher Valley, near Tours, was followed to Paris, where she was to set up a new *réseau*, Inventor, to work alongside the Prosper network. Leigh's companions were Julienne Aisner, Sidney Jones, and Marcel Clech. Aisner was to be a courier, Jones an arms instructor, and Clech a wireless operator.

On June 16, four more agents were watched upon arrival. These included Diana Rowden, an English-born journalist whom the Germans followed to her destination, and Noor Inayat Khan who, as a radio operator, would try to alert the SOE to what was happening. They would be betrayed by Henri Déricourt.

Suttill already distrusted Déricourt and arranged his own return to France on June 12, 1943. Overburdened and exhausted by running such a massive network, he was convinced his network had been infiltrated by the Germans.

It was then that the SD moved in. It arrested *résistants*, uncovered hauls of arms, and followed lead after lead. This crackdown alerted the police to look for agents matching the descriptions of Yvonne Rudellat and Pierre Culioli. They were the first agents arrested. Next came Borrel and Suttill.

By the end of August 1943 the Germans had made fifteen hundred arrests. More followed, including Noor Inayat Khan and Frager. A network designed to organize and unite Resistance in readiness for the key event of the war in the west—the invasion of France—had ceased to exist. But Vera Leigh's network had so far survived.

....

Vera Leigh had been working hard as a courier for the developing Inventor *réseau* in Paris since she arrived by Lysander on May 13, 1943. Although born in Leeds in the north of England, Leigh had been adopted, while still a baby, by a rich American who had racehorse stables near Paris. While only twenty-four she had created her own dress design company and became a society figure in the French capital. She had fled the city after the occupation and worked with the Pat evasion line with Madeleine Damerment and Virginia Hall in Lyon. Like Hall, she became a wanted figure by the Germans and fled over the Pyrenees, eventually reaching Britain, where she joined the SOE. A crack shot, she was known for a fast mind and pleasant manner. She worked closely with another SOE agent, Julienne Aisner.

From the time she had landed by moonlight she carried messages, wireless components, and sabotage materials across Paris, and, well-known there from her dress design days, she began to meet people from her past life, including some who had been involved in the "Pat" line.

Since her arrival back in Paris, the SD—thanks to Déricourt's betrayal—had known all about her. The SD and Abwehr were waiting for the other Resistance networks to develop so as to make their final haul even greater in number.

In the end it was the Abwehr, looking to match the SD's success with Prosper, that moved in. On October 30, Leigh was drinking coffee in the Café Mas near the Place des Ternes with another *résistant* when German officers strode in. At their head was Sergeant Bleicher. He walked straight to their table and placed them under arrest.

Under interrogation at 84 Avenue Foch, the SD's Paris headquarters, Leigh stuck to her cover story, that she was a milliner's assistant named Suzanne Chavanne. But the Germans already knew the truth. Inventor had been created under their gaze. All its members had been arrested by the end of December.

....

Despite their close connections to the Prosper network and to Déricourt, three agents managed to slip the net.

Claude de Baissac was in Bordeaux, where his Scientist network was not only gathering vital information on German activity in the area but also carrying out many audacious acts of sabotage. His courier, Mary Herbert, had been considered by some to be almost too fragile for the rigors of the clandestine life, but she had thrived, using her bicycle and the train to liaise with agents and *résistants* over a wide area, and to meet up with the third agent in their group, Lise de Baissac, Claude's sister.

Mary and Claude organized a series of sabotage attacks on Bordeaux docks, a port packed with submarines and cargo ships bringing supplies for the German war effort. They helped mastermind the destruction of a key radio station for Admiral Dönitz's Atlantic U-boat fleet, a power station supplying Luftwaffe airfields near Marignac, and transformers powering antiaircraft batteries in the area.

When the Germans' tightened security made further sabotage virtually impossible, they concentrated on reporting on the Reich's naval movements.

Herbert was a shy and quiet but fiercely intelligent thirty-nine-year-old. De Baissac was abrasive, proud, and determined. Their burgeoning love affair had been an attraction of opposites.

In spring, news began to trickle through from Paris about the Prosper arrests. De Baissac had met a number of the agents on visits to the capital—trips on which he had taken Herbert with him. Meantime Lise, holed up alone in Poitiers, remained the first point of contact for many Prosper agents arriving in France. It was on a visit to Lise that Mary revealed she was pregnant. Herbert changed her identity and moved house. Already members of her network had been arrested.

The danger was creeping closer. And, even without Déricourt's betrayal, the Germans had found another way to infiltrate the Scientist network: they had a local informer. A right-wing Resistance leader named André Grandclément had been persuaded by a German officer that only by working with the Nazis could he save France from the Communists. Suddenly, the SD were finding carefully hidden arms dumps and agents were being arrested.

In August 1943 London recalled Claude de Baissac. It is not clear if he knew Herbert was pregnant. He decided to take his sister, Lise, and not Mary with him, reasoning that Lise was in greater danger.

When London sent a replacement leader, Roger Landes, Mary realized Claude would not return. When she confided to Landes that she was pregnant, he wanted her to return to London. She refused and continued to work as a courier.

Landes realized that Grandclément's betrayal was already devastating; he had turned in an estimated three hundred *résistants* to the Germans. The network could not recover from such a loss.

Toward the end of November, Landes took the now heavily pregnant Herbert to a small private nursing home in a suburb of Bordeaux and left her money for her survival. She must cut all links with the Resistance to ensure the safety of her and her baby, he told her. Then he brought together a group of surviving Resistance fighters and headed for the Spanish border.

The following month Herbert's baby was born by Cesarean. With thoughts for her lover, she called the girl Claudine. Now, with the intuition of a trained spy and the protective instinct of a mother, she set about creating a new and safe life for her and her child. Deliberately neglecting to give the nursing home a forwarding address, she went to one of the flats formerly used by Lise de Baissac in Poitiers. She took on a new identity and bought ration books and papers for her child from the black market.

Then, in February 1944, the Gestapo arrested and questioned everyone in the apartment block. They kept Herbert in custody, believing she was Lise de Baissac. Herbert stuck to her new cover story, that she was visiting from Alexandria in Egypt—she spoke Arabic, one of the languages in which she was fluent—and that she did not know Lise. Her insistence—and the fact that the Germans found it hard to believe that a British agent would have a baby—convinced her interrogators.

After two months, Herbert was released. She rescued Claudine from an orphanage and went to live with friends in a country house, no longer an agent but an anonymous young mother concentrating on bringing up a baby in an occupied country.

....

The women who arrived together on June 16 included Diana Rowden, the daughter of a British army major, who had spent a great deal of her life in France and Italy. She had attended schools in Sanremo, Italy, and Cannes on the French Riviera, and continued her education at Manor House School in Surrey. She had become a soft-spoken teenager, retiring and rather stocky, with reddish hair and a pale complexion.

In 1933 she returned with her mother to France and enrolled at the Sorbonne in Paris. After graduating, she embarked on a career in journalism. On the outbreak of the war she joined the French Red Cross.

When France fell she was separated from her mother, who had fled to Britain. Rowden remained in France until the summer of 1941, when she finally escaped through Spain and Portugal to England, where she joined the WAAF. Her language skills—French, Portugese, and Spanish—resulted in her being assigned to the Intelligence Branch. From there was but a small step for the headhunters to recommend she should be enlisted in the SOE. Her training reports spoke of "high intelligence," "well motivated," and "strong hatred of the Nazis." More than one instructor's reports spoke of her leadership qualities.

Always a tomboy when she was a child, she was now in her late twenties, fit and athletic. After her arrival in France, she set off for the Jura and a hotel in Lons-le-Saunier.

Baker Street had high hopes for Acrobat, the network she was joining. The Resistance in the area was strong. But Déricourt's betrayal had ensured the SD followed her all the way to her new home.

However, when members of the network were arrested, Rowden escaped and moved east to act as a courier for another network. Together with her comrades she came up with a new development in Resistance sabotage: blackmail. The family of the Peugeot car factory in Sochaux, which was being used to make tank and aircraft parts, was approached and persuaded to create an explosion to put the facility out of action.

While Rowden appeared to have given the SD the slip, the continuing betrayal of Déricourt meant that the Germans were confident they could locate her again. In November the double agent had supervised the arrival of five agents on a Hudson aircraft. One of the men was assigned to work for Rowden. He was apprehended and persuaded to give details of where he was to meet her.

The house where Rowden was staying resembled a Swiss chalet with a wooden balcony and a cobbled road outside. She met the "new agent" in the village of Clairvaux and began to walk him up the hill to the house. As they walked he flashed a flashlight behind his back. They went inside and, a short while later, a *résistant* standing on the balcony saw three cars rushing up the hill.

Rowden managed to hide wireless crystals in a cot where a baby was sleeping, but the game was up. She had become another victim of Déricourt, although by giving the SD the runaround for three months, she had carried out valuable Resistance work.

After months in captivity and torture at the SD headquarters on Avenue Foch, she was sentenced under the "Nacht-und-Nebel-Erlass," the Night and Fog Decree. It was the code name to an order of December 7, 1941, issued by Hitler.

The decree directed that persons in occupied territories engaging in activities intended to undermine the security of German troops were, upon capture, to be brought to Germany by "night and fog" for trial by special courts. To friends and relatives they simply disappeared; no official information about the prisoners would be released.

On July 6, 1944, Diana Rowden was transferred to the men's Natzweiler-Struthof concentration camp. With her were Andrée Borrel, Vera Leigh, and Sonia Olschanezky, a twenty-one-year-old Jewish woman who had worked for the French Resistance and been recruited in France by the SOE. Olschanezky, who had refused a chance to escape to Switzerland when Prosper began to collapse, had also been betrayed.

The four were taken one by one to an isolated hut, ordered to lie down on a bed, and told they were to be injected against typhus. Instead they were given a lethal injection of phenol. Their bodies were then dragged to an oven for cremation.

Vera Atkins investigated their deaths immediately after the war and concluded, "It appears that at least one of them was still alive when she was pushed in the furnace." It is possible it was twenty-four-year-old Andrée Borrel; a Polish prisoner who witnessed the scene at the furnace said the woman scratched the face of the camp executioner and screamed, "Vive la France!"

....

Cecily Lefort had traveled south to act as courier to agent Francis Cammaerts. Lefort was London-born, forty-three years old, and of Irish descent. Before the war, she had married a wealthy French doctor and settled on the Brittany coast. She had loved sports and sailing in the couple's yacht. When the occupation came, British nationals had had to leave France.

When she returned by Lysander for the SOE, she headed south to where Cammaerts had developed Jockey, a large network of independent groups stretching through the Rhône valley and along the Riviera.

In July 1943 the Allies invaded Sicily in preparation for moving into Italy. The SOE decided to increase the amount of arms being dropped into the southeast of France, and Lefort organized a reception party for a massive drop of supplies on August 13.

Working with Pierre Reynaud, a sabotage instructor, Lefort took part in a number of operations to damage railway lines, power stations, and industrial targets.

The Resistance activity drew a corresponding increase in German retaliation. Cammaerts, one of the most security-conscious of all SOE agents in France, warned the network to stay away from particular places, including Montélimar, where they had their former headquarters. Reynaud and Lefort ignored the warning, and on September 15, 1943, they visited a local Resistance leader at his home in Montélimar.

The SD had received a tip-off from an unknown source and surrounded the house. Reynaud and the *résistant* escaped, but Lefort was found hiding in the cellar. Her Gestapo interrogators broke her alibis, but she refused to give away any of her comrades. Thanks to her courage and to Cammaerts's own security measures, Jockey survived.

Lefort did not. She arrived at Ravensbrück toward the end of 1943. During a routine medical examination in the hospital block, a doctor diagnosed stomach cancer. He operated and put her on a diet of porridge and vegetable soup. She was monitored, seemed to improve, and was returned to the main camp.

In February 1945 she was moved to a subcamp called the Jugendlager, the "youth camp," which in fact was the extermination annex created to increase the number of gassings. One prisoner later testified that the desperately ill Lefort had volunteered to move to the camp as she thought it was a rest place where she would be spared roll call.

Lefort was so sick that she was picked out for extermination almost immediately on arrival.

....

With her Asian lineage and background as a musician and author of children's stories, Noor Inayat Khan was an unlikely agent to be chosen for SOE work in France. But she was keen, brave, and fluent in French, and Buckmaster believed in her. Most of all, she volunteered at a time when F Section had desperately needed more wireless operators. She was assigned the code name Madeleine and the cover of being a children's nurse. She would work in the network known as Phono in an area to the southwest of Paris, centerd around Le Mans.

She made her first transmission on June 20, 1943, from the grounds of the Agricultural Institute at Grignon, using Gilbert Norman's radio. She did not receive her own radio until the following month.

Within a week of her arrival, the Resistance network Prosper began to disintegrate around her. And Suttill, whom she had just met, had been arrested. So too were Norman and Borrel. Khan headed to the institute and found the Germans making more arrests. She and her leader, Emile Garry, laid low. In the middle of September, having moved house again for safety, Khan radioed London to try to tell them Prosper was collapsing. She was the only radio operator at work in Paris.

But the Germans were picking up her signal loud and clear. At first their detection finders could not locate her, but they could tell from her "fist"—the way she tapped out her Morse code—that this was a single operator handling a large amount of material.

Twice Khan's courage and quick thinking helped her escape capture. Once, two Germans on the Métro became suspicious of her heavy suitcase and challenged her. She explained it contained a cinema projector, and they believed her. Soon after, she was asked to help two Canadian airmen, of whom she immediately became suspicious. She abandoned them. Her intuition was right: they were German agents.

The Germans let it be known, through the network of criminal gangs they used as thugs and informants, that they would pay 100,000 francs for information leading to Khan's arrest. Senior SD officers said they were willing to pay out ten times as much. SD headquarters received a phone call, a woman's voice telling them she could give them the radio operator's address in return for the reward. SD agent Ernest Vogt headed to the address and was shown around Khan's apartment. He flicked through her notebooks and found her wireless. One man was left in the apartment; others stood around in the street outside, trying to appear inconspicuous.

On her return Khan saw them immediately and melted back in the crowd. Alone, without her codes and wireless, she agonized over what to do. She waited until she thought enough time had passed for those watching the building to leave, and slipped inside.

Inside her apartment the SD man arrested her. She fought back so violently that he had to call reinforcements. She was taken to the fifth floor of the building at 84 Avenue Foch where, to calm her, Vogt agreed to her request for a bath. Once inside the bathroom she scrambled out of the window onto a ledge and onto the roof. But there was nowhere to go.

And so her interrogation began. SOE instructors had noted that she was not a good liar. Now she admitted she was a WAAF officer named Nora Baker but refused to say anything else at all. One SD officer reported, "She is impossible. I have never met a woman like her." Sturmbannführer Josef Kieffer, the man in charge of SD investigations into SOE agents in France, told Vera Atkins after the war: "We got absolutely no new information out of her at all."

Déricourt had already told the SD what they needed to know. Now they had Khan's wireless and code books too, which they could use in their radio game of pretense—the Englandspiel, the "English game." The Germans had been playing a similar game to devastating effect in the Netherlands, forcing a captured agent of the SOE's Dutch section to continue to transmit as if he were still free. More than fifty SOE agents would be captured during the deception.

The SD played the game with Khan's set for two months, by the end of which time she had tried another escape and been sent by train to Germany.

Suspecting that Khan might be in German hands, the SOE devised a series of personal questions for whoever was operating her radio. It took some time for the replies to come, and they seemed correct. Somehow, during hours of interrogation, Khan must have given away enough personal information to allow the Germans to fool the SOE.

The SOE checked the responses with France Antelme, who knew Khan. He agreed the responses appeared to have come from her and that she appeared to be operating freely. This miscalculation led the SOE to believe Phono was still operating, and it resulted in Madeleine Damerment, Lionel Lee, and Antelme himself dropping straight into the hands of Josef Kieffer and Ernest Vogt on the night of February 28, 1944.

10

They Serve Alone

ON MARCH 21, 1944, a Royal Navy torpedo boat cautiously made its way along the coast of Brittany, near the port of Brest, and let down a dinghy. Within a few minutes a thirty-seven-year-old woman clambered up onto the dark beach. The papers in her pocket described her as a social worker named Marcelle Montegerie, but to her handlers in London she was code-named Diane. They had ensured anyone watching her making her way inland would not have noticed a distinct limp in her left leg. She was the "limping lady" the Gestapo had been hunting in Lyon. Virginia Hall was back in France.

....

During her first week in F Section working with Buckmaster, Virginia Hall had seen that the OSS was determined to take its place alongside the SOE. David Bruce had confirmed that to her when she met him. She told Buckmaster she was going to apply for an interview with the OSS. He gave her a name to contact. Army Major Paul van der Stricht was head of the OSS legal department.

She met him in his office in Grosvenor Square. A stocky man with piercing eyes, he carefully questioned her about her family background, her work in France, and her duties in F Section. He asked her why she wanted to transfer to the OSS, and her response was brusque: "I am an American. I want to go back into France as American."

Nodding, he reached across his desk and handed her a document. "Agreement to Serve in OSS." He told her to read it. Her salary would be $336 per month. She would serve for a year on signature, and in any place ordered. Any information she obtained would be secret. She would accept the personal risk to her life. She read carefully, then spoke. There was one clause *she* wanted to insert. Reaching for her fountain pen she wrote, "All I will earn will be transferred to my mother," and signed the document. With Major Stricht's signature on behalf of the OSS, Hall was accepted as a new member of the Special Operations group.

The rest of her day at OSS headquarters was spent meeting her new colleagues and visiting the tailoring department to be fitted with clothes that would turn her into a plump, elderly woman. Later she left the building with a suitcase filled with her wardrobe of disguises and a transceiver, which could transmit and receive.

The next morning she had two medical appointments. The first was with a dentist to check her teeth and fillings. If her dental work didn't look like it had been done by a French dentist, the fillings had to be changed.

Her second appointment was with an orthopedic surgeon who would show her how she could turn her limp into a shuffle by learning to walk with an old-age stoop. By the afternoon she had managed to walk with her false leg, named Cuthbert, in a new way.

....

Having done so much formative work for the SOE, Hall's new mission was to establish an OSS network, to be called Saint, and to prepare agents and local *résistants* for the invasion.

Hall's handlers had hesitated to send her back. The Gestapo had her description from her activities in the South of France, and her leg made her more easily recognizable. But both the British and Americans desperately needed experienced agents in the field, especially since by late 1943 many of the Allied intelligence-gathering networks had been infiltrated, broken up, or were under threat of exposure. These gains by the Germans had increased pressure on agents at a time when more than ever top-class information was required from inside France. Plans for the landings on the northern coast were by then well advanced. The D-day invasion was imminent.

Hours after Motor Boat 503 left the Royal Navy base in Devon, Hall changed into her disguise. She dyed her hair and changed into a wide skirt and blouse to create an illusion of a heavier figure. She started walking with a swinging motion, like some older women did when their hips and knees were less agile and they had put on extra weight. The captain and MTB crew applauded before they helped her into the dinghy. The dawn was coming when two of the seamen rowed the dinghy up on the sand and helped her step down.

Carrying a suitcase, in which her radio set was tucked under her spare clothes, she made her way to Creuse, an area of rolling hills and steep valleys in central France, and set up home with a poor French farmer and his elderly mother. The cottage in which they lived on the edge of the village of Maidou had no water or electricity, but Hall quickly learned to adapt to the rustic lifestyle.

She worked as their cook and milkmaid, taking the cows to pasture and checking out which local fields might be suitable for drops or landing zones. She worked as her own organizer and wireless operator, and radioed London from a farmer's hayloft. It was dangerous work. F Section radio operators typically survived only about eight weeks in the field, and they tended to favor big cities rather than peaceful rural areas where people were few and far between.

Hall's mission was very much geared to the invasion, and she quickly found a way to increase the amount of information she could obtain about troop movements. The farmer's mother made cheese, and so Hall offered to help her sell it to one of her main markets: the Germans. She was able to overhear information exchanged by soldiers, who had no idea she spoke German.

Hall's messages were sent to the SOE to be relayed to the OSS. One day, she had just finished packing her radio away in the farmer's cottage when she heard a car outside. Going downstairs, she opened the door to find a group of German soldiers. An officer asked her what she was doing, and she put on her best vulnerable old lady voice to explain she was the milkmaid to the farmer and his mother. The officer waved his arm and three soldiers swept by her into the cottage. They turned over the furniture and then made their way to the room from which she had been transmitting only minutes before. Hall knew that if they found her radio she would be arrested. She eyed the open fields behind the officer and wondered how far she could get if she ran. With her wooden left leg, she was not the best equipped for such an escape.

After a few moments a soldier returned and handed a large piece of cheese to the officer. He wanted to buy it for his men. He handed over some coins and the soldiers left.

Shaken but undeterred, Hall moved from one safe house to another. In one she transmitted from an eighty-four-year-old man's attic. In another she took on a role as a goatherd and, from beneath the crinkled headscarf of a stooped peasant lady, counted the German trucks and tanks passing through the area. When London arranged a drop of arms and equipment onto one of her fields, she rode out to collect it on a hay cart with members of her Resistance team.

Hall used money sent in from London to finance a growing band of *résistants*. They already numbered in the hundreds, and urgently needed weapons. In her radio messages home, Hall kept up the pressure on London to provide more arms for them. She wanted the Resistance to be a private army by the time D-day came. She had already discussed with them an attack on the German garrison at Le Puy as part of a prelude to the invasion, which was continuing to gain momentum.

....

Meetings had already taken place in Algiers between Henri Frenay, a Resistance leader; John J. McCloy, the American assistant secretary of war; and Emmanuel d'Astier de la Vigerie, an opium-smoking former journalist who had formed one of the earliest Resistance networks. Winston Churchill had chaired discussions.

The prime minister saw the arming of the Resistance in southeastern France as essential to Allied landings on the Mediterranean coast, and he dreamed of creating an underground army like Tito's in Yugoslavia.

Caches of small arms that had been hidden after the French army's surrender in June 1940 would be supported by arms dropped from England by the SOE and OSS.

During the spring of 1943, nearly 150 tons of supplies were dropped. In the lead-up to D-day this would rise to 938 tons, each drop by either the RAF or the USAAF consisting of containers of weaponry, explosives, and ammunition, as well as smaller packages. It was a substantial increase, although still far less than Tito received.

....

Virginia Hall's activities were being repeated across France. Agents were preparing *résistants* for the coming battle and were pleading with London for more and more supplies.

Both the SOE and OSS knew they had to expand their networks through France. No one yet knew when the invasion would take place, but both Gubbins and Donovan recogized that, in the meantime, their operations in France had a special role: to prepare the path for invasion, particularly by uniting and arming the various Resistance networks.

In addition to Hall, a number of female agents were sent behind enemy lines. Their lives became increasingly dangerous. Invasion planning meant that they had to travel farther, carry more messages, meet with more contacts, and increase the number of radio messages to London.

The Prosper network had shown how damaging betrayal could be. While its tentacles had spread throughout northern France, it had been destroyed well before it could provide any meaningful help for invasion planners. Elsewhere, though, networks continued to grow, with more and more women arriving in France by moonlight to live in the shadows.

....

Away from the disaster unfolding in the north, Jacqueline Nearne and Maurice Southgate had been busy creating one of the most important *réseaux* in the unoccupied zone. Since January 1943, they had been working hard to unite various Resistance groups into a fighting force. This had been no easy task.

The area covered by their Stationer network stretched from the Massif Central, the high plateau at the heart of France, to the foothills of the Pyrenees. The pair had quickly developed a strong working relationship and, after three months when they received a wireless operator, Amédée Maingard, their ability to grow their network was enhanced further. Nearne even recruited her own brother, Francis, who lived near Grenoble with his wife and three-year-old son, as a courier. A bespectacled commercial traveler with dark brown hair and brown eyes, Francis was of a rather nervous disposition, but he desperately wanted to help his younger sister with the war effort.

The number of people joining the Resistance was increasing, a consequence of German and Vichy efforts to force young people to work for them. At the end of 1941 Hitler had decreed that fortifications should be built on the Atlantic coast to resist any invasion. The Todt organization created paid employment for local French people but also forced large numbers of Jews, North Africans, and Spanish Republicans to work for them. Increasingly, the Germans abandoned all pretense of seeking volunteers, and in September 1942 a French law allowed workers to be drafted into employment "in the national interest."

Then in February 1943, Vichy instituted Service du Travail Obligatoire (STO) requiring Frenchmen of military service age to undertake two years of compulsory labor service. Several hundred thousand Frenchmen were already working in Germany, and it was widely understood that most young men affected would be sent to join them.

Throughout the spring of 1943, the Milice also increased its activities across southern France. It evicted restaurateurs suspected of dealing in black market food and harassed and arrested Jews, Communists, and Gaullists.

This, along with the presence of the recently arrived German forces and the anger at the STO, encouraged people to take sides. It is believed that as many as 260,000 young men took to the hills and woods to escape the STO, and many ended up joining or forming Resistance groups.

This increased the work of the agents of Stationer. Nearne spent hours on the overnight train from Clermont-Ferrand to Toulouse and the morning train on to Tarbes. She carried messages for Maingard to transmit to the SOE, written on paper small enough that she could swallow it if needed. Sometimes she used a briefcase to carry documents, wireless components, or supplies that could not be easily hidden.

Often leaving a railway station was the most dangerous moment for an agent carrying incriminating material. It was here the French police and Gestapo set up their checkpoints. Nearne developed a routine at stations where she feared her luggage would be searched. She would summon a porter and have her case put in left luggage. She would return to the station when the checkpoint had been dismantled.

Autumn came, and the invasion that agents and the growing Maquis had expected did not. Then, on the night of September 22, 1943, Southgate was told to attend the drop of an agent in fields near Châteauroux. He and the reception committee watched the parachute come down some distance away, and they rushed around a large pond to find the parachutist. They eventually found a figure crouching down behind a tree urinating. Pearl Witherington had arrived.

Witherington was a clear-thinking, resourceful twenty-nine-year-old who had grown up in Paris with an alcoholic English father. Her suitcases had sunk to a bottom of the pond when she jumped, but she was used to adversity and knew how to cope when things went wrong; from the age of twelve she had had to deal with creditors chasing after her father. She had had only four years of schooling before becoming first a typist and then personal assistant to the air attaché at the British Embassy in Paris. In June 1940 she had arrived at work to discover that everybody had left and that she was trapped in Paris. When she had finally escaped from France, she had left behind her fiancé, Henri Cornioley, who had joined the army and been captured during the German invasion.

On arrival in England she contacted the Air Ministry and was given a job as a personal assistant to the director of Allied Air Forces and Foreign Liaisons. As she took shorthand notes and typed, her mind was always on Henri and returning to France. In September 1941 she received a letter from Henri's grandmother in Lausanne to say he had escaped from a prison camp and was now safe in France.

That November, having heard about the SOE through friends at the Air Ministry, Witherington met with Maurice Buckmaster. Recording the meeting in his private diary, Buckmaster later drew a circle around her name: he had found a new recruit.

Buckmaster's order to Southgate to be at Witherington's drop was a surprise for both agents. They had been in the same year at the British School of Paris. When they had met by accident later in London, it had been Witherington who had put Southgate in touch with Buckmaster. Both joined the SOE.

Now, in the darkness of occupied France, Witherington heard a low whistle. Two descending notes. She knew that Cornioley had received a message to tell him that she was coming. "Henri? Is that you?" The man's voice that came back was one that she recognized, but it was Southgate, not her fiancé. "Pearl?" came the urgent whisper. "C'est toi?"

Witherington not only would take pressure off Nearne but also would become one of the SOE's finest and most successful operatives.

....

Jacqueline Nearne's sister, Eileen, had been kicking her heels back in England, hoping Buckmaster would pluck her out of her work in decoding and send her to France to join her sister. Eileen did not know that Jacqueline had requested that he spare her younger sister from danger, an appeal which he listened to . . . for a time, at least.

But then in the autumn of 1943 Eileen was told she was being sent to the Drokes, a house on the Beaulieu estate, to be trained as a wireless operator. Instructors felt Eileen's immaturity might be a problem—Kim Philby called her "pale and wide-eyed"—and this worried Buckmaster, but he had seen her sister develop into one of his brightest agents. *Who was to say the younger sister might not do the same?* he had asked himself.

He decided to take a chance. With a cover story of a shop girl, the name Jacqueline du Tertre, and her SOE code name Rose, Eileen was trained to go to France.

....

Jacqueline Nearne and Pearl Witherington were constantly on the move. Both using the cover of traveling representatives—Witherington's cover said she worked for a cosmetics firm—they took and received messages from Resistance groups across a wide area.

They often found themselves having to command and guide the new and restless breed of men who had joined the Resistance. Most of them were in their early twenties, could be lax about security, and had egos that made them surly at having to follow a woman. Like other female agents, Nearne and Witherington were bound to face entrenched male attitudes in a country in which women had not yet even the right to vote. (Frenchwomen only got this right in time for the first election after liberation in April 1945.)

Nearne helped Southgate coordinate two of the larger, more effective Resistance subcircuits, made up of Communists and escaped prisoners of war, into sabotage parties, destroying generators, electricity pylons and a substation, trucks, and railway lines and signals.

Nearne and Amédée Maingard took joint charge of Stationer when Southgate was temporarily recalled to London in October 1943, coordinating reception committees for the weaponry being dropped by London. Southgate told his officers in Baker Street, "I could not have done half of what I have without her."

During Southgate's absence, a Communist Resistance leader whom Nearne considered a friend, Auguste Chantraine, was arrested. The network went into a security clampdown, with Nearne working hard to save Stationer from further arrests. It put her under tremendous pressure, and when Southgate returned to France in early 1944 he was shocked by how much weight she had lost and how tired she looked. Both Buckmaster and Southgate were worried about her, but she did not want to leave France with the D-day invasion so close.

In February the SOE sent a Lysander to pick her up. She went to the landing zone but allowed a French politician to take her place. Buckmaster was angry with her, but only because she was one of his best people in the field and he knew tiredness could make even the most efficient agent careless.

....

The SOE was also taking steps to strengthen its presence along the eastern side of France. On August 14, 1943, a twenty-five-year-old agent jumped from a plane near Lons-le-Saunier in the Jura mountains. She carried a briefcase containing one million French francs. The money was for the small Monk network that was based in Marseille.

The agent was a dark-haired but fair-skinned Anglo-Spanish woman named Eliane Plewman. Her brother, Albert Browne-Bartroli, would soon follow her into France, also as an F Section agent.

As she descended she could not see the lights of her reception committee. Instead, the roof of a farmhouse appeared to be drifting up toward her. A farm dog began barking wildly. She cleared the building and the yard and came down in the fields beyond.

Plewman struggled to her feet, having badly twisted her ankle on landing, and realized she had been dropped in the wrong place. She took her bearings and hid the case of money in some thick bushes and set out for help. She found her contacts had been arrested by the Germans. It took her two months to reach Marseille and, when a *résistant* was sent back for the money, he found an empty case. An opportunist passerby had obviously gotten lucky.

Plewman began a punishing work schedule, carrying messages for the leader of Monk, an agent named Charles Skepper, from his home in Marseille on a sixty-mile journey to the base used by his radio operator, Arthur Steele, at a hilltop villa owned by a Madame Régis. The cool and reliable Régis would become a local Resistance legend for her quick thinking in the face of the enemy.

On one occasion she saw a German on the terrace outside her villa just as the twenty-year-old Steele was at work in the villa. Urging him to hide his set, she went out to meet the German, who said he was on a routine check. She invited him in for a glass of homemade schnapps and introduced Steele as her son. The German was so taken with her, he often returned to enjoy a conversation and another glass of her drink. Her courage and nerve paid dividends: sometime later, when a detector van picked up a radio signal in the area, the Germans did not check her villa as they believed its occupant to be friendly to the occupiers.

Steele took the close shave as a warning though, and from then on he and Plewman would head into the hills and transmit in the shadow of a Roman aqueduct.

Plewman traveled to Roquebrune-sur-Argens, the nearest village to the villa, either by train or in a battered old truck, which was also used by the local Resistance to carry supplies and explosives. The journeys could be tense as the area was flooded with tens of thousands of German troops preparing defenses for any possible invasion in the south.

The beginning of 1944 signaled a change in the activities of Plewman and her Monk team. Sabotage was now their main priority. She trained *résistants* in how to destroy railway tracks, enabling a series of attacks on trains, including the derailing of the mainline train to Toulon inside a tunnel, which caused a holdup of four days.

During the first two weeks of January, Plewman and her team of saboteurs damaged thirty trains. The number of operations put her under strain and forced her to take risks. When her brother visited her in Marseille he was horrified to discover that she was carrying a bag of plastic explosives and that she was on her way to lay a charge. He insisted on helping her, telling her she had to take care—the success of the Monk network would bring greater attention from the Germans. His warning was eerily prophetic.

....

At the other end of the eastern side of France was a plump, fair, and rather shy woman who had married an SOE instructor shortly before arriving in France by Lysander in September 1943.

Yolande Beekman, who came from an Anglo-Swiss family and spoke French perfectly, had been put down on the same landing ground near Angers that had received Noor Inayat Khan, Cecily Lefort, and Diana Rowden three months earlier. It was to be a terrible omen.

If the double agent Déricourt had ensured she was followed on arrival, as he had the others, Beekman either shook off her tail or they lost her during her long journey to Saint-Quentin in the northeast.

Beekman was to work as wireless operator for the Musician network led by Gustave Biéler, who had been using a Prosper radio until that *réseau* collapsed. Saint-Quentin was at the heart of a key area for the Resistance. It was the center for the industrial canal and railway networks for the region, and the rail link to Lille was essential for the Germans. It was also an area busy with Luftwaffe bases, housing bombers bound for England and fighters protecting the Reich.

Musician was already under strain. The area was filled with German troops, and Resistance attacks on the railway line had increased pressure on Biéler and his men.

Beekman was known during her training for her care, but for three months during the autumn and winter she had to use the same safe house from which to transmit. For each message she made her way into the freezing cold attic of a building. She sat on a velvet divan, reading, turning the pages of the book with mittened hands, while waiting for the time to transmit or receive.

Her messages organized large and urgently needed deliveries to the twelve Maquis groups in the Musician network. She radioed for drops of Sten guns, bazookas, arms, and explosives. She also reported the increasing number of successes achieved by Musician. Bridges, gasoline pumps, tracks, signal boxes, and locomotive sheds were blown up. Working with railway workers, they added abrasive grease to lubricants and damaged ten locomotives.

Buckmaster noted that Biéler had "an amused tolerance for the women engaged in our work," but he developed a deep respect for Beekman, and she accompanied him and the others on several of the sabotage missions.

Despite the level of German activity in the area, Biéler's ambitions were high. His next plan would prove a major success, but at a terrible cost.

....

A month after Yolande Beekman's arrival, a Hudson from Tempsford, flown by Johnnie Affleck on his first such mission, circled over the village of Lons-le-Saunier searching out the same landing ground that had been used by Eliane Plewman.

Inside, the aircraft dispatcher stepped back through the fuselage and nodded at the four passengers. It was almost time. One of the passengers was a tall, athletically built woman with red-gold hair. A few hours earlier, Elizabeth Devereaux Rochester had been eating her two fried eggs at Gaynes Hall. Now she was preparing to step once more onto the soil of the country she had fled that spring.

Landing in the dark with only flashlights to guide him in, the pilot clipped a church belfry, sending cases stacked in the airplane crashing to the floor. By the time they touched down, Rochester was afraid the noise had alerted Germans in the area, and she scrambled quickly out of the plane. She fell on her face in the French mud.

One of the men with her was Richard Heslop. He was to be the organizer for a new network, Marksman, for which she would be courier. The other, Owen Johnson, was Heslop's wireless operator.

They were headed to the Haute-Savoie, an area that Rochester knew well from her days as a courier taking messages across the Swiss border. It was also the rugged mountain country that Peter Churchill and Odette Sansom had shown could be productive for the Resistance, until their capture earlier that year. Despite the collapse of Churchill's Spindle network, the Maquis had continued to grow in the area. Marksman agents would ensure they received the arms they needed.

Rochester moved into a chalet in Albigny, near Lake Annecy, and stashed a suitcase filled with plastic explosives in the cellar. Despite Heslop's concerns about her appearance—her height, in particular, made her stand out, and she always felt uncomfortable taking messages to larger towns and cities, such as Lyon and Grenoble—he later admitted that she carried out all her work with "guts and imagination." That Roedean girls' school education made her sharp under pressure, and she could memorize long messages without needing to write them down.

Early on, a young *résistant* came to talk to her about a group of his comrades who were planning a sabotage operation. She was taken aback when he said, "I suppose you'll want me to contact the boys so you can brief them?"

"You don't really think I'm going to do it?" she said.

"Why not? That's what you were trained for in England. If you can teach them how to do it, you can do it yourself."

There was something in the young *résistant*'s manner—the smile, the way the Gauloises hung almost insolently from the side of his mouth—that made Rochester think that he found it amusing to have a woman prepare and then lead the mission.

A few days later Rochester stood in the cellar, laid out detonators, time pencils, and plastic explosives, and prepared the charges. Then, under the watchful eye of the *maquisards*, she took Sten guns from where they were concealed and handed them one each.

The next day the snow fell most of the morning. When it stopped and the sun baked the mountains, Rochester led her sabotage team down a hill toward the lake. They waited until dark at the home of a contact, and then separated to make their way alone into the town of Annecy.

The streets were quiet and thick with snow. Rochester turned down a dark alley and then stepped into an abandoned warehouse, where she was due to meet her team. Stepping carefully across the debris-strewn floor, she peered out through a broken window at the station yard. Passengers were already arriving for the night train to Lyon. Rochester knew there were three locomotives just inside the terminus. These, intelligence from a railwayman told her, were unguarded before the 11:00 curfew.

Rochester dispatched a small cover party to keep guard with their Stens. The final *maquisard*—her guard—came with her to watch over her as she laid the charges. Their boots sank in the soft snow as they made their way toward the tracks and then along to the locomotives. Rochester quickly attached charges to the first and second locomotives, and then walked around the third. Just as she had finished laying the final explosives, she slipped and stumbled against a steel girder. A loud clang broke through the silence. She and her guard held their breath.

There was a noise and a shaft of light. Someone had opened a door into a back room in the terminus and was peering toward them.

"Il y a quelqu'un?"

They could not see who it was. The maquisard stood in the shadows, his Sten raised.

Rochester shouted to the man at the door that she had lost her dog and that she had tripped and hurt herself.

The man came forward to see if he could help, and she could see by his overalls and the coal dust on his wrinkled face that he must be one of the engine drivers. Her guard stepped out and shoved the gun into the man's back.

Rochester checked the third charge and all three left. Back in the warehouse the train driver explained that he wanted no part in the Resistance and had been in the back room sorting out cigarettes that he brought from Switzerland to sell locally.

One of the Resistance men took the driver under guard back to his home, while Rochester headed back up the hill toward her chalet. Leaning on the gate outside her lodgings, with her warm breath making clouds in the cold air, Rochester looked back at Annecy and waited for the charges to detonate.

As the detonation time arrived, and then passed without result, she feared she had made a mistake—perhaps she had forgotten to prime them? Or maybe they had been discovered?

She gripped her watch and stared at the dial. It was 11:00. She thought of England. It was closing time in the public houses, and she saw warm, laughing faces and beer in pewter mugs. Then the first explosion ripped through the night, and the tension disappeared from her body. Suddenly very tired, she turned, just as the second charge went off, followed immediately by the third.

Elizabeth Devereaux Rochester, who the Maquis had already honored with the nickname La Grande because of her height and bearing, was making herself known in the mountains of eastern France.

....

In Saint-Quentin, after a series of attacks on the railways, Gustave Biéler had bigger plans for Yolande Beekman and his sabotage team.

The Saint-Quentin canal was of great importance to the Germans and was used to transport submarine parts that left requisitioned factories in the north to be taken by barge to Bordeaux and the Mediterranean. The SOE saw cutting off this supply of parts as an efficient way of reducing the role U-boats could play in the harassment of ships supplying Allied armies in Italy. A plan was formed to attach limpet mines to the barges and the lock gates, and, under cover of darkness, Biéler led a team to lay the charges. When the gates next opened, the charges detonated and the canal was jammed with broken gates and the wreckage of barges. That section of the canal was out of operation for many months. The attack brought even greater attention on Musician. Beekman dyed her hair blonde and switched her identity papers and cover story but remained in her safe house.

The Gestapo realized that the Resistance must be receiving supplies from London and that a wireless operator was at work in the area. Teams of detector vans converged on the city. Beekman's landlady even saw one pass by her front window. Beekman's radio was pinpointed, and too late she decided to move. She found lodging at the Moulin Brulé, a small café by a canal bridge. The network's regular members used it as a meeting place. But by now, she and the others were under surveillance.

The next day, a frosty morning in the middle of January, Beekman came down from her room for a meeting with Biéler and another man. Two dark cars screeched to a halt outside the café and Gestapo officers ran in, guns in their hands.

According to Buckmaster, Beekman reached for her revolver but it was too late. She and Biéler were dragged into the cars and taken to Gestapo headquarters.

It was the end of the Musician network.

....

The moonlit nights of March 1944 saw a number of women arrive in France to bolster networks and take part in sabotage attacks ahead of the proposed invasion.

Twenty-eight-year-old Parisian Denise Bloch had been transferred from her work in the Resistance to work for SOE wireless operator Brian Stonehouse almost two years earlier. Having narrowly escaped arrest more than once, she had fled to London and been trained as a wireless operator. On March 2 a Lysander from 161 Squadron dropped her to work in a developing *réseau* whose role was to sabotage electricity pylons linking the Pyrenees and Brittany, and to carry out sabotage on the railway system around Nantes.

Yvonne Baseden, a twenty-two-year-old radio operator, was dropped by parachute into southwest France. She spent four days traveling to her area in the Jura, where she was to help set up a new network, Scholar, and arrange arms drops.

Patricia "Paddy" O'Sullivan was the Dublin-born daughter of an Irish journalist who had been educated by a Belgian aunt at a number of schools in Europe. Strong-willed, with a tangle of ginger hair, O'Sullivan's mission was to work a radio for the Fireman network, which was developing in the northern part of the Creuse. She almost lost her life in the drop when her parachute cords became tangled and she struggled with the lines trailing above her. Dangerously low, her parachute at last blossomed out above her, but she still hit the ground hard and was knocked unconscious.

When she came around she reckoned the two million francs packed into her backpack had saved her life. Her reception committee collected her belongings and radio, together with the containers dropped with her, and took her to a safe house where she slept for twenty hours.

O'Sullivan needed that sleep. Over the coming weeks, wireless operators were going to be busier and more important than ever.

....

The same night that Denise Bloch dropped into France, Eileen Nearne arrived onboard another black-painted Westland Lysander from Tempsford flown by Flight Lieutenant Murray Anderson.

Alongside Nearne was Jean Savy, who would lead a new circuit called Wizard to the southwest of Paris. Nearne would be his wireless operator, and they had already developed a great rapport. The thirty-seven-year-old Savy was intelligent and dependable but had two drawbacks that could affect security. As a former lawyer he was well known in Paris from his work before the war and could attract attention. The second was the reason for their arrival by Lysander rather than parachute: Savy had a withered right arm, something that made him distinctive and recognizable.

Nearne was heartened to hear their Resistance welcoming committee greet them in strong Parisian accents. They spent their first night asleep in a drafty and dirty barn. The next day at the railway station at Orléans, Nearne was so startled by her first sight of German soldiers that her companions had to tell her not to stare. In Paris, with the help of a local member of the Resistance she knew only as Louise, she found a room in Porte de Champerret and a house in the suburb of Bourg-la-Reine, from where she could transmit her messages.

The couple who owned the room, Monsieur and Madame Dubois, were taking a tremendous risk should their involvement be discovered. The Germans operated direction-finding equipment to try to capture "pianists," a major prize for the Gestapo and Abwehr, and those sheltering them faced execution or a concentration camp.

Nearne's fellow SOE radio operator Yvonne Cormeau said later, "Those who offered me a room and offered me food always knew that I had come from England. They were asked, 'Would you take a radio operator?' because that more than doubled the danger for them. And, I'll give it to these people, not once was I refused accommodation."

Cormeau, who had left her two-year-old daughter in the care of a convent when she flew from Tempsford to become the second female radio operator sent into France by the SOE, had her own remarkable escape. When her radio was uncovered by a German soldier at a roadblock, she managed to convince him that she was a district nurse and the wireless equipment in her case was an X-ray machine.

For the first few weeks there was little for Eileen Nearne to report to London, but then Jean Savy contacted her to say that he had a message for London that was too sensitive to relay by wireless. She was to request a plane for him at the earliest opportunity.

....

In Marseille, Eliane Plewman had tried to lie low after a series of successful sabotage attacks on the rail network of the southeast of France. Her fears that the Germans were actively pursuing the sabotage team had transmuted into a new concern: that there might be an informer at work in the *réseau*. It was not unusual for agents to feel a sense of foreboding, living in constant danger of discovery. She began to feel certain that something was happening to the group. One of her team suspected that the Germans had been inside his apartment, so he went to the barber's shop beneath where he lived. The barber had just smothered his face in shaving soap when two German soldiers flung open the door and looked around.

Plewman refused a suggestion to leave Marseille, saying she had too much to do. When a friend left her one day, she said, "Au revoir," to which an anxious-looking Plewman replied, "No, not au revoir—adieu."

Her network's fate was settled in a most unfortunate way. Plewman had to source some food for one of her team on the black market who had dietary issues. Her black market contact shared a mistress with an officer in the Gestapo. It was this woman who betrayed them.

Her leader, Charles Skepper, was arrested on March 23, 1944, and Plewman the next day. Within days, twelve members of the group were in cells at the Gestapo's Marseille headquarters on the Rue Paradis. Throughout horrific torture, Plewman maintained she was simply Skepper's lover and not an agent or *résistant*. At night she sang songs in her cell, to comfort herself and encourage her group not to give in.

Plewman was taken to Dachau concentration camp where, in September 1944, she was executed alongside Yolande Beekman, who had married just before leaving on her mission; Noor Inayat Khan; and Madeleine Damerment, whose capture resulted from the SOE's refusal to believe that Khan had been captured.

Also executed were Madeleine Damerment's male colleagues, France Antelme and Lionel Lee; Yolande Beekman's leader, Gustave Biéler;

Eliane Plewman's leader in the Monk network, Charles Skepper; and her radio operator, Arthur Steele.

....

Throughout the winter and early spring, battles between the Resistance and the Milice in the Haute-Savoie region had become more intense.

Formed in 1941, the Milice was a paramilitary organization whose members swore an oath against "Jewish leprosy," democracy, and opponents of Pétain's Vichy France. It was a Fascist gang, hated by the Resistance but especially dangerous to *résistants* and agents because it was made up of French men and women. By 1944 its ranks had grown to thirty-five thousand members who included the dregs of French society, often former criminals and gangsters. They were divided into gangs where they lived, making them far more efficient than the Gestapo. Unlike the Police Nationale, which sought out "enemies of the state," the Milice hunted, tortured, and killed for personal gain and satisfaction. Those with grudges against former lovers or business associates found the Milice the perfect outlet for their revenge.

The Maquis, using arms dropped by London that had often been arranged by Elizabeth Devereaux Rochester and the Marksman network, had increased its attacks. In retaliation the Milice burned down farms and shot villagers. Rochester had narrowly missed being caught—and most probably executed—when she arrived at a location late, to check a dropping area. The village's population had been wiped out by the Milice.

Despite the growing dangers, the tall American woman continued her work, carrying messages and supplies. Network leader Richard Heslop said she was unable to stay still, always pestering him for new tasks and missions.

His concerns about the fact that she looked and acted so little like a local French countrywoman still nagged at him, but it amused him too. Watching her striding toward him in the mountains, she looked so much like an English lady that he expected her to have two Labradors at her heels and to greet him with the words, "Had a bloody good walk, you know, nothing like it for keeping fit."

Another leading SOE agent, George Millar, remembered she had a "genially commanding" attitude to her *maquisards*, that she dressed in "superb" tweeds, and kept expensive luggage including gold-tipped bottles and jars in her Alpine hideouts. If the mountains gave her a feeling of security, that was about to change.

On February 2, 1944, the BBC broadcast a warning: "Attention the Maquis! Attention the Haute-Savoie! The Oberführer Joseph Darnand has decided to launch a massive attack tomorrow, February 3, against the patriots hiding out in the mountains of the Haute-Savoie. . . . There is not a minute to spare—you must take up your defensive positions!"

Hundreds of *résistants* climbed through the deep snow to join the *maquisards* who had gathered on the Glières Plateau, a vast area in the hills above Annecy, almost uninhabitable during the winter months. Here they believed that had created an "impregnable fortress." It was actually a trap.

A final reckoning on the Glières was coming, but Rochester would not be there to see it. Heslop's concerns about her appearance in these dangerous times eventually led him to act. He could no longer use La Grande for missions to the towns—she was too recognizable, too well known. She had worked hard, done her bit. He asked London to recall her. When Baker Street's message came through agreeing to his request, Rochester refused to go. Heslop reminded her that her invalid mother was in Paris, under surveillance as an enemy alien, and that her capture could put her mother in danger.

Early in March 1944, Rochester left, not for London but for Paris, where she moved into a convent. While sheltering she learned about a friend who was being held in prison. She began to plot an escape attempt.

On March 20, she visited a Swiss friend's apartment, where she had left her bicycle. There was a rapping at the door and, as she answered it, two Germans and a Milice officer pushed her back and accused her of being an American spy.

Unsure how they had found her—she later believed either she had been betrayed or a telephone call she had made in Paris had been intercepted—Rochester decided to stick near to the truth without admitting anything incriminating. She admitted to being an American but said she had recently returned to France from Switzerland. She was able to describe her life in Geneva well, as she knew the city from her days working on an escape line for Jews and airmen through the French Alps.

Unsure what to do with her but with no incriminating evidence on her person or proven links to a spy network, the Gestapo locked her up in Frèsnes prison.

....

Elizabeth Devereaux Rochester's future might have looked uncertain, but her move from Les Glières came just before a major assault by elite German mountain troops of the Gebirgsjäger. A three-thousand-strong force scaled the "citadel of Glières" on March 26 and dispersed the Maquis over four days of fighting. Heslop escaped.

More than 130 miles to the south, a second Resistance gathering on a lofty plateau also believed itself to be impregnable. The Maquis had been gathering at the immense and awe-inspiring Vercors plateau in the Rhône-Alpes region of the southeast, planning to make it a Resistance redoubt at the heart of France following an invasion.

This they would do, but like the *maquisards* of Glières they would discover that the Germans still had the will and the firepower to put down even a mass insurrection. Among the Resistance fighters of the Vercors was a female SOE agent, too—and like Rochester she was foreign born.

....

Christine Granville was an adventurer, a lover of life and of men, who had been described as "the sort of woman our mothers warned us about." She was strong-willed, multilingual, and incredibly brave. Vera Atkins called her a "beautiful animal with a great appetite for love and laughter."

Born Krystyna Skarbek in Poland, she had a Jewish mother and an aristocratic father, and was brought up a Catholic with a deep love of her country.

She had been traveling in Africa with her husband when Poland had been invaded, and had gone to Britain to volunteer to help. MI6 saw her potential, recruited and trained her, and sent her to Hungary posing as a journalist. From there she had organized a supply route for the Polish Resistance, making a series of dangerous trips across the border on her own. She also organized propaganda to persuade the Poles that the British had not abandoned them and planned acts of sabotage, with an old friend from the Polish Army, with whom she began an affair.

She was twice arrested in Hungary, but escaped. In Poland she tried to persuade her mother—her father had died before the war—to go into hiding as her Jewishness was well known. Her mother refused and was later arrested by the Gestapo. Granville never saw her again.

In February 1941, she smuggled out microfilm from Poland containing footage taken by Resistance fighters and drove it in a battered old Opel car to Sofia, the capital of Bulgaria. There she had made contact with a young air attaché at the British Legation and handed over the microfilm. It was found to contain footage of hundreds of tanks, army regiments, and Panzer divisions being amassed near the Russian border.

Granville had delivered the first intelligence showing that Hitler might be planning an attack on his ally, the Soviet Union.

She escaped through Yugoslavia, Turkey, Syria, and Palestine to Egypt, where she was recruited by the SOE under the name Christine Granville—an English-sounding name she had earlier given herself while in Hungary. Her handlers were delighted with the new intelligence she now delivered to them. Her prewar travels and aristocratic blood meant that she knew important people in many European countries and could provide information on their activities and political affiliations. She had also made a detailed study of the bridges of Syria as she had driven through.

Granville was recruited into the FANYs, although she only ever wore the uniform to have her photograph taken for her identity card.

In October 1942 she took an SOE wireless operator's course in Cairo in preparation for her planned drop on a mission into Turkey. The operation was canceled, and it was early 1944 before she completed her parachute training in Palestine at RAF airbase Ramat David, near Haifa.

In March that year she received training in elementary explosives and attended an SIS firearms course. Although she had hunted with a rifle before the war on her family's estate, she found the Sten too loud. She preferred the "ideal" fighting knife developed by SOE instructors Bill Fairburn and Eric Sykes. She had a leather sheath designed so she could strap the knife to her thigh.

Christine Granville was desperate to get back into the war and, when another mission—this time to Hungary—was canceled, she realized that France was the place that they needed to send her.

She confronted an SOE coordinator, Douglas Dodds-Parker, and told him: "I want to go to France. I *am* going to France."

He told her she was too flamboyant, too brave, and that she would get caught.

"I'll kill you," she told him.

Dodds-Parker sent her to see the new regional head of the SOE, Major General William Stawell. After dinner the pair disappeared behind a sand dune, and when Stawell returned he was said to be "knocking at the knees." Stawell instructed his officers to find Granville a mission immediately. She was going to France.

....

As D-day approached, the Stationer circuit was showing signs of strain. Jacqueline Nearne, still unaware that her sister was in France 260 miles to the north, was close to a breaking point. She had been working undercover across a huge area of the country for more than a year, carrying out sabotage operations, relaying messages, and helping to organize sometimes ragged bunches of *maquisards*.

Network leader Maurice Southgate was exhausted too, with problems arising across the circuit. One agent proved unreliable and ran off with a mistress known to have pro-Nazi sympathies. Another disappeared while searching out potential new landing zones near Poitiers and then sent a cryptic note asking Southgate or Pearl Witherington to meet him in the city. Southgate was unavailable, so Witherington made her way to Poitiers boys' school where the agent had a contact. In fact, the agent had been arrested, the note had been sent by the Germans, and Witherington was headed straight into a trap.

When she arrived at the school, she was stopped by a concierge who whispered that the building was crawling with Gestapo. Witherington realized that she had to escape calmly in case she was being watched. She took a deep breath, tied a scarf over her head, and walked away.

The pressure experienced by the leaders of Stationer would continue to take its toll on her. Having spent so much time sleeping in unheated railway carriages, she had developed rheumatism, which forced her to stop her courier work for a while.

With the network under such strain, Nearne finally agreed to follow Buckmaster's and Southgate's orders and return to London for rest. She traveled to a landing ground at Villers-les-Orme to meet a Lysander. Nearne's smile flashed in the dark when she saw the message that Buckmaster had written on the side of the fuselage in chalk: Jacqueline must come. This is an order. The inbound passengers got out, and she exchanged greetings with one: it was her friend Lise de Baissac. There was time only to embrace.

Nearne clambered into the aircraft cockpit beside a Frenchman whom she had never met. He shook her hand and introduced himself with his code name, Regis. He was Jean Savy. Nearne was seated next to her sister's leader, traveling back to London on a trip that Eileen had arranged, with his urgent message for Buckmaster.

The code name Regis meant nothing to her, and she turned her head to watch the French countryside move past the canopy as the plane lifted into the sky.

Jean Savy had discovered the Nazis' latest plan for a new Blitz on London. While traveling to the northeast of Paris, he had come upon a quarry that the Germans appeared to be using as an ammunition dump.

After liaising with local *résistants*, and taking a closer look at the site, he discovered that in fact the quarry contained around two thousand V-1 rockets. The Allies already knew about other rocket sites and, in August 1943, had launched an RAF raid on the rocket-making center at Peenemünde on Germany's Baltic coast. But the quarry Savy had found at Saint-Leu-d'Esserent contained enough firepower to perhaps bring London to its knees.

Working with Savy's intelligence, the RAF launched a series of raids that destroyed the rockets at the quarry. But it was just one site of many, and on June 13, 1944, the first of the V-1s—sometimes called doodlebugs—reigned down on London. The Nazi regime was still far from defeated.

....

Five weeks before D-day, Maurice Southgate was arrested in the town of Montluçon, sixty miles from Vichy, at the home of one of his wireless operators.

During his interrogation at Avenue Foch, the SD colonel who was questioning him asked if he knew the man code-named Claude, real name Henri Déricourt. The SD colonel already seemed to know everything about Southgate and many of his associates. "*Claude* is a very good man of ours," the colonel explained smugly. "From him we get reports, documents, and names of people."

The Germans may well have thought they were about to have another summer of success to rival the arrests of the Prosper network almost a year earlier. They surrounded Montluçon, almost trapping Southgate's courier Pearl Witherington and her fiancé, Henri Cornioley, who was now working with her. They escaped the cordon by splitting up and taking various back roads to safety.

Witherington had, by now, been in France for eight months. She had worked tirelessly, once even escaping death from members of her own side when, without a password, she arrived to collect money from a Maquis leader she did not know. They believed she was an agent of the Milice and prepared to strangle her. She only persuaded them she was SOE by giving the name of the farmer in whose field she had landed months before.

One SOE instructor had noted of Witherington: "This student, though a woman, has definitely got leaders' qualities." Despite the sexism of the qualifying phrase "though a woman," the instructor's assessment of her leadership skills was correct. Witherington's work in the field proved it. London made the decision to split the large and unwieldy Stationer circuit and make Witherington, code name Pauline, leader of the northern half. Cool and resourceful, she immediately split her circuit, dubbed Wrestler, into four subcircuits each under a lieutenant reporting directly to her.

Witherington called in fresh arms drops from London and organized her networks into something approaching a private army. The legend of Pauline, the agent for whose capture the Nazis would offer a reward of one million francs, was born. D-day was coming near and, in its wake, she would become an incomparable leader of Resistance action.

....

Nancy Wake, a woman of equally strong character, was on her way to the rugged countryside just east of Witherington. Like Pauline, Wake would become a battlefield leader. And like Christine Granville, she had caused her SOE instructors a considerable amount of trouble.

After escaping from the South of France and reaching London, Wake had approached the SOE for an interview. When she attended Orchard Court, she was delighted to realize that they knew all about the activities of the "White Mouse" who had eluded the Gestapo in Marseille.

Wake's training began with psychological examinations, which were designed to see if an agent would stand up to pressure. She loathed them. When confronted with the Rorschach inkblot test, she replied, "I see ink blots."

In Scotland, she got into an argument with a fellow trainee. Wake had been defending her friend Denis Rake, one of the SOE's most remarkable agents. Openly homosexual at a time when being gay was a criminal offense, Rake had been a circus performer before the war.

Despite hating guns and explosives, he had already worked for the SOE in France as a radio operator. He spoke French and German fluently.

The woman Wake had argued with reported her to Selwyn Jepson and raised concerns about the level of Wake's drinking. Jepson summoned her and began to reprimand her. "We don't like our girls to drink," he said. She told him "what he could do and where he could put it" and was instantly fired. When she returned to her flat in London, she received a telegram ordering her to return her FANY uniform. Wake telephoned Baker Street and said if the SOE wanted her uniform Jepson could pick it up himself. One of the SOE's most remarkable careers almost ended before it had begun.

Fortunately, Maurice Buckmaster heard about the argument. He and Wake had hit it off immediately. She saw him as "an Englishman of the old school," and they had shared their common experience as prewar journalists in Paris. Buckmaster smoothed over the situation, and Wake was rehired.

She never apologized to Jepson and saw no reason to change her behavior on her return to the SOE. At Inverie Bay in northern Scotland, she loved the weapons training but began to worry that her reports might not be good enough. Determined to find out what her instructors thought of her, she made an impression of the office key in some plasticine and had a new key cut. Then one evening she let herself into the office and rifled through the drawers. She was pleased to see that there were no negative remarks in her file; in fact, instructors felt her larger-than-life personality was "good for morale."

At Ringway, an American sergeant tried to embarrass her by passing a small package across the breakfast table with a wink. "It's a present," he smirked. Thinking it was chocolate, Wake opened it to see three condoms inside. The sergeant winked but, unperturbed, Wake began to read aloud the instructions for their use—in great detail. When the red-faced soldier left, Wake put the condoms in her pocket and finished her meal.

Outside the room an officer apologized for the sergeant's attempt to humiliate her and asked if she would like him to take the offending items back. "That's not necessary," Wake told him. "They might come in handy later on."

Her exuberance lasted right through until her last night in Britain. When she boarded a Liberator on the night of April 30, 1944, she did so with a raging hangover. She spent the flight fighting off the urge to be sick into her oxygen mask. Alongside her was Major John Farmer, who would lead the new network of which she would be a part. Code-named Freelance, the network's role would be to unite Resistance groups in the Corrèze. Denis Rake, who would be their wireless operator, had added parachuting to his list of dislikes, and was being brought in by Lysander to meet up with them later.

Over the drop zone Wake remembered the instructor's voice at Ringway as he barked in her ear, "Remember what your mother told you: keep your knees together! Now roll, *roll* as you land!"

Wake did not get the opportunity to roll—her parachute caught in a tree. A local teacher and rugby player, Henri Tardivat, who led the Resistance reception committee, helped her down, making a quip designed to charm about how all trees should bear such beautiful fruit. Wake told him to cut out "that French bullshit." They would become firm friends.

Wake and Farmer had been counting on the initial help of Maurice Southgate and were unaware of his arrest until they landed. One powerful Resistance leader, known as Gaspard, turned them away, saying he was not prepared to work with the British, but a second, Henri Fournier, offered them accommodation and help. When Rake arrived they were able to organize arms and explosives for Fournier's Maquis. Wake carried and coded the messages, using the personal code poem that she had agreed on with the SOE's codemaster, Leo Marks. He usually chose romantic poems or Biblical texts for the agents, but something more bawdy was deemed more appropriate for Wake. She agreed.

The poem she had memorized went:

She stood right there,
In the moonlight fair,
And the moon shone

Through her nightie;
It lit right on
The nipple of her tit,
Oh Jesus Christ Almighty!

Wake, Farmer, and Rake lived in the woods with a ragged bunch of *résistants*. Wake led them in weapons training, and the novelty of having a woman among them was hard to ignore—even if she wore army boots, khaki trousers, a shirt and tie, and a beret. On the first morning she went out among the pine trees to urinate, she noticed the bushes around her were moving. When she got back to camp she told the sniggering men that they had seen her peeing once and that should be enough.

From her base in the forested valley at Chaudes-Aigues, Wake became the *chef du parachutage* for the estimated seven thousand *maquisards* in the area. She chose the fields she would use for parachute drops and gave them code names so London could identify them using a Michelin map.

Early on, Wake insisted on joining a Resistance raid on a shop owned by a collaborator in the town of Saint-Flour. As she broke the window glass, helped grab handfuls of supplies, and sat in the getaway truck as it sped into the darkness, she decided that she "liked this kind of thing."

In the weeks to come, Nancy Wake would climb under bridges to set explosives and lead attacks on German convoys and a raid on a Gestapo headquarters. She was the perfect soldier-agent to be on the ground in France as the final details of the D-day landings were arranged.

11

Out of the Shadows

L ATE IN THE EVENING on June 5, 1944, agents and *résistants* were huddled around radio sets across France as the voice of BBC's French service read out a list of "personal messages." Each message had been prearranged with the various Resistance groups. All were coded differently, but they meant the same: the invasion was on its way! Le Jour J was here!

In the space of just fifteen minutes, two hundred messages were broadcast. As each group heard the words meant for them, they switched off their wireless sets and headed out into the night to play their part in the liberation of their homeland.

SOE wireless operator Yvonne Cormeau, who sent more radio messages back to London than any other F Section operative, watched the actions of the *maquisards* in her area of Gascony. "They went round, got all their matériel out of the hiding places, cleaned the weapons, stuck the ammunition in, and then they were ready to move."

Within twenty-four hours the French railway network had been paralyzed by up to one thousand acts of sabotage. It was a huge blow for the German generals planning the defense of France. Nine out of ten of the troops required to reinforce their defenses needed to be moved by rail.

....

The Wheelwright network in which Yvonne Cormeau acted as wireless operator had been developed by Cormeau and her leader, George Starr, to cover an area from the hills of the Basses Pyrenees in the southwest to the valleys of the Gironde, where the mouths of the rivers Garonne and Dordogne merge. The pair, who had a strong friendship, created a cell structure within the *réseau* that gave it an added layer of security.

Keenly intelligent, Cormeau had been in France since August 1943 and had seen the nature of the Resistance and of the occupation change. Across the months from that autumn to the summer of the invasion, the battle had come to be fought more and more out of the shadows. Explosions ripped through the rail and power infrastructure. German soldiers—sometimes Gestapo officers—were shot. The Germans retaliated by shooting hostages, burning villages, and increasing the number of radio detection vans patrolling the country and the towns.

Knowing that wireless operators had one of the most dangerous jobs in the occupied territories, Cormeau worked hard to improve her odds of survival. She used her natural skill with the wireless to keep her transmissions down to a safe duration—never more than thirty minutes at the most. The SOE noted that she was "one of the most technically efficient wireless operators we had ever sent out."

She was also observant, noting quickly that local women in the Gascogne always wore a small item of jewelry, such as a necklace or bracelet, and quickly acquiring the same. She amended her eating habits, too, when she noticed she was the only woman sipping her soup from the side of her spoon.

Cormeau, code-named Annette, had lost her husband early in the war and had a young daughter at home, but at Christmas 1943 she resisted the chance of returning to London for a short break. Seeing her little girl for a few days and then having to leave her again would have been confusing for the child and agonizing for Cormeau herself. The hope that the invasion had to come in 1944 must have provided some slight compensation; she yearned for the clandestine life to finish.

In January 1944, after appeals to London from Starr for support for the overworked Cormeau, Anne-Marie Walters joined Wheelwright.

Although only twenty years old, Walters had the determination and self-confidence one might expect from someone whose father was an Oxford don and a senior representative of the League of Nations. Raised in Geneva, she had struck SOE instructors as being "active minded" and "curious" but also "domineering." "She will not hesitate to always make use of her physical attractiveness in gaining influence over men," the trainer stated.

Her attempts to get to France had been fraught with danger and tragedy. A Halifax carrying her was forced to return to Tempsford and attempted to land in dense fog. The plane crashed and three of the crew, including the pilot, died. Walters had been saved by the padding of her helmet, parachute, and jumpsuit.

When she finally made it to French soil, she dropped from a clear moonlit sky onto a marshy field not far from the town of Condom. With her was Claude Arnault, an explosives expert.

Walters used the cover of her fake identity as a Parisian student recovering from pneumonia to carry out her courier work for Wheelwright. She was busy that spring, taking messages and instructions to Starr's many and varied bands of *maquisards* across the region, from Toulouse to Montréjeau to Tarbes. Sometimes she swung farther south into the Pyrenees to guide downed Allied airmen over the dangerous mountain paths and into Spain.

She used her looks to great effect, charming a ticket inspector who had become suspicious of the escapee she was accompanying, and making such friends with a local bus driver that he would let her off before a stop where he knew the Germans were checking papers.

In the lead-up to D-day, Wheelwright received "A" and "B" messages from London. These warned networks of the imminent invasion and included coded orders of what to do before and after. While Walters distributed these around the area, one Resistance leader was arrested with the "A" message in his possession.

Word went around her informers that the Gestapo was looking for a young, blue-eyed, fair-haired girl, and Walters went underground.

On the morning of the invasion, brimming with the confidence and cockiness of youth, she told a cautious and doubting *résistant*: "See? The Allies keep their promises after all. . . . You can hope openly now. . . . And no-one will stop you."

. . . .

Lise and Claude de Baissac were working in the southern areas of Normandy on D-day. Having escaped from France the previous summer, Lise had returned to a new region with a fresh cover name that April. She would have returned to France earlier but had broken her leg in parachute training at Ringway. The Lysander that had brought her back was flown by Squadron Leader Hugh Verity and had delivered her into a field northwest of Châteauroux. Her mission had been to work as courier for the Pimento network in Toulouse, a Socialist network under the control of an agent in Switzerland, who was suspected of not being completely loyal to the SOE. Lise had requested a transfer and headed north to work for her brother who had set up Scientist II.

Lise had arrived in Normandy early in April and had immediately begun work scouting for large landing grounds that paratroops could hold in the hours and days after the invasion. She became her brother's second in command, stepping in when his argumentative personality rubbed up against the eager and increasingly troublesome Resistance leaders. With the growing feeling that the invasion was near, there was anxiety and tension.

The Resistance, thanks to Scientist II, was now heavily armed. In the weeks before D-day, three hundred packages and almost eight hundred containers were delivered onto the local drop sites.

As D-day approached, Claude split the network between Calvados and Manche along the coast, and the Orne and Eure-et-Loir inland.

Lise was now cycling almost forty miles a day. Scientist II was so busy and in such an important area for the invasion planners that the SOE sent in a new radio operator. Phyllis Latour was a twenty-three-year-old South African with a French father. Because of the urgency of the situation, she was sent to France despite not completing her training. A resourceful agent, who had originally joined the WAAF to become a flight mechanic, Latour was motivated by a patriotic love of France, and revenge; a much-loved family friend had been killed by the Germans and his wife had committed suicide.

Lise de Baissac and Latour worked together to code and decode messages. De Baissac had a number of near misses as she cycled to Latour with messages and radio components. Sometimes she went through German checkpoints with radio crystals strapped to her legs and waist.

Latour dressed like a schoolgirl in a blue cotton dress when she had to leave her farmhouse. She stashed six bicycles at different safe houses to help her get around. When she met Germans, she pretended to be talkative and friendly, passing so well for a chatty teenager that they grew irritated and wanted to move her on.

Latour carried her codes on a piece of silk that she wound around a knitting needle and pushed through her hair, which was tied up with a shoelace. One day she was rounded up with a group of people in the street and taken to a local police station.

A female soldier made her and the other women in the group strip. The woman nodded at her hair. Latour reached up, pulled out the lace, shook her head and let her hair fall. The soldier paid no attention to the silk, and seeing that nothing was concealed in Latour's hair, nodded her away. Latour got dressed and redid her hair.

When the D-day landings took place, Latour found herself close to the battlefield. Once, she had just finished transmitting in a farmhouse when two German soldiers burst in looking for food. She flipped shut her suitcase, covering the radio set, and said she was preparing to go home as she had scarlet fever. The Germans quickly left.

De Baissac was in Paris when she heard that the D-day messages had come through. It took her three days to get back to Normandy—the roads and railways were jammed with German troops.

....

The Gestapo had circulated a WANTED picture of Virginia Hall, a sketch based on descriptions from double agents and informers. Framed by shoulder-length hair, the face in the drawing showed a firmly set jaw and a look of steely determination in her eyes. The police artist had caught the essence of the woman.

Hall had worked with OSS agent Peter Harratt to create and expand the Heckler network across the Haute-Loire region of central France. By D-day they had three units of three hundred agents taking part in sabotage across the area, and as the invasion force crossed the English Channel, she and her teams of agents began a series of attacks to destroy bridges, trains, and phone lines, and to battle and harass local German troops.

Over the coming weeks, Hall worked tirelessly, organizing sabotage, covering the hills and lanes of the area on her bicycle, watching the roadways for German troops moving north, and reporting these movements back to London.

But she wanted an even bigger army. In her messages to London, she estimated there were a couple thousand men in the mountains who just needed weapons. The men were living rough in makeshift camps; many had escaped to the hills to avoid being sent to Germany as forced laborers. All wanted to fight now that liberation was close at hand.

Hall, like many agents across France, found herself having to make repeated promises to the *maquisards* that the weapons would come, only to find herself let down by her bosses back in London. Many times she and her colleagues set off to wait for a drop and ended up waiting in vain for an aircraft that never came. This put her in the difficult position of having to placate large groups of angry and frustrated Resistance fighters.

Eventually three planes flew up a local valley to drop the delivery she had been promising for some weeks. Now, with a large armed force, she increased attacks on bridges and tunnels, creating such fear in the German garrison at Le Puy that a force of an estimated five hundred German soldiers surrendered.

....

Virginia Hall's chief, Bill Donovan, did not want to be kept out of the fight. He had come to England in the lead-up to the Normandy invasion, keen to see the troops go ashore. Understandably, he was told that having the leader of America's spy service right on the front line was a security risk that the US secretary of the navy, James Forrestal, was not prepared to take.

All the same, using a mixture of bluster and Irish charm, Donovan secured himself and his London chief, David Bruce, cabins onboard the heavy cruiser USS *Tuscaloosa*, which was part of the massive invasion force leaving the south coast of England.

At six in the morning on June 6, Donovan felt the deck of the *Tuscaloosa* tremble as its heavy guns opened up on the German defenses. The Germans quickly responded, with shells landing in the water nearby. Then there was an explosion as the destroyer USS *Corry* struck a mine.

The troops went ashore at 6:30 AM. Donovan watched through binoculars as four heavy enemy guns laid down a barrage on the beach. With the troops was a film unit from the OSS. Their work would later be screened for Roosevelt, Churchill, and Stalin.

In the skies above them, Allied bombers passed over their heads, looking to target the gun batteries inland. In one aircraft was William Stephenson. He had traveled to Europe with Donovan and had also been determined to see the results of all the intelligence planning, the culmination of the work of their agents. Stephenson was tucked into the rear gunner's seat in an RAF bomber.

Throughout D-day, Donovan hinted about going ashore. The following morning he was told he could go if he found transport. A launch was coming aside the boat carrying fliers who had been shot down near the beach and three dead bodies. Donovan and Bruce climbed down a swinging rope ladder and jumped in. The lieutenant commander eyed Donovan, who had pulled on a steel helmet and pinned his Medal of Honor to his battledress. Donovan told him to get them as close to the beach as he could.

Eventually transferring to a DUKW amphibious truck, Donovan and Bruce sat right up on the front hood and were driven up onto the sand. They jumped down and scanned a field map as men and equipment streamed ashore around them.

Casualties at Utah Beach had been lower than expected, and the men of the American First Army had began to march inland, but the Germans were still determined to push the invaders back into the sea. Donovan heard the scream of aircraft engines and looked up to see four Messerschmitts coming in to strafe the beach. He and Bruce dived for cover, with Bruce landing on top of his chief. The steel rim of Bruce's helmet gashed Donovan's chin, causing blood to gush down his neck. For one terrible moment, Bruce thought he had cut a vital artery and killed "Wild Bill" Donovan. But Donovan got up, dabbed his chin with a handkerchief, and pointed the way inland.

Perhaps unrealistically, Donovan believed he could find one of his agents or a member of the Resistance who knew one. They walked for miles before reaching a forward antiaircraft battery. When Donovan told the lieutenant in charge that he was looking for secret agents, the junior officer looked at him in surprise.

Donovan and Bruce walked on alone but then came under sustained machine-gun fire. Taking cover in the dip of land under a hedgerow, Donovan confided to his companion: "You understand, of course, David, that neither of us must be captured. We know too much."

"Yes, sir," Bruce said.

"Have you your pills with you?"

David Bruce had not been expecting to find himself in this position with Donovan. He had left his L tablet on the ship. He shook his head.

"Never mind," Donovan said, as the machine gun rattled again. "I have two of them."

Donovan pushed his hands into his battledress pockets and searched through their contents. He had his hotel keys, passport, money, and photographs of his granddaughter, but no pills. Suddenly he remembered: he had left them in the medicine cabinet in his room in Claridge's hotel in London.

He grasped Bruce's arm. "If we get out of here, you must send a message to Gibbs, the hall porter at Claridge's, telling him on no account to allow the servants in the hotel to touch some dangerous medicines in my bathroom."

Then he touched the revolver at his side. "I must shoot first," he said.

Bruce whispered, "Yes, sir. But can we do much against machine guns with our pistols?"

"Oh, you don't understand," Donovan told him. "I mean if we are about to be captured I'll shoot you first. After all, I am your commanding officer."

Suddenly, the ground around them shook as artillery shells pounded the German positions ahead of them. Both men got up and sprinted back across the field toward the beach.

On their return they found General Bradley in a barn that he had turned into his command post. Donovan told him he wanted Bruce to spend some time with the First Army.

An exhausted Bradley told him, "Bill, I would be very glad to have Bruce at my headquarters later on. But suppose you now go back to wherever you came from."

Donovan returned to the beach, where he tried out his German on a captured Wehrmacht captain who told him he was "overwhelmed" at the sight of the Allied armada and that he realized he was witnessing a historic event.

Donovan returned to Plymouth, England, on June 9. He sent a six-page memo to Roosevelt about what he had seen in Normandy, noting that the Germans did not have the resources to meet the Allied attack at every landing point. Hitler's Atlantic Wall had been breeched.

In a letter to another friend Donovan wrote, "There will be a lot of hard going [in the months ahead] but something has died in the German machine."

....

In the days and weeks after the D-day invasion, a key task for the agents and the Resistance networks was harassing and delaying German reinforcements trying to reach the Normandy battlefield. If the Nazis were able to rush enough tanks and troops into the area there was a danger that the invasion could at best become bogged down and at worst fail altogether.

One key target was the Second SS Panzer Division, known as Das Reich, which began its deadly march north from Montauban—450 miles south of the Normandy beaches—on June 8. Das Reich was made up of fifteen thousand battle-hardened men and more than two hundred tanks and self-propelled guns. British intelligence had calculated that the division could be moved onto the battlefront in three days. The SOE said that time frame had to be extended; Das Reich's arrival at Normandy must be delayed.

Carrying out that order required great courage, and the price would be paid in blood, often that of French civilians who played no part in the Resistance.

Five of F Section's networks would be deployed to stop Das Reich. Tony Brooks, an efficient and brave English-born agent who had been brought up in Switzerland, used a network of railway workers, *cheminots*, key members of the Resistance for their access and knowledge of the rail network, to sabotage flatcars that Das Reich planned to use. These flatcars were the only carriages that could pass under bridges while laden with tanks. Brooks and his team spent many dark nights using grease guns to apply an abrasive paste to the axle bearings of the flatcars, which caused them to seize up after only a few miles on the rail track.

Das Reich, which had been spread across camps over a thiry-mile area, set off by road, an immense convoy of armored cars, towed artillery, half-tracks, troop carriers, and tanks. It tore up the asphalt on the roads as it rumbled forward, the vehicles traveling three hundred feet apart in case of air attack.

The Maquis, some woefully underequipped, rose up to meet them. At the hamlet of Groléjac, fifteen men who had never seen action—one holding a 1914 French Army rifle—lay in wait next to a stone bridge. They faced a battalion of Panzergrenadiere. The action was swift. Five *maquisards* and five civilians died. This was the first violent action against Das Reich. It had been delayed by about twenty minutes, but the pattern had been set.

In another small village that the German division passed through after taking a wrong turn, it fired indiscriminately, killing thirteen unarmed people. Throughout Corrèze these acts of sacrifice and bravery continued, with Resistance men also cutting down trees and creating roadblocks to try to slow the advance.

Villages on the route north were set on fire and families shot out of hand. The saboteurs continued. When a troop train was derailed, a fierce gun battle followed between the soldiers and the Maquis. Several were killed. One was captured and was thrown into the locomotive furnace and burned to death before the locomotive continued its journey toward Normandy. Each German soldier had been read an Order of the Day from Hitler that no one should show mercy to any French man, woman, or child. Nevertheless, reports coming in increasingly showed that the Maquis actions were reaching considerable proportions.

On arrival in Tulle on June 9, Das Reich took back the town from the Resistance and began reprisals. Between four in the afternoon and seven in the evening, ninety-nine people were hanged in the streets from lampposts and balconies. The killing stopped when the Nazis realized they were running out of rope.

The following day members of Das Reich carried out an even larger massacre at Oradour-sur-Glane. The town's menfolk were herded into garages and barns and shot. Women and children were murdered in the church. More than 640 died in a few hellish hours—205 of them were children.

....

During the evening of June 9, an open Talbot car containing Major Helmut Kämpfe, who had won the Knight's Cross in Russia and now commanded a battalion of Das Reich, approached a road junction fifteen miles outside Limoges. He saw lights up ahead and stopped. He was immediately surrounded by armed *maquisards* and bundled into a truck. Kämpfe was never seen again—it is presumed he was executed shortly afterward—but his unit carried out a desperate search for him.

Shortly after ten in the next morning, soldiers from the division were combing fields and houses near the village of Salon-la-Tour when they saw a large black Citroën approach them and screech abruptly to a stop.

One man jumped out and ran away, followed by another man and a woman. Both were carrying Sten guns. The man was a *résistant* named Jacques Dufour, who had worked with the Stationer circuit. The woman was SOE agent Violette Szabo. She had arrived in France for the second time just over forty-eight hours before.

Just as a chance encounter had doomed Kämpfe the evening before, Szabo had now been caught up in the search for him. The Germans opened fire and a gun battle developed. A woman tending cows nearby was killed by a machine-gun burst from the Germans as she stepped out of a barn.

Dufour escaped, but Szabo either twisted or, according to one villager, was shot in the ankle. She continued to exchange fire from a position under an apple tree at the edge of a cornfield. It is unknown if any German soldiers were killed in the battle as there is no record of German casualties, but Szabo's courage has never been disputed. She continued firing until she ran out of ammunition. When two soldiers dragged her to an SS officer for a summary interrogation, she spat in his face.

These small battles, the actions of the Resistance, and the hours taken to "punish" the population and to sweep north in search of more "terrorists" took a toll on the Second SS Panzer Division.

Field Marshall Gerd Von Rundstedt, in charge of the Nazi defense against the invasion, urgently needed its heavy armor. He demanded it be entrained and rushed to Normandy as a priority.

....

As word spread about the massacres many in the Resistance decided the price of sabotage was too high, and Das Reich suffered few attacks on the stretch that took it through Limoges.

However, a platoon of Britain's Special Air Service (SAS) had arrived by parachute in the early hours of June 6, and it went into action,

destroying rail track and trains, mining the roads around Poitiers—
a staging and assembly point for all Axis troops in the southwest
of France—and raiding convoys in Jeeps that had been dropped by
parachute.

The SAS's greatest success—before their forest hideout was discovered and they were nearly all killed—was the identification of eleven
gasoline trains carrying vital fuel for Das Reich hidden in sidings near
Châtellerault. Using their radios, the SAS arranged for a squadron of
Mosquitoes to destroy the trains and the essential fuel they carried with
lethal accuracy.

The combined efforts to harass Das Reich had come at a huge cost,
but the delay Allied invasion planners wanted was achieved. The division only rumbled piecemeal into the rear of the Normandy battlefield
between June 15 and 30. It did not fight as a unit in Normandy until
July 10—over a month after the invasion began.

....

In the days before and after D-day, Denise Bloch had been working day
and night with her organizer, Robert Benoist, to sabotage communications installations and railway track.

They brought down high pylons at the Île Héron and cut the railway
and telephone lines coming into Nantes. A few days after the invasion,
Bloch radioed London to say that all enemy traffic in the Dourdan-
Rambouillet area was at a standstill thanks to the sabotage.

Benoist was a dashing figure. A former race-car driver, his wealthy
family owned a number of châteaus. Soon after D-day he and Bloch
headed to one of these homes, Villa Cécile, an estate southwest of Paris,
where he reckoned he could raise an army of two thousand people.

Benoist received a message that his mother was ill, and on June 18
he headed to Paris to visit her. As he left the château he told Bloch
and the others there to "scatter" if he had not returned by lunchtime
tomorrow. They took it as a joke.

By the time Benoist arrived in the city, his mother had already died.
He spent time with his family and then went to a safe house to spend

the night. As he opened the door, a pistol was pushed into his face. The Gestapo had been waiting. The group had been betrayed—to this day it is unclear by whom—and through a series of mistakes a warning that the group was blown never reached Bloch.

The next day, when Benoist did not return, Bloch was worried but not overly concerned. Having delivered her "sked" with London, she headed to the local railway station to see if Benoist was on the Paris train.

When he was not, she returned to the Villa Cécile and joined a group having an aperitif on the terrace. Soon afterward they saw a German convoy approach and turn down the long drive. The Germans began shooting before they reached the villa. Storming inside, they shouted the name "*Line!*"—one of Bloch's code names. "*Ou est Line?*"

More than forty Germans searched the house, finding Bloch's wireless and a cache of machine guns. Eventually, she had to give herself up. She and the others were loaded into trucks and driven into the night. Behind them the Villa Cécile was set alight.

Bloch was doubly vulnerable. She was not only an SOE agent; she was Jewish. Her courage held fast under interrogation, and when the Allies broke free from Normandy, she was one of thirty-seven SOE prisoners in Frèsnes, including Violette Szabo, put on a train to Germany.

....

The agents of the Wheelwright network, including radio operator Yvonne Cormeau and courier Anne-Marie Walters, had been hiding out in their headquarters in the hilltop village of Castelnau-sur-l'Auvignon, a remote location with no electricity or running water, just a well. Cormeau would head into the hills to transmit, scanning her surroundings with the binoculars she kept at her side.

Soon after the invasion, a German spotter plane circled the village and reported Maquis activity. Early the following morning, the Germans launched an attack on the plateau on which the village stood. Walters cleaned and prepared grenades as the battle developed.

She also took charge of the network's records, a bundle of papers that included details of contacts in the area. She hoped to escape with them if she could, destroy them if she could not. Slinging her Sten gun over her shoulder and pushing three magazines into her overall pockets, she made her way out of the village, which was already half-abandoned by the Resistance.

Walters scrambled through brambles and rocks to find a cave below the village church, which they had formerly used as an arms depot. She shoved the papers into an old sack, lifted stones, and scratched a hole in the earth. She buried the papers and covered them with rocks.

By the time she got back, the Germans were very close. As she made her way carefully along the side of a hill she heard a noise at her feet. Looking down she could see three men hidden in the bushes below her. They waved her down and explained that the Germans were on the crest of the hill opposite. She made the rest of the journey on her belly.

Yvonne Cormeau escaped from the village with the Resistance camp doctor, who carried her set in one hand and his medical case in the other. Cormeau carried her bag of codes and crystals.

They got away quickly, following paths and fields, posing as a rural doctor and his assistant if they were challenged. Behind them they heard the small arms and explosions of the battle. When they reached the road to Condom the doctor found a house where he had friends. Cormeau set up her wireless and told London what was happening to Wheelwright.

By one in the afternoon the battle was over and the village lost. Nineteen *résistants* were dead; the Maquis claimed to have killed more than ten times as many attackers. Their final act was to blow up an ancient tower where hundreds of pounds of high explosives had been stored.

Led by Walters, the Wheelwright team formed a long column of forty-five battered trucks and cars and wound its way southwest through country roads to Panjas and a new base. The fighters were exhausted, their legs wearily hanging off the sides of the vehicles, Stens and rifles at their sides. On top of each truck was a Bren gun and a Cross of Lorraine, which flapped proudly in the warm summer breeze. Some of the men nursed arm and leg wounds or had bandages around their heads. Most sang.

Walters prayed the column would not meet any Germans on the road—they were all too tired to fight. Her prayers were answered; the only troubles they had were getting through the crowds in each village, as women handed up wine and food and men sang "La Marseillaise."

The people of France sensed the time was right to come into the open and celebrate the coming liberation.

....

About two hundred miles northeast of the Wheelwright agents' base at Castelnau-sur-l'Auvignon, John Farmer and Nancy Wake had based their own Maquis in what seemed an even more secure hilltop retreat. Their force was huge, numbering seven thousand men scattered across camps on a plateau above the spa town of Chaudes-Aigues. In the week after D-day, Wake and radio operator Denis Rake organized four huge arms drops to their mountain army.

Wake had just returned from collecting the supplies from one of the parachute drops and was soaking in a bathtub when she heard machine-gun fire in the distance. Getting dressed quickly, she joined Farmer to hear scouts' reports that the mountain approaches to the plateau were "black" with German troops. In fact, more than fifteen thousand SS troops were besieging the area with artillery and air support.

Wake, Farmer, and Rake jumped into a car and rushed north to the village of Fridefont, where the most powerful Maquis leader, Gaspard, had his base. He had overcome his aversion to working with the British when he saw the amount of arms they could supply. However, he remained frosty to outside interference in his command. Farmer advised him to withdraw; he refused. Farmer, feeling the position was useless, got Rake to radio London to see if a Free French officer could order Gaspard to save his men.

While they waited for London to reply, Wake took the car around the Maquis positions and kept the fighters supplied with ammunition. As she drove, heavy artillery pounded the countryside and Junkers 88s swooped overhead.

On the road near Fridefont, Wake saw a shape similar to a Lysander, but she knew immediately what it was: a Henschel 126 German reconnaissance plane. As she watched it bank, she realized it planned to come in directly at her along the line of the road. As the pilot held his course he pressed the button that activated the plane's forward-firing MG 17 machine gun and the dust in the road ahead of Wake spat into the air.

Seeing the angle of the plane's descent Wake did the one thing the pilot least expected: she slowed right down. Unable to adjust the angle of the fixed gun, he flew over her head, without a round striking the car.

Now Wake accelerated. In her rearview mirror, she could see the pilot making a turn. At the side of the road a young *maquisard* she knew well waved frantically. As the Luftwaffe pilot began his new strafing run she screeched to a halt, jumped out, and ran for cover. Bullets again ripped into the roadway just a few feet from the car.

As the plane rose into the sky again, the young Frenchman tugged at Wake's arm and pointed to the woods. But her eyes were on the car. She scrambled up the grass verge, ducked inside the door, and pulled out a package from behind the driver's seat.

As the pilot opened up the machine guns in his third run, Wake jumped back into the ditch and ran into the woods. Behind her there was a flash and an explosion as a bullet ignited the car's fuel tank.

Huddled against the side of a tree the young *maquisard* looked at the package and raised his eyebrows quizzically. Wake smiled and opened it to show him what it contained: some makeup, tea, and the red satin cushion she had brought with her to make life in the forests more bearable.

....

At Fridefont Denis Rake was still waiting for the message from London that Farmer hoped would persuade the Maquis to withdraw. The Germans had secured their positions on the slopes to the plateau and were sending forward advance parties up onto the plateau itself.

Wake was with Rake as he decoded the message. As they hoped, London ordered Gaspard to save his force and withdraw. Rake prepared to take it to Gaspard, but Wake stopped him. "I want you to add something to that message," she told him. "Sign it, 'Koenig.'"

Rake knew immediately what she meant. General Marie-Pierre Koenig was one of de Gaulle's most respected generals, a man from whom Gaspard would be honored to receive any order, even an order to withdraw. The message was amended, and Gaspard agreed that his Maquis would scatter under the cover of darkness.

That night Wake herself led 120 men through the countryside. They walked for three days and nights and eventually met up with the others who had escaped in the village of Saint-Santin, near Aurillac.

Rake had feared he was about to be captured on the plateau and had buried his radio, so the unit had no way to communicate with London. Wake volunteered to cycle more than one hundred miles to where a Free French operator was known to be in contact with the SOE in Algiers. It took her three days to get there and back, passing through roadblocks and towns filled with German soldiers. Thanks to her marathon bike ride, the message to the SOE that the Resistance of Chaudes-Aigues had regrouped got through to Algiers, and two days later the SOE dropped Rake a new wireless set.

....

Pearl Witherington had been living the clandestine life of an agent since September 1943. Having taken over the Wrestler network following the arrest of Maurice Southgate in May, she found herself leading—with the support of her fiancé, Henri Cornioley—a committed force of several hundred *maquisards*. With the landings on D-day, Witherington, on whose head the Gestapo had put a bounty of one million francs, brought her force out into the open.

She had already organized and led attacks to harass the occupiers in the lead-up to D-day, disrupting supply lines through the Loire Valley, stopping German reinforcements from moving untroubled from the south to the north. Now she repeatedly cut railways and telephone lines, often doing damage that would not be repaired until after the liberation.

Such was Witherington's effectiveness that on June 11 a column of German soldiers left their barracks in Bourges and headed for her headquarters in the château at Les Souches. Witherington's Maquis had taken over the château and its outbuildings from its Pétainist owners.

Expecting trouble, the Wehrmacht commanders brought two thousand men. The château's defenses comprised only two groups of Maquis numbering about 140 men. Witherington's SOE firearms instructor in England had concluded she was "outstanding. Probably the best shot, male or female, we have yet had." All the same, that day she faced overwhelming odds.

It was a warm Sunday morning. Cornioley had just celebrated Mass with the *maquisards* in a makeshift chapel in an outbuilding when there was a bugle call from the main road. It was a warning from one of Witherington's guards to say that Germans were coming.

Under blazing sunshine a battle developed into a series of skirmishes through the houses and buildings linked to the château. When the Germans brought in a column of vehicles led by Panzer tanks, Witherington ordered her men to allow them through and hit the thin-skinned vehicles from the rear.

She escaped out the back of the house, as the Germans spread out across the gardens. Cornioley stopped and shot one of the approaching soldiers, allowing Witherington to escape. She fled into a wheat field and took cover. She watched as the Germans began to torch the buildings as the remaining *maquisards* continued to fight on.

As Witherington hugged the earth, German soldiers fired at random into the field. She was terrified for Cornioley and those *maquisards* who had been unable to disperse into the woods, but there was nothing she could do. She was armed only with a pistol.

As darkness fell, the château smoldered, and the Germans finally left. At about 10:30 PM Witherington cautiously crawled out from her hiding place. Twenty-four of her men had died. The Germans had lost more than three times as many.

She escaped through the countryside, wondering how she would contact her men, thinking about the huge amount of arms they had lost in the fire. Frustrated at having to leave behind her stock of arms and ammunition at the gutted château, Witherington was quickly on to London for further supply drops and began to reunite her *maquisards*. Recruits had already come to her. Since D-day, the number of volunteers was swelling. Men were leaving their homes to join up. The old hands referred to them sniffily as the *résistants de la dernière heure*. Witherington's army swelled to five hundred and later, by the end of August, to twenty-five hundred. She appointed four captains to command four subsections and organized huge arms drops, supplying both her Maquis and the local Communist Francs-Tireurs et Partisans (FTP).

Witherington's men referred to her as *Le capitaine Pauline*, after her code name. When she arrived at one of the many camps she had organized, they would crowd around her bicycle to hear her words of encouragement and orders. Later, with her blonde hair tucked under her beret, she would lead them to help lay charges under railway sleepers and in the span of bridges, and her men's respect grew even deeper. Throughout the forests and farmhouses of the southern Loire she was known among the population as the "Warrior Queen."

She had not only the skill of a battlefield leader but also the power to call in the RAF. After she located a gasoline train on the Vierzon-Bourges line, she had her wireless operator radio its location, and sixty wagons were blown to smithereens by the RAF.

In the middle of August, Waffen SS soldiers from Das Reich returned to the area, still intent on settling scores with the Resistance. As they searched for Maquis leader Lieutenant Louis Chauvier, who was wounded and hiding in Valençay, Witherington had him whisked to safety and hidden in the woods. In anger, the Germans torched the town.

As the Germans retreated east, they continued to execute civilians and *maquisards*. One day Witherington was taken by her men to see the mutilated bodies of their comrades. The men had had their eyes smashed with rifle butts and had been crushed beneath the wheels of a truck. Witherington later described it as "atrocious mutilation beyond recognition."

The next day she was present when a French commander ordered the execution of a captured German officer.

At the end of August, Paris was liberated, but the fighting south of the Loire continued. The Germans now had General Patton on one flank and the French First Army at their heels.

Wehrmacht general Botho Elster led a twenty-thousand-strong column of the 159th Infantry Division, a ragged procession of tanks, men on foot, horses, and carriages. Elster was a talented soldier, intent on leading them to safety so that they might regroup. His column, which stretched for miles, was being driven into the Cher valley, where Witherington's men were waiting.

She ordered bridges to be destroyed and roads blocked. *Maquisards* hid plastic explosives under horse dung and watched as the lead German trucks ran over them and exploded. Her men poured machine-gun fire onto the vehicles trapped on the narrow roads through the valley. She led a number of these attacks, organizing *maquisards* who weeks earlier had been farmhands and shop boys into a force that so harassed Elster's column that he was forced to turn it around. Too afraid to surrender to the Maquis, Elster laid down his arms for the American army. The SOE later calculated that, in battle, Witherington's men killed over one thousand Germans in five months and wounded many more.

....

On a gray Sunday morning at the end of June 1944, Yvonne Baseden sat in a culvert in an open field, her radio at her side, her eyes scanning the sky.

She heard them before she saw them: a fleet of thirty-six Flying Fortresses of the US Air Force. For the past few hours, Baseden had been on her radio, sending crack signals to guide the planes in. Using the S-phone—an SOE device that allowed an agent to have voice contact with an airplane within a range of up to thirty miles—she spoke to the lead pilot.

Within a few moments the first of the containers floated down on the parachutes, and the men and women of the Maquis ran out to collect their much-needed supplies. There were four hundred containers in all. "It was incredible," she said later. "I was jumping around, waving madly to them!"

As a jubilant Baseden, who was just twenty-two, left the drop zone she handed her wireless to a young volunteer who would cycle with it to her next location. The Resistance and the SOE put such value on a wireless operator it made sense, when possible, for them not to transport their radios themselves.

Baseden and the other central figures of the Scholar network had a meeting place just outside Dole in a tall building with a loft packed with ripening cheese. The building was empty apart from a friendly couple who acted as its caretakers. Two days after the drop the core network personnel met there to discuss plans for their newly stocked *maquisards*. As they talked they were unaware that the young man who had taken Baseden's wireless had been arrested, tortured, and given away the address.

The group was just finishing their meal when they noticed a vehicle coming toward the building. The plates were swept away and everyone went to prearranged hiding places. The building was vast and filled with empty packaging cases and stacks of wood.

The caretaker's wife answered the door, and the Germans made a cursory search. They found no one and left, leaving a sentry behind. Sometime later a larger force of Germans arrived and talked to the sentry. He had become suspicious that there were more people in the house.

This time about twenty men swept through the building, finding each of the *résistants* one by one. Baseden was yanked out of her hiding place by her hair. A fellow agent, who was still hiding, was shot in the head when a German fired randomly into the ceiling. As the prisoners were hurried out and loaded onto a horse-drawn wagon, a summer thunderstorm broke out overhead.

The Germans had no proof that Baseden was a radio operator, and her refusal to talk angered her captors. Even when they carried out a mock execution she refused to change her story: she was not an enemy agent; she was a French-born shorthand typist who had become unknowingly involved with the people with whom she was arrested.

....

Working so close to the Normandy battlefield had forced Lise de Baissac, her brother Claude, and their radio operator Phyllis Latour to abandon their previous security precautions and to share a house. They struggled for food and even ate rats but had to keep up the same intense volume of work. Latour sent 135 messages in the months before and after the invasion.

The detection vans did not stop their search with the coming of the D-day beach landings. Three were still actively searching for Latour, and the Resistance had to destroy one van. They used a grenade, and a German woman and two children were killed. Latour felt responsible for their deaths and attended their funerals.

The three were finally forced to move when German soldiers actually requisitioned their house. Lise was there alone when they arrived. She went upstairs to her room to try to rescue her sleeping bag—which was made from parachute silk—and she found an exhausted Wehrmacht soldier was already asleep in it. She did not make a fuss and left quickly.

As the Germans retreated from the Normandy coastline, the Maquis increased its attacks and Lise de Baissac became an inspiration to Resistance groups on the Orne, leading several armed raids on retreating columns. She was proficient at setting tire-bursters and laying mines in roads.

On July 8, a seven-man team of the SAS dropped from a Tempsford-based Halifax between Mayenne and Le Mans, to be met by de Baissac. Over the next four weeks she accompanied the soldiers, who were led by Captain Mike Blackman, as they scoured the area to report on enemy troop movements and identify potential targets for air attacks.

The team established a routine in which they spent one or two nights looking for targets before returning to base to code and transmit a signal. They then immediately moved to a new location. The operation, code-named Haft, was extremely successful, passing on information on forty targets before the battlefield overran the area. Blackman later recommended de Baissac for a medal for her work with his team.

....

Dublin-born Paddy O'Sullivan had not only an exceptional knowledge of languages but also the most tremendous gall and courage.

When her co-organizers, brothers Percy and Edmund Mayer, whose network was based in Angoulême, discovered she could not ride a bicycle, they instructed her to learn. Some German soldiers saw her efforts and laughed as she kept falling off. She told them if they were gentlemen they would come and help her; some of them came over and did just that.

Having learned, she cycled about forty miles a day, carrying messages between Limoges, Montluçon, and Châteauroux. Once, while carrying a radio through a checkpoint that she had been unable to avoid, she smiled and laughed with a German soldier, so charming him that he asked her out for a drink. She agreed and cycled on but never kept the date.

On another occasion she was challenged as to what was in her suitcase and answered with a laugh, "Oh, a wireless, of course!" The German waved her away.

Throughout D-day she had remained at her wireless day and night. Her network, Fireman, was one of those that had been tasked with helping to hold up Das Reich.

Later, as the Germans retreated eastward toward Germany, O'Sullivan helped organize attacks on them near Limoges. The Germans were delayed so successfully that tens of thousands of them were captured by the advancing American army.

After the liberation, O'Sullivan would return safely to England.

....

Polish-born Christine Granville had been marking time in North Africa, reading reports of the invasion and of the fighting in France.

Then, on July 7, she was driven to an airfield in Algiers and dressed in a shirt, skirt, and jacket cut to the French pattern by a tailor in London's Margaret Street. A FANY gave her some sandwiches and a flask of tea for the journey; Benzedrine to keep her awake, should she ever need it; and a cyanide pill coated in rubber so that it would not melt in her mouth unless bitten in the most desperate of circumstances. Granville's destination was the Jockey network, where its leader, Francis Cammaerts, had been working without his own wireless operator since the arrest of Cecily Lefort the previous September.

Her mission was twofold: to work with Cammaerts, a tall, loose-framed and deep-thinking Englishman whose network included a substantial force of *résistants* that had made a base high up on the Vercors plateau; and to try to subvert Polish units known to be fighting for the Germans in the region.

Granville parachuted onto the Vercors in high winds, was blown off course, and landed so heavily that she not only badly bruised her back and ankle but also smashed her revolver. She waited until morning when she was discovered by a search party of *maquisards* and taken to Vassieux-en-Vercors, the largest town on the plateau. Soon after, back out in the wild countryside, she met Cammaerts for the first time as they went to gather canisters of supplies. She was suntanned, slim, and alert following her training in North Africa, and Cammaerts was immediately impressed by her. She found him handsome too.

A few days before her arrival the Resistance had declared the plateau to be the "Free Republic of the Vercors." On July 14—Bastille Day—a fleet of seventy-five American Flying Fortresses dropped nearly nine hundred containers carrying almost ninety-five tons of arms and munitions onto the Vercors. This daylight drop was followed by a bombing raid on the Luftwaffe base at Chabeuil.

While gathering in the huge drop of arms on July 14 several *maquisards* had been wounded by two Focke-Wulf 190s that had strafed the drop zone. The planes returned later that day to attack Die, just south of the plateau, where a Bastille Day parade was taking place. But these were only minor indicators of what was about to happen. German forces were gathered around the base of the vast plateau. An all-out attack was coming.

Within days of her arrival, Granville and Cammaerts were lovers, falling into each others arms in a hotel that had been attacked by aircraft and partially destroyed. With tension so great on the plateau—Cammaerts knew the uprising and the daylight drop was something the Germans could no longer afford to ignore—both agents were, as Cammaerts later said, "absolutely certain we were going to die the next day." He knew that, despite the recent parachute drop, his men did not have the heavy artillery, mortars, and antitank weapons to repel an attack.

The following morning they were standing at a window when a German fighter with a single bomb slung underneath, came directly at them. The pair stood transfixed as the bomb left the aircraft and hurtled toward them. It slid across the roof above them and buried itself in the ground behind the hotel. Granville laughed and gripped Cammaerts's hand. "They don't want us to die," she said.

As they waited for the German onslaught, Cammaerts sent Granville on missions across the plateau, carrying messages and warnings to groups of *résistants* defending different areas. On July 18 three divisions of German soldiers—a force of ten thousand—attacked the plateau. Supported by the Luftwaffe, they quickly took the northern part of the plateau. Three days later crack SS troops landed by glider in the south and attacked Vassieux. Despite their courage, the Maquis was being overwhelmed by a superior and heavily armed enemy.

Cammaerts, Granville, and a friend made their escape from the Vercors on July 22, traveling first by car and then stumbling down through the undergrowth on the steep sides of the plateau on foot. It was a desperately difficult journey. They knew the Germans were in the area en masse and were unlikely to take prisoners. They were tired, worried for their comrades, and carried heavy radios, gear, and their personal equipment—everything they needed to continue the fight elsewhere.

They reached the road west of Die and watched from the bushes as a Wehrmacht column led by three tanks moved in. They managed to slip past the German cordon before heading south to join up with the Maquis in the Drôme.

German revenge on the Vercors was complete and ruthless. As well as the 639 *maquisards* killed, it is estimated that more than 200 civilians died. Doctors and nurses working in a makeshift Resistance field hospital were executed, as were their patients.

The two SOE agents, who had become lovers during the heady days of Vercors "independence," had had a lucky escape. But within weeks Cammaerts would be facing a German firing squad—with Granville his only chance of survival.

....

While Jacqueline Nearne was being debriefed in England—the officer who interviewed her described as "a very capable, intelligent, and highly reliable woman"—her sister had been waiting in the outskirts of Paris. Without her circuit leader Savy, Eileen Nearne had few messages to send, and she was delighted when London transferred to a new network, Spiritualist, which was active in the east of the French capital.

Spiritualist was led by a thirty-six-year-old former ski resort playboy, René Dumont-Guillemet. He had been briefed by Buckmaster to recruit those left without leadership following the arrest of Suttill, from the Prosper circuit, and others loyal to the Farmer circuit in Lille, whose leader had been killed in a gun battle with the Germans.

At Lille the Resistance had one of their greatest single successes on D-day itself, creating a traffic jam of fifty-one trains that were then picked off by RAF bombers.

Using the cover of his own haulage company, Dumont-Guillemet proved hugely successful in his task, ensuring Nearne became very busy with the radio. By late July 1944 she had sent more than one hundred messages to London. Her chances of being caught increased with each "sked." When the Germans increased the number of direction-finding vans in the area around her house in Bourg-la-Reine, she decided it was time to move with her radio.

She had just one last message to send for Dumont-Guillemet. The summer rain was heavy on the roof of the house on the morning of July 22, 1944, as she assembled her set and wound out her aerial. She tapped out the message and completed the transmission.

When she heard vehicles and shouts outside, she had to wipe the condensation from the window to see what the commotion was down in the street. The view that greeted her was the worst nightmare of every wireless operator at work in occupied Europe. The Germans had tracked her down.

Eileen Nearne just had time to burn her codes and dismantle her set before there was a loud banging on her door. She opened it to have a plainclothes Gestapo officer step into the house. Immediately, and with great presence of mind, Nearne started to shout at him, appearing confused and angry. The man stared at her before waving a number of armed men to enter. They ransacked the house, quickly found the radio, and bundled Nearne into a waiting car.

At Gestapo headquarters at 11 Rue des Saussaies, she played the role of a clueless young woman who sent messages on the radio for a mysterious boss who she thought ran some sort of company. She pretended not to care what he did and to be shocked and outraged when her interrogators suggested she was a spy. They beat her and submerged her in a bath filled with water, but her story did not change. They were unable to break her. She was put in a car bound for Frèsnes prison and a concentration camp beyond.

As the twenty-three-year-old was driven through the streets of Paris, she looked at what she thought was the most beautiful city in the world for what she feared might be the last time, and she said a silent prayer. She remained at Frèsnes until August 15, less than two weeks before the liberation of Paris, when she and hundreds of other prisoners were loaded onto a train bound for Germany.

At Ravensbrück concentration camp, she met fellow SOE agents Lilian Rolfe, Denise Bloch, and Violette Szabo, whose true identities as spies were known to the Germans. Nearne maintained her pretense that she was a simple shop girl throughout her captivity. It was a decision that saved her life. After periods in work camps, she escaped during a forced march and eventually met up with soldiers of the US First Army when they arrived in Leipzig during April 1945.

One dark evening toward the end of January 1945, Rolfe, Bloch, and Szabo were executed in the crematorium yard of Ravensbrück by an SS lance corporal with a pistol. A camp overseer who witnessed their deaths stated, "All three were very brave and I was deeply moved."

....

Senior officers at the Gestapo headquarters in the old town hall of Montluçon, where Maurice Southgate had been taken immediately after his arrest three months earlier, always met for an aperitif shortly before 12:30 PM. It was a time to discuss prisoners and plans for forthcoming arrests over a glass of schnapps.

It was a sunny day in late July 1944, and despite the fighting to the north, those officers, two hundred miles south of Paris, still felt secure enough to have only a basic guard on the door to their building. They were quite unaware of the four cars that were making their way through the streets of the medieval town. Inside were fourteen *maquisards*, armed with Sten guns and grenades.

The deadly convoy roared up to the back entrance of the town hall, and the raiders rushed inside, opening fire as they went. In a room on the first floor, the officers put down their glasses in shock. As they stood up, their chairs scuffing on the floor, the door to the room was flung open. They caught sudden sight of a figure in khaki, a beret set at an angle on her head. It was a woman. She had a machine gun over her shoulder and two hand grenades in her fists. She lobbed them forward, shut the door, and two explosions, moments apart, ripped through the room.

As the Gestapo men lay dying, the woman was already running back down the stairs. It was Nancy Wake.

....

The raid on the Gestapo headquarters was the culmination of a period of intense activity by Wake and her comrades.

After the loss of their base at Chaudes-Aigues, the Maquis had set up a series of independent camps. Wake decided to stay with her band of one hundred *résistants* in a forest near the town of Ygrande. She chose the location as it was near to the Resistance leader whom she most respected, Henri Tardivat, the man who had greeted her when her parachute had been stuck up a tree.

The schoolteacher, whom she always called Tardi, was a natural leader whose fighters were always well fed and well looked after. In the weeks after D-day, Tardi had revealed himself to be a master of planning and leading hit-and-run attacks on German convoys. Wake always accompanied him on the raids, helping him choose the location—usually a section of sunken road with wooded terrain rising on either side—and instructing the men where to lay the concealed charges.

Tardi would post a sentry up ahead who would signal with a mirror when the convoy was approaching.

As the convoy rumbled below them, Wake would signal and detonator plungers would be depressed. The raiders tried to target the escort vehicles at the front and back of the convoys first, trapping the thin-skinned trucks between the burning vehicles. Wake and the others would step out from behind trees and spray Sten and Bren gun fire onto the Germans.

With the Germans being cut down as they jumped from the trucks and unable to organize their defense, Tardi would signal the withdrawal. He and Wake had agreed never to remain too long at the scene of an ambush. A handful of men stayed behind to cover them as the main band of *maquisards* disappeared into the forest.

Now that D-day was here, Wake made no pretense to be a "secret" agent. She did not live a clandestine life in a nondescript flat; she drove through the forests in cars packed with weapons. Twice when she came to roadblocks guarded by the Milice and German soldiers, she rolled down her window and shot them with her Sten as the car sped through. So, when one night Tardi suggested the attack on the Gestapo headquarters, she was a natural choice to lead one of the raiding party's cars.

Tardi had given her the key role of attacking the room in which the senior officers met, but the others carried out grenade and machine-gun attacks throughout the building. When the four cars sped away from the old town hall, they left thirty-eight Germans dead or dying.

The residents of Montluçon came out into the streets on hearing the gun battle, believing that the liberation had arrived. Wake and the others had to lean on their car horns to move the people from the road and make their escape.

....

The Germans in central France were searching for ways to retreat east toward the Belfort Gap, a valley between the Vosges and Jura mountains. Tardivat received orders to slow up the withdrawal by blowing up the bridge over the river at Cosne-d'Allier.

Tardi and Wake went to the cave where they had stashed their explosives. They were joined by two other saboteurs and a small, tight-knit group of Spanish Republicans who had become Wake's personal bodyguards.

The bridge was unguarded. Tardi and Wake slung ropes from the barriers and tied them around their waists. With the explosives in back-packs, they climbed down the struts of the bridge to what they had adjudged to be its weakest point. They set the timers on the charges for five minutes, cleared sightseers from the town who had come to see what was going on, and took cover to watch the center of the bridge explode and fall into the river below.

Despite the German army's disarray, it needed to hit back at Nancy Wake's Maquis and sent a force into the forest to track her down. When the camp at Ygrande came under attack, the *maquisards* were pinned down by a heavy machine gun. Armed with a Colt automatic, Wake led a team of ten men through the trees to outflank the gun. She helped the *maquisard* at her side with a bazooka, and together they knocked out the gun nest.

Soon after, she took part in a raid on an armaments store near Mont Mouchet. Wake led a team to take care of the two SS sentries at the building's west gate. She and her comrades crawled through the darkness in heavy rain. They watched the two sentries meet and then turn. As the two men separated, Wake and another *maquisard* had to make their way stealthily across thirty feet of open ground and kill them silently.

She was within a few feet of her target when he turned, saw her, and began to point his rifle. She saw with horror the glint of a bayonet. Wake's actions seemed instinctive, but they were based on training drilled into her in Scotland and on a ruthlessness she had developed over her months in France. She leaped at the man and delivered a karate chop to his neck just below his ear. The man crumpled to the ground with Wake stumbling on top of him. She could feel an agonising pain where the bayonet had sliced along her right arm.

She waved her men on. They stormed the store and laid the charges. Tardi knew a friendly doctor in a nearby village who treated Wake. The wound was deep, but he stopped the bleeding and bandaged her up. She recovered well in Tardi's new base, an abandoned château, and was there at the end of August when American and Free French troops liberated Montluçon.

Only then, after liberation, determined to be reunited with her husband, did she make contact with a friend in Marseille. He told her that her husband, Henri Fiocca, who had helped her escape the Gestapo three years earlier, had been executed. He had told friends before his arrest that he had not wanted to leave Marseille, because he knew that one day Wake would come home. He had been tortured by the Gestapo, which had realized in the months after she left that Wake was the "White Mouse," but he had never revealed she had escaped to England.

....

One of the key German garrisons on the France-Italy frontier was at Col de Larche, situated high in a pass above the town of Digne. The fort was manned mainly by Poles who had been forcibly conscripted into the German army. These reluctant troops, the SOE had previously noted, took every opportunity to be made prisoners of war.

Christine Granville and a local gendarme guide spent two days climbing goat tracks through the mountains to reach the garrison. Once there, she made contact with a guard to assess how dedicated the occupants were to the coming battle. Two days later she returned alone, now with the knowledge that German forces were approaching from the Italian side of the border.

There were 150 Poles in the concrete and stone garrison, and Granville had taken with her two props to help her win them over: a bullhorn and a Polish flag. A guard let her address the men. Standing with the red-and-white flag draped around her shoulders, she told them that when the time was right they should sabotage the garrison, desert, and join the Free French. She then handed out pretyped instructions on A4 notepaper, telling them how to come down the pass carrying white flags, which would grant them safe passage as prisoners of war if they preferred not to join the Resistance.

Less than a week later, a group of *maquisards* arrived at the fort to find the garrison commander, who was unprepared to surrender, trying to control dozens of mutinous soldiers. The Maquis issued him an ultimatum and then looked on as the Poles removed the breechblock firing pins from their heavy weapons and deserted en masse, bringing mortars and machine guns with them. The SOE attributed the complete surrender of the garrison to Granville's "own personal efforts."

But, on the very day of the surrender, Granville learned that Cammaerts had been arrested. Having been informed that the Allied landings on the south coast of France were imminent, Cammaerts had been touring the *résistants* of his circuit with a new agent, Xan Fielding, and a *maquisard* named Christian Sorensen. All carried fake papers, and if they were stopped, they planned to say they were hitching rides from a driver they did not know. The driver was Claude Renoir, grandson of the Impressionist artist.

As they made their tour, Fielding realized he was carrying a lot of money on him, having brought it into France for use by the Resistance. For safety, he divided it up with Cammaerts and Sorensen. This act, designed to be cautious, in fact put all three in great danger.

All went well until they were on the return leg of their journey and almost home safe. Just outside Digne they came upon a roadblock on a bridge across one of the rivers that met in the town. Cammaerts was not concerned as it was manned by eastern European soldiers who did not speak French and who gave only a cursory glance at their papers.

Then, as Renoir was moving off, another car rushed up. Cammaerts hissed, "Gestapo!" A Milice officer got out, approached the men's car, and scrutinized their papers. Fielding's work permit had not been stamped, and he was escorted at gunpoint to the Gestapo car. Cammaerts and Sorensen, who both claimed not to know Fielding, looked uninterested as the officer searched through the items taken from their pockets. He then noticed that the banknotes in their wallets were from the same series. A strange coincidence to happen among strangers.

Cammaerts and Sorensen were arrested, too. Renoir, whose papers were in order, was permitted to drive off. He rushed to report the arrests.

. . . .

As part of their D-day operations, the SOE and OSS created special three-man sabotage teams known as Jedburghs. One team, code-named Jeremy, joined Virginia Hall's fighting force in central France during the middle of August. Hall had paved the way for their arrival, having organized twenty-two parachute drops of supplies in four weeks. One package contained tea and new stump socks for Hall. It had been sent by Vera Atkins; Hall might have been working for the OSS now, but to Atkins she was still one of her agents.

Jedburgh Jeremy based itself at Le Puy and organized three battalions of Forces Françaises d'Intérieur, numbering fifteen thousand men. Together with Hall's guerrilla fighters, the Jedburghs harassed retreating Germans and cut communication lines.

Hall led or organized attacks on bridges, freight trains, and telephone lines. The rail line between Langogne and Brassac was cut four times. A railway bridge at Chamalières was destroyed, sending a locomotive careering into the gorge below. A group of *maquisards*, carrying bazookas, destroyed a convoy of trucks and a tank on the road between Le Puy and Langeac.

Hall's force killed an estimated 150 German soldiers and forced a further 500 to surrender. She also captured nineteen members of the Milice. As the Germans themselves had noted, she was indeed one of the most dangerous of all the Allied agents at work in France during the occupation.

....

After twenty-four hours in Digne prison without food or water, Cammaerts, Fielding, and Sorensen were taken to the Gestapo headquarters in the Villa Marie-Louise.

There, in elegant surroundings, they received a brutal interrogation in which they were punched in the face and kidneys. All three said they were smugglers. The Germans were not convinced, but with fear high about a possible invasion on the south coast, they decided to condemn the men to death.

Christine Granville was working as a guide to Jedburgh teams too, and while visiting one local Resistance team she tried to persuade them to rescue Cammaerts. They decided the priorities of supporting the imminent invasion must come first, and that anyway, in the event of a commando raid, the Germans would probably execute the prisoners.

She learned that Cammaerts was to be shot on the night of August 17. She knew instantly that she had to rescue him, and if necessary, she would do it alone. Her reasons were personal and practical. Although the Germans did not know it—they had not even guessed that he was English—they had in their cells one of the SOE's leading operatives in France, a man who knew everything about the Resistance network, which would be so helpful to the Allies as their armies moved inland from the Mediterranean coast.

....

Two days before Cammaerts was due to be executed, the daily crowd of prison visitors shuffled inside the walls of Digne prison. Among them was Christine Granville. She was tired after cycling twenty-five miles but filled with determination that she would succeed in the job ahead. As she wandered around the inner walls, she whistled the tune "Frankie and Johnny," a tale of deceit and murder that she and Cammaerts liked to sing together. Inside his cell, he heard her and took it as her telling him she loved him.

She meant much more than that. Granville went to the Gestapo office at the prison and asked to see a man named Schenck, an extremely dangerous thing to do. She not only risked exposing herself—there was a price on her head—but by showing interest in Cammaerts, she risked tipping off the Germans to his importance.

She told Schenck the prisoner was her husband, adding that she was related to Field Marshal Montgomery and therefore knew that the invasion was on its way. She told Schenck he would be added to a list to be "handed over to the mob."

Uneasy, Schenck said he would talk to an interpreter from the Milice named Waem—the man who had arrested Cammaerts and the others. Schenck said he would need two million francs to persuade him. Granville agreed and told him that if he reneged on the deal she would shoot him.

She cycled out of Digne prison, and the Resistance radioed the SOE in Algiers. The SOE agreed to send the money immediately.

By the time she returned to the prison the Allies had launched Operation Dragoon, with thousands of French and American troops landing on the Mediterranean coast of France. Schenck had so far done nothing, but fearful of French retribution after the liberation he arranged a meeting with Waem. Granville gave him ten bundles of rolled banknotes.

That afternoon she went to Schenck's apartment and waited. There was a screech of tires, and her heart missed a beat as Waem came through the door, his revolver pointed at her chest. But he wanted to hear what she had to say and put the gun down on the table. Over cups of coffee made by Schenck's wife, Granville began to tell him that the Allies would soon be in Digne and when they got there he would be handed over to the Resistance authorities. He would then be treated as what he was—one of the Gestapo's chief torturers.

She admitted to him that she was a British agent and told him she could protect him. Waem listened, knowing there was little in the way of German defenses protecting him from the advancing Allies. Ensuring the safety of the three prisoners, she told him, was the only way he and Schenck could save themselves. If they helped they would receive safe passage to the nearest Allied base outside of France.

Waem nodded his agreement. He would help. It was now seven in the evening. They had two hours: the execution was set for nine.

....

With the minutes ticking down to his execution, Cammaerts—an agent who had achieved so much—thought about how close he had come to seeing the liberation of France. He did not feel fear; he just felt that to be shot now was such a pity.

He, Fielding, and Sorensen received what seemed like a decent last meal of vegetable soup and brown bread, and then the man who had arrested them came to take them from their cells. There was a summer drizzle in the air as they crossed the prison courtyard at gunpoint.

Cammaerts had been in France for the best part of a year and a half. As he walked, he realized the potential fate of all agents, the one he had pushed to the back of his mind for so long, was about to become his reality. He and the others savored the sound of their feet on the stone, the thin rain on their face, as last reminders of what it meant to be alive.

Outside the prison gates they stopped, the men's heads turning toward the athletic field, where the firing squad usually carried out its orders.

And then, suddenly, Waem turned to him and said, "What a wonderful woman you have," and herded all three toward a waiting Citroën. The driver, whom none of them knew—it was Schenck—screeched off through the growing gloom and into the countryside. Cammaerts and the other two had no idea what was happening. Then the Citroën slowed where a woman was standing against the wall of a barn.

The door opened and the woman got in. It was Granville.

Arriving back at their Resistance hideout in Seynes-les-Alpes, Cammaerts felt unable to say anything to the remarkable woman who had saved his life.

He simply held her hand.

12

Afterward

AFTER HER ROLE IN stealing the Vichy French naval codes from its embassy in Washington, Betty Pack had been considered for a mission in occupied France.

William Stephenson pondered the idea of having Pack brought to Britain for training, but there remained work for her to do spying on the by now interned Vichy diplomats in the United States. When her cover had been blown, she settled into a life away from the service, living with Charles Brousse as if they were husband and wife, despite the fact that they were both still married to other people.

Pack did make it to France, but not until after the liberation. By the winter of 1944 she and Brousse were living in Paris, and after the war they settled in an old château in the tiny village of Castellnou in the Pyrenees. Arthur Pack had always promised to grant Betty her divorce when the war was over. The week after VE day, proceedings were opened in an English court, and a couple of months later the divorce was granted. On the night of November 1, 1945, Arthur shot himself.

Betty had her daughter Denise join her in France. Her son Tony joined the British Army and fought in the Korean War. He won the Military Cross for bravery but was shot dead on July 10, 1952, before he had the opportunity to receive it. Both children had suffered emotionally because of the way their parents had abandoned them. While Betty was a resourceful and brave agent, she was a terrible parent.

During Betty's stay in Paris she had met Charles's first wife's sister, who had had a relationship with a senior Gestapo officer during the occupation. It became apparent that information about Pack had been passed to the Germans after her cover had been blown in the United States, and that the Gestapo were expecting her to eventually come to France as an agent, as Stephenson had once planned. They had a full description of her and Brousse, and they were waiting. Had that mission gone ahead, agent Cynthia might well have found herself facing a Nazi firing squad. In the end, it was cancer that killed her, on December 1, 1963. She was fifty-three.

....

Following her arrest in Paris in 1944, Elizabeth Devereaux Rochester was taken to Frèsnes prison, where she maintained the story that she was a US citizen who had recently returned to France from Switzerland. When the Germans withdrew from Paris they left her in prison, and she was released when the city was liberated. She remained in France for the rest of her life and enjoyed a career in advertising.

....

On her return to the United States, Virginia Hall received a Distin-guished Service Cross in a simple ceremony in Donovan's office. She went on to work for the CIA, where one colleague suggested her incred-ible war service made her a "sort of embarrassment to the non-combatant CIA types," and she never achieved the promotions she was perhaps due. She died in 1982.

....

Andrée Borrel's colleague Gilbert Norman, who had also tried to alert the SOE to his own capture, was hanged at Mauthausen. His circuit leader Francis Suttill died in Sachsenhausen.

Yvonne Rudellat and Pierre Culioli, who had made such a successful team but had been caught after a gunfight at a roadblock, were both sent to concentration camps.

Culioli survived Buchenwald; he was the only male agent caught during the Prosper betrayal who escaped execution.

Rudellat arrived at Ravensbrück toward the end of August 1944 but was later transferred to Belsen, where starvation, typhus, and dysentery condemned thousands to a terrible death. Already weak, Rudellat survived until liberation on April 5, 1945, but died a few weeks later. After the war Vera Atkins tracked down a Polish woman who remembered Rudellat. The woman told her, "She arrived morally strong but became very ill and by April 10, she knew she was dying. I do hope she lived to know the camp was liberated so she rested quietly knowing her work had been of use and rewarded."

....

The female agents of the SOE-NKVD pact also paid dearly for their bravery. Francine Fromont, who spent more than sixteen months as a wireless operator in southern France, was executed on August 5, 1944. A number of streets in France and a school in Paris bear her name. Her colleague Guyot, who it was later revealed was her husband, returned to France after the war and became a prominent politician in the French Senate.

After being incarcerated in Ravensbrück, Else Noffke—who had tried and failed to commit suicide to avoid being arrested by the Gestapo—was shot in November 1943.

Emilie Boretzky, who had confessed all to the Gestapo, was later sent to Ravensbrück, where she was liberated by Soviet forces only to be deported as a traitor to a labor camp. Her comrade, Hermann Köhler, was executed in Mauthausen concentration camp in 1945.

....

Others survived.

Brian Stonehouse, who had been arrested in October 1941, was at Natzweiler-Struthof when Andrée Borrel arrived. He was later moved to Dachau, where he was liberated by American troops at the end of April 1945. After the war he returned to his work as an artist, and died in 1998.

Blanche Charlet, with whom he had been arrested, was held in the prison in Castres for more than a year. Having made friends with a sympathetic wardress, she got hold of pistols and spare keys and took part in a mass breakout. She found refuge in a monastery and was eventually picked up in a boat arranged by the SOE from the coast of Brittany.

Maurice Southgate survived Buchenwald concentration camp and later settled in France. He died in 1990.

. . . .

Mary Herbert, who had given birth while an agent in France, was reunited with her lover, Claude de Baissac, soon after the liberation of Paris. It was then that Claude first set eyes on his baby daughter, Claudine. They were married in November 1944 in London.

Claude and his sister Lise were liberated by the British Army in Normandy in July 1944. Lise de Baissac died in 2004, age ninety-eight.

Their wireless operator, Phyllis Latour, was liberated by the Americans early in August 1944. When the troops arrived she stood in the street with local villagers and waved them in.

. . . .

Three female SOE agents survived Ravensbrück.

Odette Sansom and Peter Churchill managed to communicate after their arrest, and she persuaded him to say that they were married and that he was Winston Churchill's nephew. It was a piece of bravura that saved her life.

Sansom was imprisoned in Frèsnes and brought to the Avenue Foch a number of times for interrogation and torture. In June 1943 she was informed that she had been officially condemned to death. She was eventually moved to Ravensbrück, where she was kept in an underground isolation cell. In April 1945 the camp commandant, who believed her story about her link to Churchill, drove her to the advancing Americans, using her as a hostage for his own life.

After the war, Sansom received the George Cross. Violette Szabo and Noor Inayat Khan were awarded theirs posthumously.

Yvonne Baseden, who had been arrested in July 1944, and Eileen Nearne survived Ravensbrück by maintaining their cover stories that they were French and not British.

Baseden developed tuberculosis during her incarceration, and the intervention of the Swedish Red Cross in April 1945 saved her life.

Eileen Nearne died in 2010, age eighty-nine. Her sister, Jacqueline, who served for a nerve-shredding fifteen months in France, went on to work for the United Nations Organization in New York. She died in 1982.

....

After returning from France, Anne-Marie Walters attempted to return to active service in August 1944, but was unsuccessful. She resigned her commission and left the SOE. She spent her life in France and Spain, working as a translator, and died in 1998.

....

After the war, despite her service to Britain, Christine Granville struggled to make a life in the country. She found work as a stewardess on an ocean liner, where she met a man who became obsessed with her. In June 1952, the man arrived at her lodgings in the Shelbourne Hotel in Kensington, London, and stabbed her to death.

Francis Cammaerts returned to his former career as a teacher after the war. He retired to France and died in 2006.

Neither of the two men promised safety in return for Cammaerts's life are believed to have survived for long. The Gestapo man, Schenck, returned to his apartment—against Cammaerts's advice—and was shot by the Resistance. Granville had reported to the SOE that it was important her promise to Waem, the man from the Milice, was honored. Exactly what happened to him is unclear, but he was probably executed by the French.

....

The death of Franklin D. Roosevelt in April 1945 left Bill Donovan without his political patron just as the war was coming to a close and the US government was reassessing its intelligence capability for the years ahead. The new president, Harry S. Truman, disliked Donovan and disbanded the OSS soon after VJ Day. Donovan returned to the law and was a special assistant to the chief prosecutor at the Nuremburg War Crimes Tribunal. He died in 1959, age seventy-six.

Although Donovan had no official role to play in the CIA—the successor to the OSS—Allen Dulles did. Dulles went on to be its director from 1953 until he was forced to resign after the failed Bay of Pigs invasion of Cuba in 1961. He died in 1969.

Maurice Buckmaster went back into civilian life and returned to a job with the Ford Motor Company. He died at age ninety in 1992.

Colin Gubbins was knighted in 1946. The SOE was disbanded the same year, and Gubbins retired to work as a textile merchant. He retired to a home in the Hebrides and died in 1976, age seventy-nine.

Selwyn Jepson returned to writing crime novels after the war. He died in 1989.

Following the disbandment of the SOE, Vera Atkins headed to Germany in search of her missing agents. She compiled information on those who had been incarcerated in camps and had been executed, and was a prosecution witness at the trials of Nazi officers. She worked hard to ensure that memorial plaques were installed to remember the agents killed at Natzweiler-Struthof, Dachau, and Ravensbrück. She died in a nursing home in June 2000.

....

Henri Déricourt, whose work as a double agent had enabled the SD to destroy the Prosper network, survived the war. Most of those he betrayed did not. Déricourt was put on trial in a French court after the war. There was little information in the public arena at the time, and although the circumstantial evidence against him was immense, there was no definite proof. He was acquitted. In 1962, having returned to his work as a pilot, his plane went missing over Laos. He was presumed dead.

Roger Bardet, who also betrayed his comrades in the Resistance, was convicted of treason and served a prison sentence.

....

In October 1942 Hitler gave his so-called "commando order," instructing that all such personnel as spies "are to be exterminated." A supplementary directive added that "all sabotage troops will be exterminated, without exception. . . . The chance of their escaping with their lives is nil." The instruction confirmed that agents would face no mercy, only torture and death; even the Hague Convention offered no protection for those captured as spies.

As Selwyn Jepson told prospective agents during their interviews, "I have to decide whether I can risk your life and you have to decide whether you're willing to risk it." SOE historian M. R. D. Foot recorded that 117 of the 470 agents of F Section who went into the field did not come back. Thirteen of the section's thirty-nine female agents died.

After the war, Francine Agazarian went to the cell in Flossenberg concentration camp where her husband, Jack, had been held. She then walked to the spot where he had been executed. It was an agonizing and courageous thing to do, but it had to be done—his sacrifice had to be remembered.

Agents had known the dangers they faced as they carried out their undercover work, but most claimed to be concentrating so hard that the fear seldom came through. Francine herself said, "Germans were everywhere in Paris; one absorbed the sight of them and went on with the job of living as ordinarily as possible and applying oneself to one's job."

Lise de Baissac recalled, "You know that you're in danger all the time but you always think that you will go through. I have never been afraid, really, that I should be caught. It never occurred to me. I think that we're all like that. If you're frightened, you can't do anything."

Women agents in the field, particularly those who took part in the open warfare that followed D-day, witnessed the violence of battle that had previously typically been experienced only by men. Phyllis Latour found it particularly difficult to deal with the devastating damage caused by bombers in the streets where she lived her secret life. "I can imagine the bomber pilots patting each other on the back and offering congratulations after a strike," she said. "But they never saw the carnage that was left. I always saw it, and I don't think I will ever forget it."

....

Instructors' and male agents' early impressions were that women could help men become more "invisible." Peter Churchill noted that "there is no better cover in this country [France] than to be seen in the company of a girl." Once they had seen women at work in the field, opinions changed. Another agent, Philippe de Vomécourt, concluded that women "showed more single-mindedness in their duties" than men.

The women in this book showed that they were every bit as skilled as male agents—and often combatants—during World War II. Never again would a counterintelligence force naively assume that a woman could not be a dangerous agent.

After the war Nancy Wake, who received medals from Britain, the United States, France, Australia, and her native New Zealand, said, "I hate wars and violence, but if they come then I don't see why we women should just wave a proud goodbye and then knit them balaclavas."

Her role in khaki put her on an equal footing with the men at a time when such equality was possible in few areas of society. When Wake realized her fellow *maquisards* were watching her take a pee in the woods, she understood but did not want it to affect her standing in the group. "They were men living in the forest without women," she said, "so my presence among them caused quite a stir, so I could sort of understand them wanting to do that, *once* . . . but I also had to put a stop to it. I wanted their respect, not their leering eyes, and I couldn't have both."

The Maquis leader, Henri Tardivat, confirmed after the war that Wake had been accorded the respect she deserved: "She is the most feminine woman I know until the fighting starts. Then she is like five men."

When Wake died in 2011, age ninety-eight, her ashes were scattered in the forests near Montluçon where she had proved herself among the bravest of the brave during 1944.

....

Pearl Witheringon, who married her fiancé, Henri Cornioley, after the war and settled in France, had seen gun battles and the execution of a German prisoner by the Maquis. Through her planning and battlefield leadership, she was responsible for the deaths of many enemy soldiers, and although she said she could have killed if she was threatened, she added: "I didn't go out and fight with a gun. I don't think it's a woman's job. We're made to give life, not take it. I couldn't have stood up and coldly shot somebody."

Most of the SOE women received awards and medals of some kind—and many received the Croix de Guerre from France—but the protocol that governed military decorations was not laid out to recognize their contribution.

Pearl Witherington's story is instructive. She was recommended for the Military Cross but was ineligible because she was a woman.

She was then awarded the civilian MBE, a medal usually given to people for work in their community. She returned it with the note:

> The work which I undertook was of a purely military nature in enemy occupied country. When the time for open warfare came we planned and executed open attacks on the enemy. I spent a year in the field and had I been caught I would have been shot, or worse still, sent to a concentration camp. I consider it most unjust to be given a civilian decoration. The men received military decorations. Why this discrimination with women when they put the best of themselves into the accomplishment of their duties?

There was nothing "civil" about her work, she said. The men—and it was mostly men—who had arranged for women to be armed agents during the Second World War had never planned for them to be "civil."

They were trained to fight and kill, to bring bombing raids down on targets, to lead sabotage operations, and to turn large, sometimes vast numbers of men into underground armies.

They were soldiers, taking the fight to the enemy where he least expected it.

They were warriors. Brave, intelligent, resourceful. Living life in the shadows and helping to bring light to those living in the darkness of Nazi tyranny.

Glossary of Acronyms

ADF–Association des Dames Française
ATS–Auxiliary Territorial Service
BSC–British Security Coordination
CIA–Central Intelligence Agency
COI–Coordinator of Information
    MO–Morale Operations
    MU–Maritime Unit
    R&A–Research and Analysis
    SO–Special Operations
    X-2–Counter Intelligence
CSP–Contact and Source in Place
FANY–First Aid Nursing Yeomanry
FBI–Federal Bureau of Investigation
FTP–Francs-Tireurs et Partisans
MI5–Security Service
MI6–Secret Intelligence Service (SIS)
NAAFI–Navy, Army and Air Force Institutes
NI–Navy Intelligence
NKVD–Soviet intelligence; translates to People's Commissariat for Internal Affairs
ODA–Order of Departure of Agents
OSS–Office of Strategic Services
    OSS London:
    Communications and Propaganda
    Country Units
    R&A–Research and Analysis
    Sabotage

SI–Secret Intelligence

SO–Special Operations

X-2–Counter Intelligence

RAF–Royal Air Force

SAS–Special Air Service

SD–Sicherheitsdienst, the intelligence branch of the SS

SIS–Secret Intelligence Service (MI6)

SLU–Special Liaison Unit

SOE–Special Operations Executive

SS–Schutzstaffel

STO–Service du Travail Obligatoire

USAAF–United States Army Air Force

WAAF–Women's Auxiliary Air Force

Bibliography

Allan, Stuart. *Commando Country*. Edinburgh: National Museums Scotland, 2007.

Ashdown, Paddy. *The Cruel Victory: The French Resistance, D-day, and the Battle for Vercours 1944*. London: William Collins, 2014.

Atwood, Kathryn J. *Women Heroes of World War II: 26 Stories of Espionage, Sabotage, Resistance, and Rescue*. Chicago: Chicago Review Press, 2011.

Bailey, Roderick. *Forgotten Voices of the Secret War: An Inside History of Special Operations in the Second World War*. London: Ebury, 2008.

Buckmaster, Maurice. *They Fought Alone*. London: Odhams, 1958.

Clark, Freddie. *Agents by Moonlight: The Secret History of RAF Tempsford During World War II*. Stroud, UK: Tempus, 1999.

Clutton-Brock, Oliver. *RAF Evaders: The Complete Story of RAF Escapees and Their Escape Lines, Western Europe, 1940–1945*. London: Grub Street, 2009.

Escott, Squadron Leader Beryl E. *The Heroines of SOE: Britain's Secret Women in France*. Stroud, UK: History Press, 2011.

Fitzsimons, Peter. *Nancy Wake: A Biography of Our Greatest War Heroine*. London: Harper-Collins, 2001.

Foot, M. R. D. *SOE: An Outline History of the Special Operations Executive 1940–1946*. London: Bodley Head, 2014.

Foot, M. R. D. *SOE in France: An Account of the Work of the British Special Operations Executive in France 1940–1944*. London: HMSO, 1966.

Ford, Roger. *Fire from the Forest: The SAS Brigade in France, 1944*. London: Cassell, 2003.

Ford, Roger. *Steel from the Sky: The Jedburgh Raiders, France 1944*. London: Cassell, 2004.

Hastings, Max. *Das Reich: The March of the 2nd SS Panzer Division Through France*. London: Pan Books, 1983.

Helm, Sarah. *A Life in Secrets: The Story of Vera Atkins and the Lost Agents of SOE*. London: Abacus, 2005.

Heslop, Richard. *Xavier: A British Agent with the French Resistance*. London: Biteback, 2014.

Hodgson, Lynn Philip. *Inside Camp X*. Port Perry, ON: Blake Book Distribution, 2002.

Howarth, Patrick. *Undercover: The Men and Women of the Special Operations Executive*. London: Routledge & Kegan Paul, 1980.

Hue, André, and Ewen Southby-Tailyour. *The Next Moon: The Remarkable True Story of a British Agent Behind the Lines in Wartime France*. London: Penguin Books, 2005.

Hyde, H. Montgomery. *Cynthia*. London: Hamish Hamilton, 1965.

Jackson, Robert. *The Secret Squadrons: Special Duty Units of the RAF and USAAF in the Second World War*. London: Robson Books, 1983.

Jones, Liane. *A Quiet Courage: The Story of SOE's Women Agents in France*. New York: Bantam, 1990.

Kramer, Rita. *Flames in the Field: The Story of Four SOE Agents in Occupied France*. London: Michael Joseph, 1995.

Lovell, Mary S. *Cast No Shadow: The Life of the American Spy Who Changed the Course of World War II*. New York: Pantheon Books, 1992.

Macksey, Kenneth. *The Partisans of Europe in the Second World War*. New York: Stein & Day, 1975.

Marks, Leo. *Between Silk and Cyanide: A Codemaker's War, 1941–1945*. London: HarperCollins, 1998.

Mauch, Christof. *The Shadow War Against Hitler: The Covert Operations of America's Wartime Secret Intelligence Service*. New York: Columbia University Press, 2003.

McIntosh, Elizabeth P. *Sisterhood of Spies: The Women of the OSS*. Annapolis: Naval Institute, 1998.

Merrick, K. A. *Flights of the Forgotten: Special Duties Operations in World War II*. London: Arms and Armour, 1989.

Miller, Russell. *Behind the Lines: The Oral History of Special Operations in World War II*. London: Secker & Warburg, 2002.

Moorehead, Caroline. *A Train in Winter: A Story of Resistance, Friendship and Survival*. London: Chatto & Windus, 2011.

Mulley, Clare. *The Spy Who Loved: The Secrets and Lives of One of Britain's Bravest Wartime Heroines*. London: Pan Books, 2013.

O'Connor, Bernard. *Women of RAF Tempsford: Churchill's Agents of Wartime Resistance*. Stroud, UK: Amberley, 2011.

O'Donnell, Patrick K. *Operatives, Spies and Saboteurs: The Unknown Story of the Men and Women of WWII's OSS*. New York: Citadel, 2004.

Oliver, David. *Airborne Espionage: International Special Duty Operations in the World Wars*. Stroud, UK: Sutton, 2005.

Ottaway, Susan. *Sisters, Secrets and Sacrifice*. London: Harper, 2013.

Ottaway, Susan. *Violette Szabo: The Life That I Have*. Barnsley, UK: Leo Cooper, 2002.

Overton Fuller, Jean. *The German Penetration of SOE: France, 1941–44*. London: William Kimber, 1975.

Pattinson, Juliette. *Behind Enemy Lines: Gender, Passing, and the Special Operations Executive in the Second World War*. Manchester: Manchester University Press, 2007.

Payment, Simone. *American Women Spies of World War II*. New York: Rosen, 2004.

Pearson, Judith L. *The Wolves at the Door: The True Story of America's Greatest Female Spy*. Guilford, CT: Lyons, 2005.

Persico, Joseph. *Piercing the Reich: The Remarkable True Story of Allied Undercover Operations in World War II That Rivals "A Man Called Intrepid."* London: Sphere Books, 1980.

Rochester, Elizabeth Devereaux. *Full Moon to France*. London: Robert Hale, 1968.

Saward, J. *The Grand Prix Saboteurs: The Extraordinary Untold Story of the Grand Prix Drivers Who Became British Secret Agents in World War II*. London: Morienval Press, 2006.

Seymour-Jones, Carole. *She Landed By Moonlight: The Story of Secret Agent Pearl Witherington: the Real 'Charlotte Gray.'* London: Hodder & Stoughton, 2013.

Srodes, James. *Allen Dulles: Master of Spies*. Washington, DC: Regnery, 1999.

Suttill, Francis J. *Shadows in the Fog: The True Story of Major Suttill and the Prosper French Resistance Network*. Stroud, UK: History Press, 2014.

Tickell, Jerrard. *Odette*. London: Pan Books, 1976.

Verity, Hugh. *We Landed By Moonlight*. Crécy, 2000.

Vinen, Richard. *The Unfree French: Life Under the Occupation*. London: Pengiun Books, 2006.

Walker, Robyn. *The Women Who Spied for Britain: Female Secret Agents of the Second World War*. Stroud, UK: Amberley, 2014.

Waller, Douglas. *Wild Bill Donovan: The Spymaster Who Created the OSS and Modern American Espionage*. New York: Free Press, 2011.

Walters, Anne-Marie. *Moondrop to Gascony*. Wiltshire, UK: Moho Books, 2009.

Wilkinson, Peter, and Joan Bright Astley. *Gubbins & SOE*. Barnsley, UK: Pen & Sword Military, 2010.

Yarnold, Patrick. *Wanborough Manor: School for Secret Agents*. Guildford, UK: Hopfield, 2009.

About the Authors

GORDON THOMAS is the author of fifty-six books. Several were Main Selections for the US Book of the Month Club, the Literary Guild, and the Readers Digest Book Club. He has received two Mark Twain Society Awards for Reporting Excellence. Seven of his books are major motion pictures, including *Voyage of the Damned*, which was nominated for three Academy Awards, and the TV movie *Enola Gay*. *Experiences* won the Jury's and Critics' prizes at the Monte Carlo TV Festival.

He holds an Edgar Award for *Shipwreck*. In April 2006 he received the Citizens Commission for Human Rights Lifetime Achievement Award for Investigative Journalism.

He has written extensively on all aspects of the work of the global intelligence community for over forty years.

His *Gideon's Spies: The Secret History of the Mossad* became a major documentary, which he wrote and narrated for Britain's Channel 4, and was later shown worldwide. It followed three years of research during which he was given unprecedented access to Mossad's key personnel. The book has been published internationally and is in its seventh edition.

Thomas writes on intelligence matters for the *Daily Telegraph* (UK), *Welt Am Sonntag* and *Bild* (Germany), *Wprost* (Poland), and the *Daily Telegraph* (Australia). He has been a regular broadcaster on current affairs for the BBC and US networks and has lectured widely on the intelligence world.

....

GREG LEWIS is a journalist, documentary maker, and writer. He has written a dozen nonfiction books on a variety of subjects, including history, popular culture, and sports. He also works as a ghostwriter.

He has produced more than sixty documentaries for television and radio and has won major broadcast awards from BAFTA Cymru and the Guild of Health Writers UK.

His biography of Irish American prizefighter Tom Sharkey, *I Fought Them All*, which Lewis wrote with his wife, Moira Sharkey, won a Wishing Shelf nonfiction award.

His journalism has appeared in a variety of newspapers and magazines, including the *Times* (UK), *Private Eye* (UK), and *Military History* (US).

Greg lives in Wales with Moira and their two children, Evan and Caoimhe.

Also available from Amberley Publishing

Foreword by HRH The Princess Royal

THE WOMEN WHO SPIED FOR BRITAIN

Female Secret Agents of the Second World War

ROBYN WALKER

Available from all good bookshops or to order direct
Please call **01453–847–800**
www.amberley-books.com